Media Fr

Media French

A Vocabulary of Contemporary Usage

Adrian C. Ritchie

University of Wales Press
Cardiff
2008

www.uwp.co.uk

British Library Cataloguing-in-Publication Data
A catalogue record for this book is available from the British Library.

ISBN 978-0-7083-2098-3

Typeset by Etica Press Ltd
Printed in Great Britain by Antony Rowe Ltd, Chippenham, Wiltshire

Contents

Introduction

Purpose and scope

In this revised edition of my handbook of French idiom, *Newspaper French* (first published in 1990), I have tried to group together some of the more useful terms and idioms that the reader of contemporary French will regularly encounter.

For the translator and the advanced user of French in today's world, familiarity with specialized vocabulary in fields such as administration, economics, the law, social and political affairs is essential. In order to read, understand and use the French language of today, one needs a knowledge of these registers.

Words are always best understood in context, and so in this guide to contemporary French usage each headword is illustrated by one or more examples of its use, drawn from a wide range of situations and contexts.

How to use this vocabulary

A strict alphabetical order has been adopted for all entries: thus **conseil, conseil général,** and **conseiller** occur as separate entries and in that sequence.

Headwords are printed in **bold type,** as also are those words and phrases within the illustrations that correspond precisely to the headword [e.g. **action** (*nf*): une **action** de 24 heures paralyse les transports parisiens (*industrial action, strike*)]. In more extended collocations, the whole sense-group is emboldened in order to highlight the use of the headword in context, as under **consentir** (*vt*), where the key element of the sentence: **un effort important est consenti** (*a major effort has been made*) is highlighted, as also is the expression **aboutir à une paix durable** (*achieve a lasting peace*) under **aboutir** (*vi*).

Illustrative examples are given under each headword in order to clarify its use, in one or more contexts. *Translations,* in round brackets and italicized, are given for headwords, e.g. **audition** (*questioning*), when they appear in the illustrative examples. In the case of phrases incorporating the headword, e.g. **audition de témoins**, the whole sense group (*questioning of witnesses*) is translated. For certain peculiarly French concepts [often legal or political terms such as **bâtonnier, cohabitation,** or **îlotier**], the nearest cultural equivalent in English is given. *Commas* are used to separate equivalents and near equivalents in the target language; a *semi-colon* indicates a clear shift in meaning.

Cross-referencing is used extensively throughout in order to widen the scope for comparing and contrasting uses of a given word. Under **civil** (*adj/nm*), there are cross-references to other expressions to be found, for example, under **code, désobéissance, partie, procédure, société,** and **union.** Similarly, under **grève** (*nf*), I have drawn attention to other collocations under **consigne, mot d'ordre, mouvement, piquet** and **préavis.**

Certain French words appear *very frequently as an element in a set phrase or other common expression,* among them the following: **charge, chômage, congé, contrat, direction, droit, emploi, état, exploitation, guerre, impôt, logement, marché, peine, politique, pouvoir, social, syndical, taux, terre, titre, travail** and **voie.** In such cases, cross-references are unavoidably numerous: under **emploi** (*nm*), the reader is alerted to the existence of collocations under **atypique, bassin, contrat, cumuler, familial, insécurité, perspective, précarité, sécurité,** and **suppression.** Under **pouvoir** (*nm*) likewise, to expressions to be found under **accaparer, accrocher, coulisse, décision, écarter, élargi, étendu, éviction, fondé, inféoder, maintenir, noyautage, partage, passation, porter, usure** and **venue.** As a general principle, compound words that consist of attributive uses of French nouns, for example **article de fond** (*feature article*) or **garde à vue** (*period of police custody*), are put under the first word in the expression.

Phrases built on common verbs such as **donner, faire, mettre** or **prendre** are cross-referred to the more 'significant' component:

hence **donner lecture** appears under **lecture** (*nf*), and **mettre en place** under **place** (*nf*). The same principle is followed in the case of the nouns **mise** and **prise**, on which a large number of compounds are built: hence **mise au point** and **prise en compte** are ranged under **point** (*nm*) and **compte** (*nm*) respectively.

Adjectives in French commonly – though not always – are placed after the noun, and so decisions about how to deal with *noun+adjective groups* must be taken. In the majority of cases, such pairs of words are given under the noun: so **agitation sociale** (*social unrest*) goes under **agitation** (*nf*), and **flux migratoire** (*immigration*) appears under **flux** (*nm*). An adjective like **fiscal** (*fiscal, tax*) occurs as a qualifier in so many compounds and collocations that it seems wise to place it under **abattement**, **deduction**, **évasion**, **foyer**, **paradis**, **pression**, **recette** etc.

In some cases, however, such as **sujet conflictuel** or **commerce dominical**, where the adjective or other qualifier could be perceived as *the most significant element in the word group*, the reader will find the expression under the adjective, but with suitable cross-referencing under **sujet** (*nm*) and **commerce** (*nm*). There is inevitably an element of editorial choice in these matters, and decisions may sometimes strike the reader as arbitrary.

A number of past participles, which commonly have adjectival force, such as **accru**, **avarié**, **éclaté**, or **expérimenté**, are given separate entries in this glossary. Headwords which can be both noun and adjective, e.g. **clandestin**, **concurrent**, or **horaire** are marked (*adj/ nm,f*) or variants of same. Verb/noun homographs, e.g. **conseiller**, are, however, kept separate.

Symbols and abbreviations

In the interest of clarity and ease of reference, much lexicographical data normally provided in dictionaries [phonetic transcription of headwords, semantic categories, field and style labels etc.] has been omitted. I have however incorporated a minimum of information, indicating the main parts of speech, the number [where necessary] and the gender of French nouns.

The following are the most commonly used symbols:

(*nm*)	masculine noun
(*nf*)	feminine noun
(*nmf*)	masculine and feminine nouns with invariable form
(*nm,f*)	masculine or feminine noun
(*nmpl*)	masculine plural noun
(*pl*)	plural
(*adj*)	adjective
(*adj/nm*)	adjective or masculine noun
(*adj/nf*)	adjective or feminine noun
(*adj/nm,f*)	adjective or masculine or feminine noun
(*adj/nmf*)	adjective or invariable masculine and feminine noun
(*adv*)	adverb
(*inv*)	invariable
(*pref*)	prefix
(*prep*)	preposition
(*v impers*)	impersonal verb
(*vpr*)	reflexive verb
(*vi*)	intransitive verb
(*vt*)	transitive verb
(*excl*)	exclamation
[*fam*]	familiar/informal
[*fig*]	figurative use
[...]	extra information, illustrations, etc., are given inside square brackets

Adrian C. Ritchie
Bangor, October 2007

Acronyms and Abbreviations

Besides the most commonly met acronyms and abbreviations, the following list contains addresses of ministries, headquarters of political parties, trade unions, etc. These are widely used as convenient shorthand for the bodies, offices and organizations to which they refer.

Certain acronyms referring to new taxes, social security or housing benefits, or recently formed political parties may prove ephemeral and disappear rapidly from common use, but they are included here for reasons of completeness.

AFNOR	Association française de normalisation
AFP	Agence France Presse
AFR	Allocation formation-reclassement
AGIRC	Association générale des institutions de retraite des cadres
ALPE	Association laïque des parents d'élèves
AME	Aide médicale d'Etat
ANPE	Agence nationale pour l'emploi
APA	Aide personnalisée à l'autonomie
APE	Allocation parentale d'éducation
APEL	Association des parents d'élèves de l'école libre
APL	Aide personnalisée au logement
ARRCO	Association des régimes de retraite complémentaire
ASSEDIC	Association pour l'emploi dans l'industrie et le commerce
BCE	Banque centrale européenne
Beauvau	[place] Ministère de l'Intérieur
BEP	Brevet d'études professionnelles
BEPC	Brevet d'études du premier cycle
Bercy	[rue de] Ministère de l'Economie et des Finances

BERD	Banque européenne pour la reconstruction et le développement
BIT	Bureau international du travail
BNP	Banque Nationale de Paris
BO	Bulletin officiel
Bourbon	[palais] Assemblée nationale
BPF	Bon pour francs
Branly	[quai] Conseil supérieur de la Magistrature
Brienne	[hôtel de] Ministère de la Défense
Brongniart	[palais] Bourse de Paris
BSP	Brigade des stupéfiants et du proxénétisme
BT	Brevet de technicien
BTP	bâtiment et travaux publics
BTS	Brevet de technicien supérieur
CA	Conseil d'administration
CAC	Compagnie des agents de change
CAC 40	Paris Stock Exchange 40 Share Index
CAF	Coût, assurance, fret; Caisse d'allocations familiales
Cambon	[rue] Cour des Comptes
CAP	Certificat d'aptitude professionnelle
CC	Corps consulaire
CCI	Chambre de commerce et d'industrie
CCP	Compte chèque postal; centre de chèques postaux
CD	Corps diplomatique
CDD	Contrat à durée déterminée
CDI	Contrat à durée indéterminée
CDS	Centre des démocrates sociaux
CE	Comité d'entreprise
CEDEX	Courrier d'entreprise à distribution exceptionnelle
CERC	Centre d'études des revenus et des coûts
CERN	Conseil européen pour la recherche nucléaire
CES	Conseil économique et social
CESU	Chèque-emploi service universel
CET	Collège d'enseignement technique
CF	Communauté française
CFA	Centre de formation d'apprentis
CFAO	Conception et fabrication assistées par ordinateur

CFDT	Confédération française démocratique du travail
CGE-CGC	Confédération générale des cadres
CFI	Crédit (de) formation individualisé
CFTC	Confédération française des travailleurs chrétiens
CGC	Confédération générale des cadres
CGT	Confédération générale du travail
CGT–FO	Confédération générale du travail – Force ouvrière
CHU	Centre hospitalier universitaire
Cie	Compagnie
CIF	Congé individuel de formation
CNAL	Comité national d'action laïque
CNCL	Commission nationale de la communication et des libertés
CNI	Centre national des indépendants
CNPF	Conseil national du patronat français
CNRS	Centre national de la recherche scientifique
COB	Commission des opérations de Bourse
CODER	Commission de développement économique régional
CODEVI	Compte pour le développement industriel
Conti	[quai] Académie française
CPA	Classe préparatoire à l'apprentissage
CPAM	Caisse primaire d'assurance maladie
CPNT	Chasse, pêche, nature et tradition
CREDOC	Centre de recherches, d'études et de documentation sur la consommation
CRIF	Conseil représentatif des institutions juives de France
CRS	Compagnie républicaine de sécurité
CSA	Conseil supérieur de l'audiovisuel
CSG	Contribution sociale généralisée
CSM	Conseil supérieur de la magistrature
CU	Communauté urbaine
DAB	Distributeur automatique de billets
DATAR	Délégation à l'aménagement du territoire et à l'action régionale
DDASS	Direction départementale à l'action sanitaire sociale

DES	Diplôme d'études supérieures
DEUG	Diplôme d'études universitaires générales
DGE	Dotation globale d'équipement
DGF	Dotation globale de fonctionnement
DGSE	Direction générale de la sécurité extérieure
DOM	Département d'outre-mer
DPU	Droit de préemption urbain
DSQ	Développement social des quartiers
DST	Direction de la surveillance du territoire
DUEL	Diplôme universitaire d'études littéraires
DUES	Diplôme universitaire d'études scientifics
DUP	Déclaration d'utilité publique
DUT	Diplôme universitaire de technologie
EDF	Electricité de France
Elysée	[palais de l'] Présidence de la République
ENA	Ecole nationale d'administration
ENS	Ecole normale supérieure
ESC	Ecole supérieure de commerce
ESSEC	Ecole supérieure des sciences économiques et sociales
ETAM	Employé, technicien, agent de maîtrise
E-U	États-Unis
Fabien	[pl. du colonel] siège de la CGT
FCP	Fonds commun de placement
FD	Force démocrate
FDES	Fonds de développement économique et social
FED	Fonds européen de développement
FEN	Fédération de l'éducation nationale
FFA	Forces françaises en Allemagne
FIS	Front islamique du salut
FMI	Fonds monétaire international [UK: IMF)
FN	Front national
FNS	Fonds national de solidarité
FO	Force ouvriére
GDF	Gaz de France
GE	Génération écologie
GIE	Groupement d'intérêt économique
GIGN	Groupe d'intervention de la gendarmerie nationale
Grenelle	[rue de] Ministère des Affaires Sociales; Ministère de l'Industrie; Ministère du Travail

HEC	[école des] hautes études commerciales
HLM	Habitation à loyer modéré
IFOP	Institut français d'opinion publique
IGAME	Inspecteur général de l'administration en mission extraordinaire
IGF	Impôt sur les grandes fortunes
IGR	Impôt général sur le revenu
INSEE	Institut national de la statistique et des études économiques
INSERM	Institut national de la santé et de la recherche médicale
IRPP	Impôt sur le revenu des personnes physiques
IS	Impôt sur les sociétés
ISF	Impôt de solidarité sur la fortune [ex-IGF]
IUT	Institut universitaire de technologie
IVD	Indemnité viagère de départ
IVG	Interruption volontaire de grossesse
JCR	Jeunesse communiste révolutionnaire
JEC	Jeunesse étudiante chrétienne
JO	Jeunesse ouvrière; Journal officiel; Jeux Olympiques
Lassay	[hôtel de] résidence du Président de l'Assemblée nationale
LEP	Livret d'épargne populaire; Lycée d'enseignement professionnel
Lille	[rue de] siège du RPR
LO	Lutte ouvrière
Luxembourg	[palais du] Sénat
MATIF	Marché à terme international de France; Marché à terme d'instruments financiers
Matignon	[hôtel] résidence du Premier ministre
MJC	Maison des jeunes et de la culture
MOCI	Moniteur officiel du commerce et de l'industrie
MPF	Mouvement pour la France
MRAP	Mouvement contre le racisme, l'antisémitisme et pour la paix
MRG	Mouvement des radicaux de gauche
MST	Maladie sexuellement transmissible
NDLR	Note de la rédaction [Brit: Editor's note]
NF	Norme française

OCDE	Organisation de coopération et de développement économique
OFPRA	Office français de protection des réfugiés et apatrides
OLP	Organisation de libération de la Palestine [Brit: PLO]
OMS	Organisation mondiale de la santé [Brit: WHO]
ONG	Organisation non gouvernementale [Brit : QUANGO]
ONU	Organisation des Nations Unies [Brit: UNO]
OPA	Offre publique d'achat
OPEP	Organisation des pays exportateurs de pétrole [Brit: OPEC]
Orfèvres	[quai des] Police judiciaire de Paris
Orsay	[quai d'] Ministère des Affaires étrangères
ORSEC	[plan] Plan d'organisation des secours
OTAN	Organisation du Traité de l'Atlantique Nord [Brit: NATO]
PAC	Politique agricole commune [Brit: CAP]
PACS	Pacte civil de solidarité
PAF	Paysage audiovisuel français; Police de l'air et des frontières
Palais-Royal	[rue du] Conseil d'Etat
PAP	Prêts aidés pour l'accession à la propriété
PC	Prêt conventionné; Parti communiste Poste de commandement
PCF	Parti communiste français
P-DG	Président-directeur général
Pet C	Ponts et chaussées
PEEP	Fédération des parents d'élèves de l'enseignement public
PEL	Plan d'épargne-logement
PER	Plan d'épargne-retraite
PIB	Produit intérieur brut [Brit: GDP]
PIL	Programme d'insertion locale
PJ	Police judiciaire
PLA	Prêt locatif aidé
PLM	Paris-Lyon-Marseille
PLU	Plan local d'urbanisme
PME	Petite[s] et moyenne[s] entreprise[s]

PMI	Petite[s] et moyenne[s] industrie[s]
PMU	Pari mutuel urbain
PNB	Produit national brut [Brit: GNP]
POS	Plan d'occupation des sols
PR	Parti républicain
PS	Parti socialiste
PSU	Parti socialiste unifié
PTT	Postes, télécommunications et télédiffusion
PV	Procès-verbal
QG	Quartier général
RAID	Recherche, Assistance, Intervention, Dissuasion
RATP	Régie autonome des transports parisiens
RC[S]	Registre du commerce [et des sociétés]
RDS	Remboursement de la dette sociale
R et D	Recherche et développement
RER	Réseau express régional
RES	Rachat d'entreprise par les salariés [Brit: MBO]
RF	République française
RG	Renseignements généraux
RIB	Relevé d'identité bancaire
RIP	Relevé d'identité postal
Rivoli	[rue de] Ministère de l'Economie et des Finances
RMI	Revenu minimum d'insertion
RN	Route nationale
RPR	Rassemblement pour la République
RTT	Réduction du temps de travail
SA	Société anonyme
SAFER	Société d'aménagement foncier et d'établissement rural
Sàrl	Société à responsabilité limitée
SDAU	Schéma directeur d'aménagement et d'urbanisme
SDECE	Service de documentation extérieure et de contre-espionnage
SDF	[personne] sans domicile fixe
Ségur	[avenue de] Ministère de la Santé
SEITA	Société nationale d'exploitation industrielle des tabacs et allumettes

SEM	Société d'économie mixte
SERNAM	Service national des messageries
SFIO	Section française de l'internationale ouvrière
SGDG	Sans garantie du gouvernement
SICAV	Société d'investissement à capital variable
SICOB	Salon des industries du commerce et de l'organisation du bureau
SIDA	Syndrome d'immunodéficience acquise [Brit: AIDS]
SIVOM	Syndicat intercommunal à vocation multiple
SIVOS	Syndicat intercommunal à vocation spécialisée
SIVP	Stage d'initiation à la vie professionnelle
SIVU	Syndicat intercommunal à vocation unique
SMIC	Salaire minimum interprofessionnel de croissance
SNCF	Société nationale des chemins de fer français
SOFRES	Société française d'enquêtes par sondage
Solférino	[rue de] siège du Parti socialiste
SR	Service des renseignements
SS	Sécurité sociale
TGI	Tribunal de grande instance
TGV	Train à grande vitesse
TIG	Travail d'intérêt général
TOM	Territoire d'outre-mer
TTC	Toutes taxes comprises
TUC	Travaux d'utilité collective
TVA	Taxe sur la valeur ajoutée [Brit: VAT]
UDC	Union du centre
UDF	Union pour la démocratie française
UE	Union européenne
UER	Unité d'enseignement et de recherche
UFR	Unité de formation et de recherche
Ulm	[rue d'] siège de l'Ecole normale supérieure
UNAPEL	Union nationale des associations de parents d'élèves de l'école libre
UNEDIC	Union nationale pour l'emploi dans l'industrie et le commerce
URSSAF	Union pour le recouvrement des cotisations de sécurité sociale et d'allocations familiales
UV	Unité de valeur
Valois	[rue de] Ministère de la Culture et des Arts

Varenne	[rue de] Hôtel Matignon; Ministère de l'Agriculture
Vaugirard	[15 rue de] Sénat
Vendôme	[place] Ministère de la Justice
Vivienne	[rue] Bourse de Paris
VRP	Voyageur représentant placier
ZAC	Zone d'aménagement concerté
ZAD	Zone d'aménagement différé
ZAE	Zone d'activité économique
ZEP	Zone d'environnement protégé; Zone d'éducation prioritaire
ZI	Zone industrielle
ZIF	Zone d'intervention foncière
ZUP	Zone à urbaniser en priorité

A

abaissement (*nm*): depuis l'**abaissement** de l'âge légal des relations homosexuelles (*lowering*)

abaisser (*vt*): faut-il **abaisser** la majorité à 16 ans? (*lower, bring down*); le nouveau gouvernement a promis d'**abaisser les taux d'intérêt** (*reduce interest rates*)

abandon (*nm*): un projet européen qui exigera des **abandons de souveraineté** (*giving up of [national] sovereignty*)

abandonner (*vt*): il va **abandonner** son mandat de sénateur (*give up*)

abattement (*nm*): les **abattements fiscaux** en matière de succession (*tax allowance*); un **abattement de zone** pour compenser la cherté de la vie en Corse (*allowance granted on a regional basis*)

abattre (*vt*): la négociation des prix permet d'**abattre** de 20% le tarif théorique (*lower, reduce*); **abattu** dans une fusillade rue de Clichy (*shot, gunned down*)

abonder (*vi*): le parquet semble **abonder dans leur sens** (*be in full agreement with them*)

abonné, -e (*nm,f*): le câble a gagné 245.000 **abonnés** en 2003 (*subscriber; customer*); les **abonnés** ont priorité pour la location des places (*season ticket holder*)

aborder (*vt*): il faut **aborder** la question sociale (*tackle; broach*)

aboutir (*vi*): cette manœuvre pour isoler l'Iran pourrait **aboutir** (*succeed*); le meilleur moyen d'**aboutir à une paix durable** (*achieve a lasting peace*)

aboutissement (*nm*): l'**aboutissement** d'une lutte de trente ans (*[successful] outcome, conclusion*)

abrogation (*nf*): l'**abrogation** d'une mesure (*repeal, rescinding*); un projet de loi visant l'**abrogation de la loi de 1986** (*repeal of the 1986 act*)

abroger (*vt*): ils ont **abrogé** les récentes mesures de bannissement (*rescind, repeal [measure/law]*)

abstenir [**s'**] (*vpr*): les députés MoDem **s'abstiennent** sur le vote de confiance au gouvernement (*abstain*); le porte-parole du gouvernement **s'est abstenu de tout commentaire** (*decline to comment*)

abstention (*nf*): l'**abstention**, 45% chez les moins de trente ans (*abstention [from voting]*); un **taux d'abstention** très élevé (*abstention rate*)

abus (*nm*): une loi qui peut donner lieu à des **abus** (*abuse; injustice*); huit employés ont été inculpés d'**abus de confiance** (*fraud and deception*); l'**abus de biens sociaux**, ou l'utilisation de l'argent de l'entreprise pour des fins autres que son activité (*fraudulent use of company assets*); la question des **abus sexuels sur les enfants** (*child molesting*)

abuser (*vt*): soupçonné d'avoir **abusé** de 17 élèves, garçons et filles (*[sexually] abuse*)

abusif, -ive (*adj*): des indemnités de rupture **abusive** du contrat de travail (*wrongful*)

abusivement (*adv*): les journalistes **abusivement** assimilés à des fauteurs de troubles (*wrongfully*)

académie (*nf*): un enseignant qui s'estime lésé peut s'adresser à l'**académie** (*[Fr] regional education authority*); SEE ALSO **inspecteur**, **recteur**

accablant, -e (*adj*): un rapport qui s'avère **accablant**; le témoignage était **accablant** pour lui (*damning*); SEE ALSO **élément**

accabler (*vt*): l'accusé, **que nombre d'indices accablent** (*against whom there is overwhelming evidence*)

accalmie (*nf*): l'**accalmie** sur la Bourse de Paris n'a été que de courte durée (*lull, period of quiet trading*)

accaparer (*vt*): les militaires ont **accaparé le pouvoir** depuis le putsch (*seize power*)

accédant, -e (*nm,f*): un effort a été fait en faveur des **accédants à la propriété** (*house buyer; new homeowner*)

accéder (*vt*): 1960: le Congo belge **accède à l'indépendance** (*attain independence*); il faut que la femme puisse **accéder** aux postes de responsabilité (*rise/attain [to]*); l'an dernier 50.000 ménages **ont accédé à la propriété** (*became homeowners*)

acceptation (*nf*): l'**acceptation** par l'Irak du plan de paix soviétique (*acceptance*)

accès (*nm*): le **libre accès** des femmes au planning familial (*free access*); SEE ALSO **bretelle**

accession (*nf*): après l'**accession à l'indépendance** de la Namibie (*attaining independence*); depuis son **accession au pouvoir** en 1985 (*coming to power*); un prêt à taux zéro destiné à relancer l'**accession à la propriété** (*home ownership*)

accompagnement (*nm*): l'importance de l'**accompagnement** social et psychologique des sidéens (*support*)

accompagner (*vt*): pour **accompagner** avec succès la réinsertion des chômeurs de longue durée (*give support, assist*)

accord (*nm*): aucun **accord de paix** n'a été signé (*peace agreement*); **accord salarial** dans la Fonction publique (*pay/wage settlement*); SEE ALSO **amiable, conclure, parapher, protocole, rompre, valider**

accorder (*vt*): une solution qui n'**accorde** pas immédiatement l'indépendance au Kosovo (*grant*); [**s'**] (*vpr*): le PD-G **s'accorde une augmentation** de 37% (*award oneself a pay rise*); les négociateurs ont pu **s'accorder sur un calendrier** de retrait des troupes (*agree on a timetable*); SEE ALSO **autonomie**

accroc (*nm*): un nouvel **accroc** dans la cohabitation (*hitch, difficulty*)

accrochage (*nm*): des **accrochages** ont opposé manifestants et forces de l'ordre (*clash, incident*)

accrocher [**s'**] (*vpr*): sa volonté de **s'accrocher au pouvoir** (*hang on to power*)

accroissement (*nm*): un **accroissement** de la corruption en France (*increase, growth*)

accroître (*vt*): l'Etat a progressivement **accru** son rôle (*increase, strengthen*); [**s'**] (*vpr*): le nombre des emplois **s'est accru** en douze ans de plus de 20 millions (*increase, grow*)

accru, -e (*adj*): il promet un **engagement accru** des Etats-Unis au Proche-Orient (*greater commitment*); SEE ALSO **compétition**

accueil (*nm*): de pays d'immigration, le Portugal devient **pays d'accueil** (*country of refuge*); SEE ALSO **famille, structure, terre**

accueillir (*vt*): l'OTAN **accueille** favorablement le projet français (*greet, welcome*); **accueilli** dans un centre d'hébergement (*accommodated*); on **accueillait** de plus en plus d'immigrés clandestins (*admit*); **mal accueillis** au début, les Maghrébins ont réussi à s'intégrer (*[made] unwelcome; unpopular; ill received*)

accusation (*nf*): il conteste en bloc les **accusations** dont il fait l'objet (*charge, accusation*); l'**accusation** a fait valoir que l'inculpé avait été pris en flagrant délit (*prosecution*); la **mise en accusation** du Président des Etats-Unis (*impeachment; indictment*); SEE ALSO **chambre**

accusé, -e (*nm,f*): l'**accusé** nie avoir été mêlé à un trafic de devises (*accused, defendant*); envoyer un **accusé de réception** (*acknowledgement of receipt*); SEE ALSO **banc, box**

accuser (*vt*): le juge les **accusa** de meurtre (*indict, accuse, charge*); son parti **accuse** un retard de 21 points sur les travaillistes (*show, register*); [**s'**] (*vpr*): le décalage entre les deux partis **s'accuse** (*grow, increase*); SEE ALSO **mutuellement**

acheminement (*nm*): les combats gênent l'**acheminement de l'aide humanitaire** (*transport/distribution of humanitarian aid*)

acheminer (*vt*): afin d'**acheminer** l'aide humanitaire (*forward, transport*); [**s'**] (*vpr*): les négociations **s'acheminent** vers leur conclusion prévisible (*head/move [towards]*)

achèvement (*nm*): les sommes nécessaires à l'**achèvement** des travaux (*completion, conclusion*)

achever (*vt*): la police semble avoir **achevé** la première phase de son enquête (*complete*); [**s'**] (*vpr*): l'année 1982 vit **s'achever** le programme de nationalisations (*come to completion, conclude*)

achoppement (*nm*): le principal **point d'achoppement** concerne l'agriculture (*stumbling block*); SEE ALSO **pierre**

achopper (*vi*): les discussions risquent d'**achopper** sur ce dossier difficile (*hit a snag*); la contestation risque de **faire achopper** les pourparlers de paix (*derail; bring to a halt*)

acompte (*nm*): verser un **acompte** de 30% du prix d'achat (*down payment, deposit*)

acquéreur (*nm*): chercher un **acquéreur** pour son unité de Kentucky (*buyer, purchaser*); **se porter acquéreur** d'un terrain (*offer to buy*)

acquérir (*vt*): des sociétés ont été cédées et d'autres **acquises** (*acquire; take over*); [**s'**] (*vpr*): les titres peuvent **s'acquérir** aux guichets de la Poste (*be obtained*)

acquêts (*nmpl*): les **acquêts**, les biens acquis pendant la durée du mariage (*estate comprising only property acquired after marriage*)

acquis, -e (*adj*): sa réélection **est acquise** (*is a certainty*); d'ores et déjà **il est acquis au projet** (*he is in favour of the plan*)

acquis (*nm*): les **acquis** – modestes – de la politique sécuritaire (*successes; achievements*); les **acquis sociaux** auxquels tous ont droit (*social benefits/entitlements*)

acquisition (*nf*): une véritable fièvre d'**acquisitions** a gagné les pays membres (*takeover [esp. of company]*)

acquittement (*nm*): la cour d'assises prononce un **acquittement** (*verdict of not guilty*); un contrôle de l'**acquittement** des droits d'entrée sera instauré (*payment*); SEE ALSO **plaider**

acquitter (*vt*): le tribunal correctionnel relaxe, la cour d'assises **acquitte** (*acquit, discharge*); les entreprises **acquittent** la taxe professionnelle (*pay*); [**s'**] (*vpr*): **s'acquitter** d'une facture impayée (*pay, pay off, settle*); SEE ALSO **loyer**

acte (*nm*): l'usage de la langue arabe dans les **actes** officiels (*deed; document*); la revalorisation de l'**acte médical** (*medical treatment*); SEE ALSO **prendre**

actif, -ive (*adj/nm,f*): les **actifs**, qu'ils soient chômeurs ou salariés (*active/working population*); SEE ALSO **population, vie**

action (*nf*): acquérir des **actions** en Bourse (*share*); une **action** de 24 heures paralyse les transports parisiens (*industrial action; strike*); sa décision d'**engager une action en justice** (*take legal action*); SEE ALSO **émission, journée, redresser**

actionnaire (*nmf*): son premier **actionnaire**, l'Etat (*shareholder*)

actionnariat (*nm*): partisan de l'**actionnariat du personnel** (*employee share ownership*)

activité (*nf*): la société de Lille a vendu ses **activités** de peignage et de tissus (*interests; operations*); la croissance de l'**activité féminine** (*female employment, women in work*); SEE ALSO **appoint, artisanal, cesser, délictueux, manufacturier, parc, salarié, séparer, zone**

actualisation (*nf*): l'**actualisation** d'une loi vieille de cent ans (*updating*)

actualiser (*vt*): pour **actualiser** ces chiffres, il faut les multiplier par deux (*update, bring up to date*)

actualité (*nf*): la question retrouve tout à coup toute son **actualité** (*topicality, relevance*); un sujet qui en 2004 était **d'une brûlante actualité** (*the burning issue of the day*); l'**actualité politique** est peu fournie en ces mois d'été (*political news*)

actuel, -elle (*adj*): l'**actuelle** majorité au parlement (*present, current*)

actuellement (*adv*): le parti **actuellement au pouvoir** (*currently in power*)

adaptation (*nf*): après un long processus d'**adaptation** (*adjustment*); l'**adaptation** de l'emploi aux aspirations des femmes (*adaptation, adapting*)

adapté, -e (*adj*): rechercher des solutions **adaptées** à chaque situation (*appropriate*); la justice pénale est **mal adaptée** au monde des affaires (*ill-suited; inappropriate*)

additif (*nm*): un **additif** au règlement intérieur de l'école (*additional clause*)

adduction (*nf*): emporter un important marché d'**adduction d'eau** (*water supply*)

adepte (*adj/nmf*): une secte qui compte trois millions d'**adeptes** au Brésil (*follower, disciple; member*); l'idée **fait des adeptes** dans les rangs socialistes (*gain support*)

adéquat, -e (*adj*): la demande sera examinée par la commission **adéquate** (*appropriate; relevant*)

adéquation (*nf*): une meilleure **adéquation** entre l'offre et la demande (*matching*)

adhérent, -e (*adj/nm,f*): financé par les cotisations des 5.000 **adhérents** (*member [trade union/political party]*); l'adoption de l'euro par les **nouveaux adhérents** de l'UE (*new members*)

adhérer (*vt*): pourquoi tant d'ouvriers hésitent-ils à **adhérer**? (*become a member, join [union/political party]*)

adhésion (*nf*): depuis l'**adhésion** de la Pologne à l'Union européenne (*joining, accession*); l'enjeu de l'**adhésion** de la Turquie à l'UE (*membership*); l'idée **a recueilli une très large adhésion** (*gained widespread support*); SEE ALSO **traité**

adjoint, -e (*adj/nm,f*): employé en tant qu'**adjoint** au directeur (*assistant; deputy*); les **adjoints au maire** font le gros du travail (*deputy mayor*)

admettre (*vt*): seulement 34% des candidats ont été **admis** (*pass [examination]*)

administrateur (*nm*): l'Assemblée générale désigne les **administrateurs** (*director; trustee*); les affaires en dépôt de bilan sont confiées à l'**administrateur judiciaire** (*official receiver*)

administratif, -ive (*adj*): SEE **lourdeur**

administration (*nf*): un désaccord avec un particulier ou une **administration** (*government service*); mars 1982 donna à l'**administration locale** un regain de vie (*local government*); SEE ALSO **conseil, pénitentiaire**

administré, -e (*nm,f*): le maire est soutenu par ses **administrés** (*citizen; constituent*)

administrer (*vt*): une collectivité **s'administrant** librement dans le cadre de la République (*running its own affairs; self-governing*)

admissible (*adj*): il y avait 76% de candidats **admissibles à l'oral** (*eligible to sit the oral part of an exam*)

admission (*nf*): l'**admission** de l'Autriche dans la Communauté européenne (*admission, entry*)

adopter (*vt*): le projet de loi a été **adopté** en première lecture (*pass, carry*)

adoptif, -ive (*adj*): sa famille **adoptive**, dont il ne voulait plus porter le nom (*adoptive*); SEE ALSO **parent**

adoption (*nf*): l'**adoption** du projet de loi sur l'avortement (*adoption/passage [of bill]*); vérifier si l'**adoption** est conforme à l'intérêt de l'enfant (*adoption, fostering*)

affaiblir (*vt*): déjà **affaibli** politiquement (*weakened*)

affaiblissement (*nm*): l'**affaiblissement** de la monnaie nationale (*weakening*); avoir pour effet un **affaiblissement** du rôle du gouvernement (*diminishing, diminution*)

affaire (*nf*): une **affaire de mœurs** (*sex scandal; sex case*); Paris n'a pas l'intention de se mêler des **affaires intérieures** du Canada (*internal affairs*); SEE ALSO **chiffre, expédier, milieu, quartier, retour, tribunal**

affairisme (*nm*): l'inquiétude de la gauche face aux accusations d'**affairisme** (*shady dealing; [political] racketeering*)

affaissement (*nm*): l'**affaissement** du chiffre d'affaires des journaux (*fall, collapse*); on craignait un nouvel **affaissement des cours** à Wall Street (*fall in share prices*)

affaisser [s'] (*vpr*): le terrain **s'était affaissé** par endroits (*subside, give way*)

affectation (*nf*): 20% des recrues auront une **affectation** civile (*posting*); l'opposition s'inquiète de l'**affectation** du produit de ces privatisations (*allocation [of funds]*)

affecter (*vt*): les objecteurs de conscience, **affectés** dans une formation militaire non-armée (*attach; assign*); **affecter** les sommes économisées à l'aide au tiers-monde (*allocate; earmark*)

affectif, -ive (*adj*): SEE **carence**

affichage (*nm*): une campagne d'**affichage** à l'échelon national (*bill-sticking; placarding*)

affiche (*nf*): dans la presse écrite et **par voie d'affiche** (*using posters/ by poster*)

affiché, -e (*adj*): son approbation **affichée** de la politique du gouvernement (*open, declared*)

afficher (*vt*): **afficher** un antiaméricanisme virulent (*display*); les statistiques récentes **affichent** une diminution de 5% du chômage (*reveal, show*); SEE ALSO **désaccord**

affiliation (*nf*): la loi de 1972 rend obligatoire l'**affiliation** à un régime de retraite complémentaire (*registration [with]*); le Premier ministre **n'a pas d'affiliation partisane** (*belongs to no particular party*)

affilié, -e (*adj/nm,f*): le TUC représente 66 syndicats rassemblant 6,7 millions d'**affiliés**; les **affiliés** du régime général de la Sécurité sociale (*[affiliated] member*)

affilier [s'] (*vpr*): 20.000 membres supplémentaires **se sont affiliés** cette année (*join, become a member*)

affluer (*vi*): les réfugiés continuent d'**affluer** aux frontières (*arrive in great numbers*)

afflux (*nm*): l'**afflux** des demandeurs d'asile (*influx, inflow*)

affranchir [s'] (*vpr*): les républiques veulent **s'affranchir** de la tutelle de Moscou (*break free*)

affranchissement (*nm*): son **affranchissement** de la tutelle russe (*freeing, emancipation*); l'**affranchissement** est à la charge de l'expéditeur (*postage*)

affrètement (*nm*): un contrat portant sur l'**affrètement** de trois supertankers (*chartering*)

affréter (*vt*): un avion gros porteur **affrété** par la Croix-Rouge (*charter*)

affrontement (*nm*): violents **affrontements** entre l'OTAN et les talibans (*clash*); SEE ALSO **poursuite**

affronter (*vt*): des jeunes émeutiers **affrontent** les forces de l'ordre (*confront; clash with*); [**s'**] (*vpr*): les Etats-Unis et l'Iran **s'affrontent** déjà en Israël (*confront each other*)

âge (*nm*): SEE **classe**, **discrimination**, **limite**, **pyramide**, **tranche**, **troisième âge**

agenda (*nm*): l'**agenda** du retrait des forces américaines en Irak (*timetable*)

agent (*nm*): le quart des **agents de l'Etat** travaillent en Ile-de-France (*state employee; civil servant*); l'arrestation de 19 courtiers et **agents de change** (*exchange broker*); une vingtaine d'**agents de maîtrise** ont été licenciés (*supervisory staff*)

agglomération (*nf*): une commune de l'**agglomération rennaise** (*Rennes and its suburbs*); en zone rurale et dans les **petites agglomérations** (*small urban area*)

aggravation (*nf*): Fidji: **aggravation** de la crise (*worsening*); face à l'**aggravation** du déficit extérieur (*increase*)

aggravé, -e (*adj*): une peine maximale de deux ans pour les délits, même **aggravés** (*with aggravating circumstances*); SEE ALSO **peine**

aggraver (*vt*): la politique qu'il propose **aggraverait les inégalités** (*exacerbate inequalities*); [**s'**] (*vpr*): 500 morts au Pérou, où la situation **s'aggrave** dans le sud (*worsen, deteriorate*)

agir (*vi*): SEE **délégation**, **illégalité**

agissement (*nm*): ces **agissements** sont le fait d'une minorité (*behaviour; actions*); les **agissements suspects** du député socialiste (*schemes, intrigues*)

agitation (*nf*): depuis le début de l'**agitation** islamiste (*unrest*); une recrudescence de l'**agitation sociale** (*social unrest*)

agité, -e (*adj*): SEE **rentrée**

agréé, -e (*adj*): faire effectuer des travaux par un professionnel **agréé** (*authorized; accredited*)

agréer (*vt*): l'Allemagne ne saurait **agréer** à une baisse artificielle de ses taux d'intérêt (*agree [to], accept*)

agrément (*nm*): l'**agrément** des pouvoirs publics est nécessaire pour procéder (*consent, approval*)

agresser (*vt*): Tunisie: un journaliste **agressé** par des policiers en civil (*attack*)

agression (*nf*): des enfants victimes d'**agressions sexuelles** de la part de parents ou de proches (*sexual abuse*)

aide (*nf*): des sommes allouées au titre de l'**aide extérieure** (*foreign aid*); environ 100 milliards d'euros d'**aides publiques** (*government aid; public money*); un quartier où 51% des habitants **vivent des aides sociales** (*live on state benefits*); l'emploi d'une **aide à domicile** est facilité par l'exonération de cotisations sociales (*domestic help*); SEE ALSO **acheminement, bénéficiaire, dépendance, exportation, venir**

aile (*nf*): avec l'accord de l'**aile modérée** du parti (*moderate wing*)

aisance (*nf*): vivre dans une relative **aisance** (*prosperity, affluence*)

aisé, -e (*adj*): les ménages les plus **aisés** (*wealthy, well-off*)

aléa (*nm*): comme tous les placements, il est soumis aux **aléas** de la Bourse (*uncertainties; ups and downs*)

aléatoire (*adj*): le caractère **aléatoire** des contrats avec l'étranger (*risky*); distribution **aléatoire** d'eau et d'électricité (*unreliable*); fouilles **aléatoires** des véhicules, contrôles des voyageurs (*random*)

alerte (*nf*): **alerte à la bombe** sur un avion d'Air France (*bomb scare*); décréter l'**état d'alerte** (*state of emergency*); SEE ALSO **cote**

aliéner [s'] (*vpr*): au risque de s'**aliéner** les organisations syndicales (*alienate, antagonize*)

alignement (*nm*): un **alignement** sur les normes occidentales demandera du temps (*bringing into alignment*)

aligner (*vt*): on essaie d'**aligner** la pratique française sur les dispositions en vigueur à l'étranger (*align; bring into alignment*); [s'] (*vpr*): la loi belge s'**aligne** sur la directive européenne (*conform [with]*); l'opposition l'accuse de s'**aligner sur Washington** (*align oneself with America*)

alimentaire (*adj*): SEE **autosuffisance, carence, pension**

alimentation (*nf*): les sociétés ont la responsabilité de l'**alimentation en eau potable** de la ville (*supply of drinking water*)

alimenter (*vt*): attirer les investissements et **alimenter** la croissance (*feed, sustain*); payer des impôts et **alimenter les caisses de l'Etat** (*be a source of revenue for the state*)

alinéa (*nm*): le gouvernement fait grand usage de l'article 49, **alinéa** 3 de la Constitution (*paragraph*)

alléchant, -e (*adj*): des perspectives **alléchantes** pour les entreprises (*very attractive*)

allégation (*nf*): il dément formellement les **allégations** portées contre lui (*allegation, accusation*)

allégement (*nm*): un **allégement** des contrôles aux frontières (*lightening; relaxing*); annoncer de nouveaux **allégements d'impôts** (*tax cuts*); SEE ALSO **enveloppe**

alléger (*vt*): **alléger** des programmes trop lourds (*reduce content of, lighten*); la volonté du gouvernement d'**alléger les impôts** (*reduce taxation*); [**s'**] (*vpr*): la procédure de nos jours **s'est allégée** (*has become simpler*)

alléguer (*vt*): faire la preuve de la vérité des **faits allégués** (*allegations*)

alliance (*nf*): le chef d'Etat **fait alliance** avec l'armée (*ally oneself [with]*); SEE ALSO **progressiste**

allié, -e (*adj/nm,f*): la Russie, **alliée** traditionnelle de la Serbie (*ally*)

allier [**s'**] (*vpr*): le finlandais Nokia **s'allie** à Warner Music (*link up [with]*)

allocataire (*nmf*): les **allocataires** du Fonds de solidarité (*recipient [of allowance]; beneficiary*)

allocation (*nf*): toucher l'allocation de solidarité à la suite de l'**allocation de fin de droits** (*final unemployment benefit entitlement*); réservant les aides sociales et **allocations familiales** aux seuls Français (*family allowance; child benefit*); SEE ALSO **caisse, veuvage**

allocution (*nf*): au cours de son **allocution** radiophonique hebdomadaire (*speech, address*)

allongement (*nm*): préconiser un **allongement** de l'année scolaire (*lengthening; extension*)

allonger (*vt*): un décret **allongeant** le temps de travail des enseignants (*lengthen, extend*); [**s'**] (*vpr*): la durée de vie qui **s'allonge** (*get longer, increase*)

allouer (*vt*): le gouvernement va **allouer** une nouvelle aide aux paysans (*allocate*)

alourdir (*vt*): le gouvernement a choisi d'**alourdir l'impôt** (*increase taxes*); [**s'**] (*vpr*): affrontements à Gaza: **le bilan s'est alourdi** (*the death toll has risen*)

alourdissement (*nm*): malgré l'**alourdissement** des impôts locaux (*increase, rise*)

alternance (*nf*): la première **alternance** droite-gauche (*changeover of political power*); on lui a proposé une **formation en alternance** (*block-release training*)

amalgame (*nm*): un monde qui ne cesse de **faire l'amalgame entre Islam et terrorisme** (*lump Islam and terrorism together*)

ambiance (*nf*): l'**ambiance** à Alger est plutôt à l'apaisement (*mood, atmosphere*)

ambiant, -e (*adj*): sa proposition reflète le discours libéral **ambiant** (*prevailing*)

aménagement (*nm*): le projet de loi sur l'**aménagement du temps de travail** (*flexible working hours*); l'**aménagement du territoire** vise à remédier aux déséquilibres régionaux (*regional development*)

aménager (*vt*): **aménager le temps de travail** pour créer des emplois (*adopt flexible working hours*)

amende (*nf*): SEE **onéreux, passible**

amendement (*nm*): l'**amendement** de la loi sur la presse (*amendment*)

amender (*vt*): un décret **amendant** la loi de 1988 (*amend*)

amenuiser [**s'**] (*vpr*): l'écart **s'amenuisa** encore l'année dernière (*reduce, become less*)

amiable (*adj*): Panama: **accord à l'amiable** avec Washington (*amicable agreement*); le **règlement à l'amiable** d'un dossier (*out-of-court settlement*)

amicale (*nf*): une **amicale** de locataires (*association; club*)

amorce (*nf*): l'**amorce** d'une décrue du chômage (*beginnings, first signs*); on a trouvé une **amorce de solution** (*initial elements of a solution*)

amorcer (*vt*): l'Ethiopie **amorce** un rapprochement avec les Etats-Unis (*begin, initiate*); [**s'**] (*vpr*): on ne voit pas encore **s'amorcer** la reprise tant attendue (*begin; get under way*)

amortir (*vt*): pour **amortir** les effets de la crise (*cushion*); le prêt sera **amorti** en cinq ans (*pay off, repay*)

amortissement (*nm*): l'**amortissement de la dette** exigera de longues années d'efforts (*paying off the debt*)

ampleur (*nf*): révélant l'**ampleur** du malaise qui traverse la société française (*scale*); devant l'**ampleur des combats** (*scale of the fighting*)

amplifier [**s'**] (*vpr*): cette disparité ne cesse de **s'amplifier** (*increase*); SEE ALSO **appeler**

amputer (*vt*): le gouvernement a décidé d'**amputer de moitié** les salaires des fonctionnaires (*cut by half*)

ancien, -ienne (*adj/nm,f*): la France, **ancienne** puissance coloniale (*former*); les **anciens** des grandes écoles prestigieuses (*former student*); SEE ALSO **bâti**, **habitat**

ancienneté (*nf*): la progression automatique, **à l'ancienneté** (*by virtue of length of service*); SEE ALSO **bonification**, **prime**

ancrage (*nm*): Bretagne: le vote **confirme l'ancrage à gauche de la région** (*confirms that the region is a left-wing stronghold*)

animateur, -trice (*nm,f*): les élus locaux sont de plus en plus les **animateurs** de leur communauté locale (*leader; driving force*)

animation (*nf*): contribuer à l'**animation touristique** de la ville (*promotion of tourism*); **faire de l'animation sociale** dans les Maisons de jeunes (*take a lead in community activities*)

annexe (*adj/nf*): renvoyer une déclaration de revenus et les **pièces annexes** (*enclosures*)

annonce (*nf*): l'**annonce** de nouvelles mesures de compression du personnel (*announcement*); **passer une annonce** dans la presse locale (*place an advertisement*)

annoncer [**s'**] (*vpr*): la rentrée **s'annonce chaude** dans les lycées (*seems likely to be turbulent*); SEE ALSO **rude**

annuité (*nf*): une économie de 62.000 euros sur les **annuités des prêts** (*annual loan repayment*)

annulation (*nf*): l'**annulation** en 2003 des lois d'amnistie (*quashing*); des rumeurs d'**annulation des élections** avaient couru avant le premier tour (*calling off of the elections*); en raison des **annulations de commandes** des derniers mois (*cancelled orders*)

annuler (*vt*): le maire **annule** son arrêté anti-mendicité (*repeal*); on **annula** le verdict sur un vice de procédure (*quash*); Paris décide d'**annuler les dettes restantes** de ces pays (*cancel outstanding debts*)

anonymat (*nm*): selon un maire du Calvados, qui **requiert l'anonymat** (*asks to remain anonymous*); préférant **garder l'anonymat** par peur de représailles (*remain anonymous*)

antécédent, -e (*adj/nm*): compte tenu des **antécédents judiciaires** du prévenu (*criminal record*)

antenne (*nf*): les locaux abritent l'**antenne** parisienne du mouvement (*agency; branch*); le **temps d'antenne** accordé aux petits partis (*broadcasting time*)

anticasseur (*adj*): les dispositions de la **loi anticasseurs** (*law banning violent behaviour during demonstrations*)

anticipé, -e (*adj*): SEE **élection**, **libération**, **retraite**

apaisement (*nm*): il faut aussi qu'Israël contribue à l'**apaisement** (*reduction of tension*); tout cela **va dans le sens de l'apaisement** (*is a move in the direction of peace*)

apaiser (*vt*): Washington a besoin d'**apaiser la tension** avec la Corée du Nord (*ease tensions*); [**s'**] (*vpr*): la tension en Cisjordanie a semblé **s'apaiser** depuis (*die down; calm down*)

apatride (*adj/nmf*): l'Office français de protection des réfugiés et **apatrides** (*stateless person*)

apolitique (*adj*): les Français, de plus en plus **apolitiques** (*apolitical; indifferent to politics*)

appareil (*nm*): l'immobilisme de l'**appareil du parti** et de son leader (*[political] party apparatus*)

appareiller (*vi*): le porte-avions **appareillera** lundi matin (*cast off, get under way*)

apparenté, -e (*adj/nmf*): les Socialistes et leurs **apparentés** ont voté l'amnistie (*political ally*)

appartenance (*nf*): l'**appartenance** à une ethnie, une nation ou une race (*belonging [to]*); inculpé d'**appartenance à un groupe terroriste** opérant à l'étranger (*membership [of]*)

appauvrir (*vt*): enrichir les très riches et **appauvrir** les très pauvres (*impoverish; make poorer*); [**s'**] (*vpr*): la France **s'appauvrit-elle**? (*become poorer*); l'Afrique **s'appauvrit** aussi par ses sols (*become more impoverished*)

appauvrissement (*nm*): l'**appauvrissement** des classes moyennes (*impoverishment*)

appel (*nm*): **appel à témoins** après une tentative d'enlèvement d'une fillette (*appeal for witnesses*); **faire appel** de la décision du tribunal de Rennes (*appeal/lodge an appeal*); **lancer un appel d'offres** pour la construction de l'autoroute (*invite tenders*); SEE ALSO **cour, interjeter, procès**

appelant, -e (*nm,f*): l'appel étant injustifié, l'**appelant** est condamné aux dépens (*appellant against a judgment*)

appelé (*nm*): 400 postes de militaires de carrière et 2.183 postes d'**appelés du contingent** (*conscript; national serviceman*)

appeler (*vt*): un jeune Français était normalement **appelé** à l'âge de 19 ans (*conscript, call up for service*); **appeler** à un changement de régime (*appeal/call [for]*); SEE ALSO **grève, vœu**

appellation (*nf*): des personnes répondant à cette **appellation** (*label, name, title*)

application (*nf*): la **mise en application** du protocole de Kyoto (*implementation*); le dispositif devrait **entrer en application** début 2008 (*come into force*)

appliquer (*vt*): le règlement a été **appliqué** dès le premier jour (*implement*); la loi **sera appliquée** sans faille (*will be enforced*)

appoint (*nm*): les petits partis servent souvent d'**appoint** au gouvernement minoritaire (*extra support*); une **activité d'appoint** à domicile (*second job*)

appointements (*nmpl*): recevoir des **appointements** (*emoluments; salary attached to a post*)

appointer (*vt*): les maires, élus mais fonctionnaires **appointés** par l'Etat (*paid by the state*)

apport (*nm*): l'**apport** du tourisme étranger (*contribution; input*); faute d'**apport personnel** suffisant (*personal contribution; down payment*)

appréciation (*nf*): à Paris et à Bonn on a des **appréciations** assez différentes sur cette affaire (*view; assessment*); l'**appréciation** du dollar favorise les achats à l'étranger (*appreciation; rise in value*)

apprécier (*vt*): la justice aura pour tâche de désigner les responsables et d'**apprécier les conséquences** (*decide what action to take*); [**s'**] (*vpr*): le prix du baril de brut **s'est apprécié** de quatre dollars (*rise in value/price*)

apprenti, -e (*nm,f*): faire bénéficier les **apprentis** d'aides de l'Etat (*apprentice*)

apprentissage (*nm*): Emploi: mesures pour développer l'**apprentissage** (*apprentice training, apprenticeship*); partisan de l'**apprentissage précoce** de l'anglais (*early learning of a skill*)

approbation (*nf*): son **taux d'approbation** dépasse les 50% (*approval rating*); la politique des Etats-Unis **rencontre une large approbation** (*meet with general approval*)

approfondi, -e (*adj*): une étude **approfondie** de la question (*in-depth*)

approfondir [**s'**] (*vpr*): la récession économique **s'approfondit** (*deepen, get worse*); les disparités entre riches et pauvres ne cessent de **s'approfondir** (*become more pronounced*)

approfondissement (*nm*): un **approfondissement** du fossé entre gauche et droite (*widening [gap/gulf]*)

approvisionnement (*nm*): les pays qui dépendent de la Russie pour leur **approvisionnement pétrolier** (*oil supplies*)

approvisionner (*vt*): les stocks permettent d'**approvisionner la demande** (*satisfy demand*); aubaine qui lui permit d'**approvisionner son compte en banque** (*pay money into a bank account*)

appui (*nm*): Bagdad compte sur l'**appui** de la France (*support, backing*); le président cherche des **appuis diplomatiques** (*diplomatic backing*)

appuyer (*vt*): pour **appuyer** leurs revendications, ils menacent de faire grève (*support, back*)

apurement (*nm*): assurer l'**apurement** des dettes de l'entreprise (*discharging [of debt]*)

apurer (*vi*): le déficit ne sera pas **apuré** avant l'année 2006 (*discharge [debt]*); augmenter les impôts de 10% pour **apurer le passif** (*pay off the debt*)

arbitrage (*nm*): soumettre un litige à l'**arbitrage de l'ONU** (*UN arbitration*); **faire appel à l'arbitrage** pour éviter la publicité des tribunaux (*go to arbitration*)

arbitraire (*adj/nm*): arrestations **arbitraires** et exécutions sommaires (*arbitrary*); dans aucun pays le citoyen n'est à l'abri de l'**arbitraire de l'internement** (*arbitrary internment*)

arbitrer (*vt*): le FN pourrait **arbitrer les élections** dans les circonscriptions urbaines (*decide the election result*)

ardoise (*nf*): effacer une **ardoise** énorme (*debt; deficit*)

argent (*nm*): sans avoir recours à l'**argent public** (*public funds*); SEE ALSO **recycler**

arguer (*vi*): il veut faire annuler les élections, **arguant de fraudes** (*on the grounds of electoral fraud*)

argumentaire (*nm*): les juges ont refusé l'**argumentaire** de la défense (*plea, argument*)

argumenter (*vi*): le ministre de l'Intérieur avait **argumenté dans le même sens** (*put forward the same argument*)

armateur (*nm*): les **armateurs** veulent briser la grève des marins (*shipowner*)

arme (*nf*): l'ETA a donc décidé de **déposer les armes** (*lay down its arms*); SEE ALSO **commerce**, **embargo**, **livraison**, **lobby**, **pourvoyeur**

armé, -e (*adj*): SEE **branche**, **bras**

armée (*nf*): cette réforme devrait toucher d'abord l'**armée de terre** (*army*); d'ici à 2015, l'**armée de l'air** perdra quelque 26.000 hommes (*air force*); les partisans d'une **armée de métier** (*professional army*); SEE ALSO **heurter**

armement (*nm*): nos **ventes d'armements** sont en hausse de 13% (*arms sales*); un important **armement allemand** suspend ses escales au port du Havre (*German shipping company*); SEE ALSO **course**

armer (*vt*): faudrait-il **armer** la police municipale? (*arm, equip with arms*); avec 90 thoniers **armés** par 2.000 marins (*man, crew [boat, ship]*)

arnaque (*nf*): une belle histoire d'**arnaque** et de magouilles politiciennes (*swindling; dishonesty*); une tortueuse affaire d'**arnaque immobilière** (*property fraud*)

arnaquer (*vt*): **se faire arnaquer** par un démarcheur peu scrupuleux (*be swindled*)

arraisonnement (*nm*): premier **arraisonnement** d'un pétrolier irakien par la marine américaine (*boarding and inspection*)

arraisonner (*vt*): les garde-côtes grecs ont **arraisonné** en mer Egée un navire battant pavillon américain (*board [and inspect]*)

arranger (*vt*): le report du sommet **arrangerait** tout le monde (*suit, be convenient*); [**s'**] (*vpr*): les choses vont **s'arranger** d'ici à la date de la réunion (*improve; be settled*)

arrérages (*nmpl*): s'acquitter des **arrérages de loyer** et des factures impayées (*arrears of rent*)

arrestation (*nf*): trois **arrestations** à la suite d'émeutes (*arrest*)

arrêt (*nm*): le tribunal a enfin rendu son **arrêt** (*judgment, decision*); prononcer un **arrêt de mort** (*death sentence*); une journée d'action, avec **arrêts de travail** et manifestations (*stoppage; stopping work*); SEE ALSO **maison**

arrêté (*nm*): encore sous le coup d'un **arrêté d'expulsion** (*expulsion order*); le Smic sera augmenté **par arrêté du ministre** si l'indice des prix augmente de 20% (*by ministerial decree*); des **arrêtés municipaux** interdisant la mendicité publique (*local by-law*); SEE ALSO **préfectoral**

arrêter (*vt*): le gouvernement **arrête** un plan d'aide aux agriculteurs (*decide on; finalize*)

arrhes (*nfpl*): le paiement des **arrhes** engage l'acheteur et le vendeur (*deposit*); **verser des arrhes** pour l'achat d'un terrain (*pay a deposit [esp. for purchase of property]*)

arriéré, -e (*adj/nm*): la Chine et l'Inde plus **arriérées** que puissantes (*backward*); le fisc lui réclame 1.000 euros d'**arriérés d'impôts** (*unpaid taxes*); SEE ALSO **recouvrer**

arrière-pays (*nm*): un port maritime doit disposer de liaisons avec un **arrière-pays** le plus large possible (*hinterland*)

arrière-pensée (*nf*): cette initiative n'est certes pas sans **arrière-pensées** politiques (*ulterior motive*)

arroger [**s'**] (*vpr*): les pleins pouvoirs qu'il **s'était arrogés** en 2005 (*assume [without right]*)

arrondissement (*nm*): huit **arrondissements** de Paris ont élu un nouveau maire (*administrative district [of Paris, Marseille, Lyon]*); SEE ALSO **chef-lieu**

artère (*nf*): l'avenue de l'Indépendance, l'**artère** la plus importante de la ville (*main road, thoroughfare*)

article (*nm*): dans son **article de fond**, l'éditorialiste traite longuement de cette question (*feature article*); l'**article de tête** du *Figaro* était consacré au Darfour (*leader, leading article*); SEE ALSO **réprimer**

artisan (*nm*): les petits commerçants et les **artisans** sont les plus nombreux (*craftsman; self-employed person*)

artisanal, -e *mpl* **-aux** (*adj*): des fromages français fabriqués **de façon artisanale** (*by small-scale production methods*); SEE ALSO **fabrication**

artisanat (*nm*): le ministre des PME, du commerce et de l'**artisanat** (*artisan class; self-employed craftsmen*); un actif sur dix vit de l'**artisanat** (*craft industries*)

ascendance (*nf*): l'association des Français **d'ascendance polonaise** (*of Polish descent*)

ascension (*nf*): le chômage **poursuit son ascension** (*continues to rise*)

asile (*nm*): SEE **demande, requérant, terre**

asphyxie (*nf*): face à l'**asphyxie des transports** en Ile-de-France (*paralysis of the transport system*)

assainir (*vt*): **assainir** les eaux du lac (*purify, treat*); il voudrait **assainir les relations** russo-ukrainiennes (*improve relations*); [**s'**] (*vpr*): la situation des entreprises **s'est assainie** depuis lors (*improve; become more healthy*)

assainissement (*nm*): une directive qui rend obligatoire l'**assainissement des eaux usées** (*waste water treatment*)

assassin (*nm*): les **assassins** et violeurs de mineurs (*murderer, killer*); SEE ALSO **présumé**

assassinat (*nm*): en cas d'**assassinat** de mineur (*murder, killing*)

assemblée (*nf*): les salariés de France 2 réunis en **assemblée générale** (*[annual] general meeting*); lors du débat à l'**Assemblée nationale** (*National Assembly*)

assentiment (*nm*): obtenir par voie de référendum l'**assentiment** de la population (*assent, consent, approval*)

asseoir (*vt*): utiliser sa fortune pour **asseoir** son influence (*consolidate, strengthen*)

assermenté, -e (*adj*): étant donné sa qualité de fonctionnaire **assermenté** (*on oath*)

assesseur (*nm*): le Président de la cour d'assises, flanqué de deux **assesseurs** (*assessor; assistant judge*)

assiette (*nf*): l'**assiette** de l'impôt sur le revenu est devenue trop étroite et injuste (*tax base; tax bands*)

assignation (*nf*): le divorce prend effet dès la date de l'**assignation** [**à comparaître**] devant le tribunal (*summons, issue of a writ*); quatre **assignations à résidence** après le coup manqué d'hier (*house arrest*)

assigner (*vt*): la société a été **assignée en justice** pour rupture de contrat (*serve writ on; summons*); **être assigné à résidence** depuis trois ans (*be placed under house arrest*)

assimilé, -e (*adj/nm,f*): sans compter les modérés et **assimilés** (*ally*)

assise (*nf*): soucieux de ménager son **assise électorale** (*electoral base*); (*pl*) la **juridiction d'assises**, avec son jury populaire (*criminal court; [Brit] Crown court*); en 1974, lors des **assises nationales** du mouvement (*national conference*); SEE ALSO **juré**

assistanat (*nm*): comment sortir d'une condition d'**assistanat** (*living on state aid/handouts*)

assistance (*nf*): un accroissement de l'**assistance** technique et militaire (*aid, help*); il veut valoriser le travail plutôt que l'**assistance** (*[living on] state benefits*); ses quatre enfants, **placés à l'Assistance publique** (*[placed] in care*); SEE ALSO **non-assistance**

assistant, -e (*nm,f*): **assistant social** dans un quartier ouvrier de Mulhouse (*welfare/social worker*); faire garder son enfant à domicile par une **assistante maternelle** (*childminder*)

assisté, -e (*adj/nm,f*): encourageant ainsi une **mentalité d'assisté** (*dependency culture; a belief that one can live on state handouts*)

associatif, -ive (*adj*): mettre tout en œuvre pour favoriser la **vie associative** dans les villes neuves (*community life*); SEE ALSO **local**

association (*nf*): la ville ne subventionne plus les **associations caritatives** (*charity agency, charitable body*); accusés de meurtre et d'**association de malfaiteurs** en relation avec une entreprise terroriste (*criminal conspiracy*)

associé, -e (*adj/nm,f*): **associé** dans un cabinet d'avocats (*partner*)

associer [**s'**] (*vpr*): la France **s'associe** aux autres pays occidentaux (*associate with, join*)

assortir (*vt*): une peine de six mois avec sursis, **assortie** d'une amende de 5.000 euros (*with an additional fine*); [**s'**] une condamnation **qui s'assortit d'une période de mise à l'épreuve** (*together with a period of probation*)

assouplir (*vt*): le chancelier n'envisage-t-il pas d'**assouplir sa position**? (*become less rigid*); accepter d'**assouplir les règles** sur la TVA à taux réduit (*relax the rules*); [**s'**] (*vpr*): de nos jours, la procédure **s'est assouplie** et allégée (*become simpler*)

assouplissement (*nm*): aller plus loin dans l'**assouplissement des 35 heures** (*a more flexible approach to the 35-hour working week*); Hongkong: l'**assouplissement de la censure** irrite Pékin (*relaxing of censorship*)

assujetti, -e (*adj/nm,f*): les **assujettis au régime ordinaire de la Sécurité sociale** y ont droit (*persons registered with the French health and pensions scheme*); taxe à laquelle **sont assujetties** les entreprises (*are liable*); le nombre de contribuables **assujettis à l'ISF** (*[Fr] liable to pay wealth tax*)

assujettissement (*nm*): en principe, l'**assujettissement à l'impôt** dépend du lieu de domicile (*[tax] liability*)

assurance (*nf*): un préjudice qui n'est pas couvert par les **assurances** (*insurance policy*); le fret et les **assurances** (*insurance*); SEE ALSO **munir, police, souscripteur**

assurer (*vt*): être prêt à **assurer la direction du pays** (*take over the government of the country*); [**s'**] (*vpr*): **s'assurer** contre le vol (*take out insurance*); SEE ALSO **intérim, suivi**

astreindre (*vt*): pour **astreindre** Jérusalem à négocier (*compel, oblige*)

astreinte (*nf*): un métier qui implique jusqu'à 120 heures d'**astreinte** par semaine (*being on stand-by/on call*); **verser une astreinte** de 30.000 euros par infraction constatée (*pay financial penalty [for failure to comply with court order etc]*)

atelier (*nm*): **à l'atelier** comme à l'usine (*in the workplace*); une partie du colloque sera consacrée à des **ateliers de travail** (*workshop; working group*)

atermoiement (*nm*): après dix ans d'**atermoiements**, ils ont paraphé les accords (*procrastination, delaying tactics*)

atonie (*nf*): Suisse: **atonie** persistante de l'économie helvétique (*sluggishness*)

atout (*nm*): cette région a de sérieux **atouts** pour l'industriel (*advantage, asset*)

attaque (*nf*): SEE **éventuel**

attaquer (*vt*): il menace de les **attaquer en justice** (*take to court*); le maire a annoncé son intention de l'**attaquer en diffamation** (*bring a libel action [against sb]*); SEE ALSO **front**

atteinte (*nf*): une **atteinte** au principe de l'égalité entre les sexes (*attack [on]*); les **atteintes aux personnes** [coups et blessures, viols] continuent à progresser (*attacks on the person*); SEE ALSO **crédibilité, environnement**

attendu (*nm*): le juge donne, dans son **attendu [de jugement]**, une justifiction raisonnée de sa sentence (*explanation [of verdict]*)

attentat (*nm*): un **attentat** à l'explosif contre la mairie de Calvi (*[terrorist] attack*); auteur de plusieurs viols et d'**attentats à la pudeur** (*indecent assault*); SEE ALSO **outrage**

attente (*nf*): l'école est loin de répondre aux **attentes** des entreprises (*expectations*); **contre toute attente** élue sénatrice de New York (*contrary to expectation*); des personnes **en attente d'expulsion** (*awaiting expulsion*); SEE ALSO **prévenu**

attentisme (*nm*): **attentisme** et prudence à Amman (*wait-and-see attitude*)

attentiste (*adj*): la Russie adopte une position **attentiste** (*cautious; wait-and-see*)

atténuant, -e (*adj*): SEE **circonstance**

attestation (*nf*): il faut joindre au dossier l'**attestation de prise en charge Sécurité sociale** (*proof of social security entitlement*)

attester (*vt*): on doit **attester** de cinq ans de résidence (*furnish proof*); **attester** du caractère libre et équitable des élections (*certify, attest; vouch for*)

attitré, -e (*adj*): le négociateur **attitré** de la CFTC (*officially recognized; accredited*)

attractif, -ive (*adj*): les salaires de la fonction publique ne sont pas très **attractifs** (*attractive*)

attribuer (*vt*): le meurtre d'un Israélien **attribué** à l'OLP (*impute, attribute*); [**s'**] (*vpr*): ETA **s'attribuait** l'attentat de Madrid (*claim responsibility for*)

attributaire (*nmf*): c'est la préfecture qui établit la liste des **attributaires** des tickets de rationnement (*recipient [of a state benefit]*)

attribution (*nf*): l'**attribution** du prix Nobel de la paix (*award*); les conditions d'**attribution des marchés** ne respectent pas la législation (*awarding of contracts*); quatre ministres **conservent leurs attributions** dans le nouveau cabinet (*retain their post*)

atypique (*adj*): une protection sociale pour les **emplois atypiques** (*temporary/seasonal/part-time employment*)

audience (*nf*): lors de la dernière **audience** du procès (*[court] hearing*); la **salle d'audience** était pleine à craquer (*court room*); premier groupe radiophonique avec 8,9% de **part d'audience** (*audience share*)

audiovisuel, -elle (*adj/nm*): SEE **paysage, redevance**

audit (*nm*): un **audit** a mis en lumière de graves irrégularités de gestion (*audit; financial analysis*); SEE ALSO **cabinet**

audition (*nf*): après une ultime **audition de témoins** (*questioning of witnesses*); être conduit à la gendarmerie **pour audition** (*for questioning*)

auditionner (*vt*): 97 personnes ont été **auditionnées** par la commission (*hear; question*); **auditionner un témoin** en présence de ses conseils (*question/examine a witness*)

auditoire (*nm*): exposer les faits devant un **auditoire** très attentif (*audience*)

augmentation (*nf*): les suicides de policiers **en augmentation** (*on the increase*); réclamer de fortes **augmentations salariales** (*pay rise*); procéder à une **augmentation de capital** (*issue of share capital*); SEE ALSO **accorder, fort**

augmenter (*vi*): les droits d'inscription vont **augmenter** de 5% (*rise*); (*vt*): les employés **augmentés** le mois dernier (*awarded a pay rise*); Phénix **augmente son capital** (*raise fresh capital*)

austérité (*nf*): en 1998, **en pleine austérité** (*in a period of austerity measures*); SEE ALSO **budget, cure**

auteur (*nm*): quelque 220 **auteurs** de crimes et délits (*perpetrator*)

authentifier (*vt*): la signature permet d'**authentifier** la carte lors de son utilisation (*authenticate, validate; prove the validity of*)

autochtone (*adj/nmf*): les **habitants autochtones** de la région (*indigenous population*); les **autochtones** insistent sur leur identité (*native inhabitant*)

autodétermination (*nf*): il était hostile à l'idée du référendum d'**autodétermination** (*self-determination*)

autogestion (*nf*): dans l'**autogestion** l'entreprise est gérée et contrôlée par les travailleurs (*worker management, worker's control*)

autonome (*adj*): une liste centriste **autonome** aux élections européennes (*separate; independent*); une grève des conducteurs CFDT, CGT et **autonomes** (*independent; unaffiliated*)

autonomie (*nf*): Espagne: nouveau statut d'**autonomie** pour l'Andalousie (*autonomy; self-government*); Blair **accorde une autonomie partielle** à l'Ecosse (*grant devolved status*);

autonomiste (*adj/nmf*): les **autonomistes** basques revendiquent l'attentat (*separatist*)

autoproclamer [**s'**] (*vpr*): il **s'est autoproclamé** hier président par intérim (*proclaim oneself*); une région autonome **autoproclamée** au nord du pays (*self-proclaimed*)

autorisation (*nf*): posséder un titre de séjour et une **autorisation de travail** (*work permit*); obtenir une **autorisation de séjour** (*residence permit*)

autorisé, -e (*adj*): SEE **milieu**

autoriser (*vt*): une situation dans laquelle le code civil **autorise** l'avortement (*permit, allow*); autant d'éléments qui l'**autorisent à être confiant** dans l'avenir (*entitle one to be confident*)

autorité (*nf*): l'**autorité parentale** est en général conjointe (*parental authority*); (*pl*) les **autorités** empêchent les journalistes de faire leur travail (*authorities*)

autosatisfaction (*nf*): il leur reste deux motifs d'**autosatisfaction** (*satisfaction, self-congratulation*)

autosuffisance (*nf*): ce pays mène une politique d'**autosuffisance** (*self-sufficiency*); compromettant l'**autosuffisance alimentaire** de ces pays (*self-sufficiency in food*)

autosuffisant, -e (*adj*): le continent africain pourrait être **autosuffisant** en matière alimentaire (*self-sufficient*)

auxiliaire (*adj/nmf*): des emplois d'**auxiliaire**, de vacataire, ou de contractuel (*temporary worker*)

aval (*nm*): Washington donne son **aval** à l'accord (*consent; endorsement*)

avaliser (*vt*): le Conseil constitutionnel doit **avaliser** le découpage électoral (*endorse*)

avance (*nf*): la droite **prend une sérieuse avance** dans les sondages (*build up a considerable lead*); une **avance** sur la prime d'intéressement sera distribuée aux salariés (*advance on salary/ payment*)

avancée (*nf*): une nouvelle **avancée** dans le traitement du sida (*advance*); le **manque d'avancées** dans la gestion commune de l'immigration (*lack of progress*)

avancement (*nm*): le conseil municipal sera informé de l'**avancement** des négociations (*progress*); l'**avancement** est à l'ancienneté (*promotion*)

avancer (*vi*): pour **faire avancer** le processus de paix (*move forward, advance*); (*vt*): personne ne souhaite **avancer** les élections (*bring forward*); **avancer** des propositions concrètes et crédibles (*put forward*)

avanie (*nf*): une nouvelle **avanie** infligée à la France par ses partenaires (*snub*)

avant (*prep/adv*): la direction **met en avant** une diminution des agressions dans le métro (*point to*); autre sujet **mis en avant**, celui de l'environnement (*put forward, emphasize*); la **mise en avant** des produits régionaux (*promotion*); SEE ALSO **bond, fuite, minorité**

avantage (*nm*): le cumul des **avantages en nature** représente le quart du salaire d'un cadre (*perk, payment in kind*); SEE ALSO **bénéficier, donner**

avantageux, -euse (*adj*): proposer des marques **à prix avantageux** (*at attractive prices*)

avant-projet (*nm*): l'**avant-projet** de rapport, publié en 2003 (*first draft*)

avarie (*nf*): subir des **avaries** (*damage*); **constater une avarie** dès réception des marchandises (*report damage*)

avenant (*nm*): les syndicats ont obtenu un **avenant** à l'accord (*additional clause; codicil*)

avènement (*nm*): seul un changement de gouvernement permettra l'**avènement** d'une France plus juste (*advent*)

avéré, -e (*adj*): s'il s'agit de cas de dopage **avérés** pendant le Tour (*confirmed, proven*)

avérer (*vt*): même si l'authenticité du document **est avérée** (*is proved/confirmed*); [**s'**] (*vpr*): la rentrée sociale **s'avère** chaude cette année (*prove/turn out to be*); SEE ALSO **déterminant**

avertissement (*nm*): un **avertissement** au gouvernement à deux ans des élections (*warning*); SEE ALSO **multiplier, musclé**

aveu *pl* **-x** (*nm*): des **aveux** extirpés sous la torture (*confession*); les *mafiosi* qui **sont passés aux aveux** (*confess, make a confession*); SEE ALSO **extorquer, revenir**

avis (*nm*): un texte voté par les députés contre l'**avis** du gouvernement (*advice*); le Conseil d'Etat **rendra son avis** avant la fin du mois (*give a ruling*); un **avis de concours** pour la réalisation de quinze logements neufs (*invitation to tender*)

aviser (*vt*): **aviser** le client de la date de livraison (*notify, advise*)

aviver (*vt*): ce qui ne fait qu'**aviver les tensions** entre pays voisins (*fuel/stir up tension*)

avocat (*nm*): un échange d'arguments entre le ministère public et les **avocats** (*defence lawyer*); l'**avocat général** a demandé une peine de dix ans (*public prosecutor [in Assize/Crown court]*); [*fig*] Romano Prodi **se fait l'avocat** de la transparence financière (*make a plea [for]*)

avoir (*nm*): après le gel des **avoirs panaméens** aux Etats-Unis (*Panamanian assets*)

avoisiner (*vt*): la population **avoisine** les 300.000 (*be in the region of*)

avorté, -e (*adj*): coup d'Etat **avorté** au Bénin; détournement **avorté** d'un avion turc (*failed, unsuccessful*)

avoué, -e (*adj/nm*): les partisans **avoués** de l'Europe y dominent (*avowed, declared*); les fonctions d'un *solicitor* s'apparentent à celles de l'**avoué** (*solicitor [Brit]*)

avouer (*vi*): les auteurs des attentats ont **avoué** (*confess*); (*vt*): les trois adolescents ont **avoué les faits** (*confess [to the deed/crime]*)

axe (*nm*): l'importance de l'**axe** germano-nippon (*axis*); le discours du président Bush sur l'**axe du Mal** (*the axis of evil*); il précisera alors les **grands axes** de sa politique (*main thrust, main themes*)

axer (*vt*): il **axe** son projet autour de deux thèmes (*focus*); une campagne électorale **axée sur l'emploi** (*focused on employment issues*)

ayant droit (*nm*): l'abaissement de l'âge de la retraite augmente le nombre d'**ayants droit** (*beneficiary; person entitled to receive a benefit*)

azimut (*nm*): [*fig*] **enquête tous azimuts** sur le crime de Bobigny (*wide-ranging investigation*); **bombardements tous azimuts** sur le Liban (*all-out bombardment*)

B

baccalauréat (*nm*): titulaire d'un **bac[calauréat]** option Sciences économiques (*[Fr] secondary school examination allowing entry into higher education*); diplômé d'une école de commerce (**bac + 5**) (*having done 5 years of post-Bac studies*); les lycéens manifestent pour **passer le bac blanc**, annulé en raison du boycott de certains enseignants (*[Fr] sit 'mock' Bac examinations*)

bachelier, -ière (*nm,f*): des **bacheliers**, tous types de bacs confondus (*holder of baccalaureat*)

bafouer (*vt*): **bafouant** une loi inscrite dans la constitution (*flout, defy*); les Albanais de Macédoine **se sentent bafoués** par la majorité slave (*feel slighted; feel their rights are flouted*)

bail *pl* **baux** (*nm*): **prendre un bail** de dix ans sur une propriété (*take out a lease*); SEE ALSO **prorogation, renouvellement**

bailleur, -euse (*nm,f*): le **bailleur** va être en droit de relever le loyer de 3,19% (*lessor; landlord*); ses **bailleurs de fonds** étrangers qui lui ont apporté leur aide (*[financial] backer; sponsor*)

baisse (*nf*): nette **baisse** de la production (*downturn, fall*); préférer des **baisses de salaire** à des licenciements (*wage/pay cut*); SEE ALSO **diffusion, ponction, réviser**

baisser (*vi*): le chômage **baisse** aussi en Espagne (*fall*); (*vt*): il ne faudrait pas **baisser** l'impôt sur le revenu (*lower, reduce*)

baissier, -ière (*adj*): la tendance reste donc globalement **baissière** (*bearish [stock market]*)

balance (*nf*): un excédent record de la **balance commerciale** allemande (*trade balance*); la **balance des paiements courants** est déficitaire pour le mois de mai (*balance of payments*)

ballon (*nm*): un simple **ballon d'essai** pour tester les réactions de l'opinion (*test of public opinion; trial run*)

ballottage (*nm*): le voici **en ballottage serré** dans sa circonscription de Sarcelles (*facing a tight second ballot*)

ban (*nm*): un enfant déscolarisé, **en rupture de ban avec la société** (*a social reject; rejected by society*)

banalisation (*nf*): la **banalisation** des rapports sexuels avant le mariage (*generalization*)

banalisé, -e (*adj*): deux policiers à bord d'un **véhicule banalisé** (*unmarked car*)

banaliser [se] (*vpr*): une violence qui **se banalise** (*become commonplace*)

banc (*nm*): la présence du Premier ministre **au banc du gouvernement** (*on the government front bench*); **sur le banc des accusés** aux assises de Rouen (*in the dock*)

bancaire (*adj*): SEE **virement**

banditisme (*nm*): la création d'une unité de répression du **grand banditisme** (*organized crime*)

banlieue (*nf*): la gauche est majoritaire dans les **banlieues ouvrières** (*working class suburbs*); les Minguettes, **banlieue sensible de Lyon** (*problem area on the outskirts of Lyon*); SEE ALSO **mal**

banque (*nf*): une des principales **banques de dépôt** (*clearing bank*); une **banque de données**, accessible en ligne (*data base*)

banqueroute (*nf*): mener son pays au bord de la **banqueroute** (*bankruptcy*); inculpé d'escroquerie et de **banqueroute** (*[fraudulent] bankruptcy*)

barème (*nm*): les tranches du **barème des impôts** ont été relevées de 3,3% (*tax scale*)

baron (*nm*): la puissance des **barons de la presse** (*press baron/ magnate*); parmi les **grands barons** du régime (*political heavyweight*)

barrage (*nm*): se désister en faveur du centriste, afin de **faire barrage** au Front national (*foil, block*)

barre (*nf*): les témoins se succèdent **à la barre** (*in the witness box*); dans l'une des **barres** HLM de cette cité difficile (*high-rise apartment block*)

barreau *pl* **-x** (*nm*): **reçu au barreau** en 2001 (*called to the bar*); la cour d'assises l'a **renvoyé derrière les barreaux** (*send to prison*)

barrière (*nf*): une industrie protégée par des **barrières douanières** (*customs/tariff barriers*)

bas, basse (*adj*): la concurrence des **pays à bas salaires** (*low-wage country*); les compagnies aériennes **à bas coûts**, particulièrement touchées (*low-cost*); (*adv*): tenter de **mettre à bas** le régime des mullahs (*overthrow, topple*); SEE ALSO **nivellement**

basculement (*nm*): le **basculement** de l'opinion en faveur des républicains (*swing*)

basculer (*vi*): depuis trois ans, l'opinion publique a **basculé** (*shift, undergo radical change*); les Etats-Unis pourraient **basculer dans la récession** (*go into recession*)

base (*nf*): un accord doit encore être ratifié par la **base** (*rank-and-file members*); une réunion pour **jeter les bases** d'une politique de l'emploi (*lay the foundations [for/of]*)

bassin (*nm*): des aides à la formation dans les **bassins d'emploi** du Nord (*regional employment area*); dans le **bassin minier** de la Lorraine (*coalfield*)

bastion (*nm*): dans ce **bastion socialiste** qu'est le Nord-Pas de Calais (*Socialist stronghold*)

bâti, -e (*adj/nm*): la **taxe sur le foncier bâti** est payée par les propriétaires (*property tax paid on buildings*); la préservation du **bâti ancien** (*old/historic buildings*)

bâtiment (*nm*): la bonne activité du **bâtiment** profite à de nombreux secteurs (*building/construction*)

bâtir (*vt*): essayer de **bâtir des ponts** entre ZEP et Grandes Ecoles (*build bridges*); SEE ALSO **terrain**

bâtonnier (*nm*): une plainte a été déposée par le **bâtonnier** du barreau de Tours (*[Fr] president of the bar/barristers*)

battage (*nm*): pour comprendre le **battage médiatique** autour des immigrés bulgares en Grande-Bretagne (*media hype*)

battre (*vt*): SEE **pavillon**

bavure (*nf*): l'hypothèse d'une **bavure policière** n'est pas écartée (*police blunder*)

belligérant -e (*adj/nm*): des discussions entre les représentants des **belligérants** (*warring party/faction*); SEE ALSO **partie**

bémol (*nm*): le seul **bémol** de ce débat a été donné par les Socialistes (*discordant note*)

bénéfice (*nm*): hausse de 20% du **bénéfice semestriel** (*half-yearly profits*); l'impôt sur les **bénéfices des sociétés** (*company profits*); les libéraux pourraient **tirer bénéfice** de la crise (*gain advantage [from]*); SEE ALSO **dégager, optimiser**

bénéficier (*vt*): les Français **bénéficient d'avantages sociaux** largement supérieurs (*enjoy welfare benefits*)

bénévolat (*nm*): le **bénévolat**: service assuré par une personne bénévole, sans obligation et gratuitement (*system of voluntary work*)

bénévole (*adj/nmf*): une équipe d'amateurs dirigés par des **bénévoles** (*unpaid voluntary worker*)

benjamin, -e (*adj/nm,f*): **benjamin** d'une famille de six enfants (*youngest [child]*)

beur (*adj/nm*): les **beurs**, ou les Français issus de l'immigration maghrébine (*second generation North African living in France*)

bien (*nm*): hausse des importations de **biens de consommation** courante (*consumer goods*); les importations de **biens et services** ont progressé de près de 15% (*goods and services*); maisons, terrains ou autres **biens fonciers** (*real estate*); tous ses **biens mobiliers** ont été saisis par la justice (*personal estate; moveables*); SEE ALSO **mener**, **séparation**

bienfait (*nm*): profitant des **bienfaits** de la politique agricole commune (*benefit*)

bien-fondé (*nm*): convaincre les compagnies du **bien-fondé** de sa stratégie (*validity*); au-delà du **bien-fondé** ou non de la sentence (*rightness*)

bilan (*nm*): le **bilan** de quatre jours d'affrontements s'élève à 44 morts (*final toll [accident/conflict]*); le **bilan du gouvernement** est globalement positif (*the government's track record*); SEE ALSO **alourdir**, **déposer**, **dépôt**

billet (*nm*): un vendredi noir pour le **billet vert** (*US dollar, greenback*)

bimensuel (*adj/nm*): *L'Actualité*, un **bimensuel** politique canadien (*fortnightly paper*)

blanc, blanche (*adj/nm,f*): certains électeurs ont préféré **voter blanc** (*return a blank vote*); SEE ALSO **baccalauréat**, **bulletin**, **col**, **livre**, **mariage**

blanchiment (*nm*): le **blanchiment** de fonds d'origine criminelle (*laundering [of money]*)

blanchir (*vt*): une loi d'amnistie est venue **blanchir** les coupables (*clear, exonerate*); [*fig*] soupçonné de **blanchir** de l'argent en provenance des pays de l'Est (*launder [money]*)

bleu, -e (*adj*): SEE **casque**

bloc (*nm*): les pays de l'ancien **bloc soviétique** (*Soviet bloc*)

blocage (*nm*): enfin l'Europe est sortie de son **blocage** institutionnel (*impasse; stalemate*); le gouvernement opte pour un **blocage des prix** (*price freeze/controls*); la Pologne dispose d'un **pouvoir de blocage** équivalent à celle de l'Allemagne (*blocking powers*); SEE ALSO **minorité**

blocus (*nm*): mettre fin au **blocus** aérien et maritime (*blockade*); les Etats-Unis **décrètent un blocus naval** d'Haïti (*decide a naval blockade*)

bloqué, -e (*adj*): les négociations sont **bloquées** (*deadlocked*); les salaires sont de fait **bloqués**, mais les prix restent libres (*frozen*)

bloquer (*vt*): il faudrait **bloquer les pensions** pendant trois années consécutives (*freeze pensions*)

bombardement (*nm*): la reprise des **bombardements** (*bombing raid*); SEE ALSO **azimut**

bombarder (*vt*): [*fam*] **être bombardé** ministre de l'enseignement supérieur (*be catapulted [into a job]; be nominated unexpectedly*)

bond (*nm*): un **bond en avant** grâce à l'ADN et aux fichiers informatiques (*leap forward*); en 2007, **les prix ont fait un bond** (*prices have shot up*)

bondir (*vi*): les investissements étrangers ont **bondi** de 44% (*shoot up*)

bonification (*nf*): départ à 55 ans avec **bonifications d'ancienneté** (*long-service bonus*)

bonus (*nm*): un **bonus** de fin d'année de 1.000 euros (*bonus*)

boom (*nm*): l'économie britannique est **en plein boom** (*in a period of expansion*); pendant le **boom immobilier** des années 90 (*real estate/property boom*)

bord (*nm*): regagner la confiance des Irakiens **de tous bords** (*of every party; on all sides*)

bouclage (*nm*): l'allégement du **bouclage** de la bande de Gaza (*sealing off*)

boucler (*vt*): le dossier doit être **bouclé** avant 2009 (*complete, close*); le pacte nucléaire **bouclé** fin juin avec les Etats-Unis (*sign [agreement]*); tout le quartier **fut bouclé par les forces de l'ordre** (*was sealed off by the police*)

bouclier (*nm*): les Etats-Unis projettent d'installer un **bouclier antimissile** en Europe centrale (*missile defence shield*); SEE ALSO **levée**

bouder (*vt*): le Canada menace de **bouder** le sommet de la francophonie (*refuse to attend*); les électeurs bulgares **boudent l'Europe** (*show little interest in/spurn Europe*); SEE ALSO **urne**

boulot (*nm*): les moins de 35 ans qui galèrent dans les **petits boulots** (*odd jobs, casual work*)

bourg (*nm*): ce gros **bourg rural** de quinze mille habitants (*market town*)

bourgade (*nf*): une **bourgade** de 1.500 âmes, dans le Lot (*village, [small] town*)

bourse (*nf*): la reprise a été confirmée à la **Bourse de Londres** (*London Stock Exchange*); les retraités CGT d'Orléans, réunis à la **Bourse du travail** (*trades' council*); SEE ALSO **coter**, **introduction**

boursier, -ière (*adj/nm,f*): les **gains boursiers** sont imposables (*Stock market gains/profits*); des **boursiers** dont les études sont financées par l'Etat (*student in receipt of grant*); SEE ALSO **krach**, **raid**

box (*nm*): dans le **box [des accusés]**, la jeune femme se défend vaillamment (*dock*)

boycottage (*nm*): les appels au **boycottage** de produits français (*boycotting*)

boycotter (*vt*): la ménagère française **boycotte** la viande importée (*boycott*)

bradage (*nm*): l'opposition crie au **bradage** du patrimoine national (*selling off*); le **bradage** de ces territoires (*abandoning*)

brader (*vt*): accusé de **brader** l'héritage du général de Gaulle (*squander*); des exportations **à des prix bradés** sur le marché mondial (*at rock-bottom prices*)

braderie (*nf*): l'Opposition dénonce la grande **braderie** de l'industrie de la défense (*clearance sale; selling off*)

branche (*nf*): les **branches** les plus touchées par la crise (*[industrial] sector*); la **branche armée** du mouvement palestinien, Hamas (*armed wing*)

bras (*nm*): l'agriculture manque de **bras** (*manpower*); la menace que représente le FIS et son **bras armé** (*military wing [of political movement]*); [*fig*] **bras droit** du Premier ministre (*right-hand man*); [*fig*] la Maison-Blanche engage un **bras de fer** avec le Congrès (*trial of strength*)

brèche (*nf*): profiter d'une **brèche** dans la législation (*gap, loophole*)

bretelle (*nf*): la réalisation d'une **bretelle de raccordement** à la RN124 (*connecting/linking section of road*)

brevet (*nm*): décrocher son **brevet [d'études]** (*[Fr] school-leaving certificate*); payer une redevance pour l'utilisation de **brevets d'invention** (*patent*)

breveter (*vt*): **faire breveter** un nouveau procédé (*patent, take out a patent for*)

briguer (*vt*): Hachette **brigue** le troisième rang mondial de l'édition (*strive/bid [for]*); avoir la ferme intention de **briguer l'Elysée** en 2007 (*[Fr] stand for president*); SEE ALSO **succession**

brouille (*nf*): une normalisation, après des années de **brouille** (*quarrel, disagreement*)

bruit (*nm*): des **bruits** sans fondement, déjà amplement démentis (*rumours*)

brûlant, -e (*adj*): autre **dossier brûlant**: le projet d'autoroute (*controversial subject*)

brut, -e (*adj/nm*): le prix du **brut** est en chute libre (*crude oil*); le deuxième **exportateur de brut** du monde (*oil exporting country*); SEE ALSO **produit**

budget (*nm*): le **budget d'austérité** est vivement contesté (*austerity budget*); SEE ALSO **insuffisance**

bulletin (*nm*): déposer dans l'urne son **bulletin de vote** (*ballot/ voting paper*); l'accroissement des **bulletins blancs ou nuls** (*blank or spoiled ballot paper*); la possibilité de voter **à bulletins secrets** la poursuite d'une grève (*by secret ballot*); SEE ALSO **élire**

buraliste (*nm*): le **buraliste**, à la fois préposé de l'administration et commerçant; la vignette auto est en vente chez les **buralistes** (*[Fr] newsagent [also selling cigarettes, stamps etc]*)

bureau *pl* -**x** (*nm*): les timbres fiscaux s'achètent au **bureau de tabac** (*tobacconist*); le **bureau exécutif** du parti, réuni hier (*executive board*); au cours du **bureau national** de la centrale syndicale (*national congress*); SEE ALSO **immeuble**

bureaucratie (*nf*): l'énorme **bureaucratie** des organismes sociaux (*bureaucracy; bureaucratic machine*)

but (*nm*): SEE **lucratif**

buter (*vi*): les négociations **butent** sur des problèmes de souveraineté nationale (*founder*)

butin (*nm*): en vue de l'importance du **butin** dérobé (*[stolen] goods; haul*); **butin de guerre**, le pétrole irakien aux multinationales (*spoils of war*)

butoir (*nm*): SEE **date**

C

cabale (*nf*): la **cabale** montée contre lui par l'aile gauche du parti (*plot; intrigue*)

cabinet (*nm*): former un nouveau **cabinet** (*cabinet [in ministry or government]*); le **cabinet fantôme** du groupe parlementaire socialiste (*shadow cabinet*); un important **cabinet d'audit** de Londres (*accountancy firm*)

cacique (*nm*): son projet de réforme a heurté les **caciques du parti** (*party bosses*)

cadastral, -e *mpl* **-aux** (*adj*): l'établissement et la mise à jour du **plan cadastral** de la commune (*land register*)

cadastre (*nm*): consulter le **cadastre** pour établir les limites exactes de la commune (*land register*)

cadence (*nf*): les syndicats dénoncent les **cadences trop élevées** à l'usine du Mans (*excessive production rates*)

cadre (*nm*): le nombre de femmes **dans les postes de cadre supérieur** (*in senior executive positions*); l'amélioration du **cadre de vie** rural ou urbain (*[living] environment*); SEE ALSO **accord**

caduc, caduque (*adj*): un traité jugé **caduc** à Jérusalem (*null and void*); l'OPA **devient caduque** ce vendredi (*expire; lapse*)

cahier (*nm*): la stricte contrainte des **cahiers des charges** (*schedule of conditions; specifications*); les syndicats remettent leur **cahier de doléances** au ministre du Travail (*[list of] grievances/ demands*)

caillasser (*vt*): les véhicules des pompiers **se font souvent caillasser** (*are often the target of stone-throwing*)

caisse (*nf*): l'expansion actuelle apporte d'abondantes recettes fiscales dans les **caisses de l'Etat** (*the coffers of the state*); des organismes comme les **caisses d'allocations familiales** (*child benefit office*); des achats financés par la **caisse noire** (*slush fund*); SEE ALSO **alimenter**, **facilité**, **livret**

calendrier (*nm*): aucun accord sur un **calendrier** du retrait des forces d'intervention (*timetable*); SEE ALSO **accorder, redécoupage**

calomnie (*nf*): la **calomnie** et la diffamation sont des infractions pénales (*slander, calumny*)

calomnier (*vt*): un avocat condamné pour avoir **calomnié** un magistrat (*slander; libel*)

cambiste (*nm*): d'après les **cambistes**, la baisse de la devise américaine continuera (*foreign exchange dealer/trader*)

camouflet (*nm*): le Bundestag **inflige un camouflet** au gouvernement (*deliver a snub*); la Chine **essuie un camouflet** à Hongkong (*receive a snub/insult*)

campagne (*nf*): il y avait une sur-représentation des **campagnes** dans l'assemblée départementale (*rural areas*); la **campagne électorale** bat son plein (*election campaign*); SEE ALSO **référendaire**

candidat, -e (*nm,f*): deux fois il **fut candidat à la présidence** (*ran for president*); SEE ALSO **députation, porter, pressenti**

candidature (*nf*): il va **poser sa candidature** pour le poste (*apply [for job/post]*)

canton (*nm*): le **canton**, circonscription pour les élections au conseil général (*[Fr] electoral constituency; district*)

cantonal, -e *mpl* **-aux** (*adj*): leurs chances d'emporter les [élections] **cantonales** (*[Fr] elections to the council of the* département); SEE ALSO **consultation**

cantonner [**se**] (*vpr*): la France **se cantonne** dans un rôle de gendarme (*confine/restrict oneself*)

capacité (*nf*): la **capacité** de l'Europe à résister à la compétition américaine (*capability*); sans réduire les **capacités de défense** de la France (*defence capability*)

capital *pl* **-aux** (*nm*): prendre 25% du **capital social** d'une entreprise (*share capital*); Honda **entre dans le capital** de Rover à hauteur de 25% (*buy into; take a stake in*); Sarkozy accroît son **capital confiance** (*popular support*); SEE ALSO **hémorragie**

capitalisation (*nf*): nos entreprises souffrent d'une trop faible **capitalisation** (*capital base*)

capoter (*vi*): l'accord avait **capoté** au dernier moment (*collapse, fall through, fail*)

carcéral, -e *mpl* **-aux** (*adj*): les **conditions carcérales** déplorables des détenus (*prison conditions*); SEE ALSO **surpeuplement**

carence (*nf*): la **carence** des pays socialistes dans ce domaine (*shortcomings; deficiency*); ces pays n'ignorent pas la **carence alimentaire** (*food shortages*); des jeunes **en grande carence affective** (*emotionally deprived*)

caritatif, -ive (*adj*): des opérations caritatives ou humanitaires (*charitable*); SEE ALSO **association**

carnet (*nm*): depuis un an, le **carnet de commandes** s'est rempli (*order book*)

carrière (*nf*): les grévistes réclament une augmentation de 1.000 euros et des **améliorations de carrière** (*better career prospects*); SEE ALSO **déroulement, évolution**

carte (*nf*): l'obtention d'une **carte de séjour** (*residence permit*); le trafic de **cartes grises** d'épaves (*car registration papers; [Brit] vehicle log book*); SEE ALSO **horaire**

cartel (*nm*): l'**office des cartels**, chargé de faire respecter la libre concurrence (*[Brit] monopolies board*)

cas (*nm*): son **cas** a été réexaminé par la cour d'appel (*case*); depuis 1860, ce **cas de figure** s'est présenté huit fois (*case, instance; scenario*); un centre de réinsertion pour **jeunes cas sociaux** (*underprivileged children*)

caser (*vt*): il n'est pas facile de **caser** un jeune Maghrébin (*place in a job*); **[se]** (*vpr*): les diplômés ont moins de problèmes pour **se caser** (*obtain employment*)

casier (*nm*): son **casier judiciaire** est déjà fourni (*criminal record*)

casque (*nm*): incidents entre **casques bleus** et Chypriotes turcs (*UN peace-keeping force*)

cassation (*nf*): dans la perspective d'une éventuelle **cassation** (*quashing [of verdict]*); la **Cour de cassation**, la juridiction suprême (*Supreme Court of Appeal*); SEE ALSO **pourvoi, pourvoir**

casse (*nm*): pillages et **casses** se sont multipliés lors des manifestations (*break-in [house, property]*)

casser (*vt*): la Cour de cassation **cassa** le verdict (*overturn, quash*); obligés de **casser les prix** pour rester compétitifs (*slash prices*)

casse-tête (*nm*): ce dossier est un vrai **casse-tête** pour le ministre (*headache; brain-teaser*); Etats-Unis: **le casse-tête iranien** (*the Iranian problem*)

casseur (*nm*): la présence de **casseurs** dans un défilé pacifique (*rioting demonstrator*); les **casseurs de prix** venus d'Allemagne (*price-buster; hard-discounter*)

catégoriel, -ielle (*adj*): SEE **revendication**

cause (*nf*): l'enquête risque de **mettre en cause** des personnalités importantes (*implicate; incriminate*); des tests ADN l'ont **mis hors de cause** (*clear, exonerate*); cette agitation va **remettre en cause** la croissance de l'économie (*jeopardize, put at risk*); la CGT refuse toute **remise en cause** du Smic (*reconsideration [of]*); SEE ALSO **fait, gain**

caution (*nf*): verser une **caution** de 250 euros (*deposit, down payment*); votre débiteur, ou la personne qui **porte caution** pour lui (*stand surety*); **être laissé en liberté sous caution** pendant toute la durée du procès (*be freed on bail*); les statistiques officielles, bien qu'elles soient **sujettes à caution** (*unreliable; unconfirmed*); SEE ALSO **libérer**

cautionnement (*nm*): chaque candidat paye un **cautionnement** de 1.000 euros (*surety; guarantee*)

cautionner (*vt*): se refuser à **cautionner** la politique du maire (*back, support*)

céder (*vt*): le groupe vient de **céder** sa filiale suisse (*dispose of, sell*); les habitants n'ont pas **cédé** devant le terrorisme (*give in*)

ceinture (*nf*): la progression du Front national dans la **ceinture** parisienne (*peripheral area; belt*); la **ceinture verte** du Val-de-Marne (*green belt*); dans la **ceinture rouge** des Hauts-de-Seine (*Communist belt*)

célibataire (*adj/nmf*): les enfants majeurs **célibataires** (*single, unmarried*); **célibataire**, divorcé ou séparé (*single person*); SEE ALSO **mère**

cellule (*nf*): une **cellule de crise** a été réunie (*crisis/emergency team*); les cinq **cellules de réflexion** mettent en place un plan d'action (*think tank*); les conditions du maintien de la **cellule familiale** (*family unit*)

censure (*nf*): SEE **assouplissement, motion**

central, -e *mpl* **-aux** (*adj/nm,f*): quatre prisonniers s'évadent de la **centrale** de Melun (*prison*); les **centrales [syndicales]** réclament une hausse du pouvoir d'achat (*confederation of trade unions*)

centralisme (*nm*): le trop grand **centralisme** de l'Education nationale (*centralism, control from the centre*)

centre (*nm*): SEE **disputer, hébergement, réinsertion, urbain, urgence**

cerner (*vt*): les manifestants **cernent** le siège du gouvernement (*surround, encircle*)

cessation (*nf*): un plan franco-américain de **cessation** des hostilités (*suspension; cessation*); recourir à la **cessation de travail** pour appuyer une revendication (*stoppage*); **en cessation de paiements**, la société dépose son bilan (*unable to meet its financial obligations*)

cesser (*vt*): les salariés ont **cessé le travail** (*stop work, down tools*); la société en difficultés **cesse ses activités** (*cease trading*)

cessez-le-feu (*nm*): SEE **rompre**

cession (*nf*): la **cession** à la Russie de la flotte ukrainienne (*transfer; handover*); la **cession** de leurs activités minières (*sale, disposal*)

chaîne (*nf*): la suppression du **travail à la chaîne** est l'objectif prioritaire (*assembly-line production*)

chambre (*nf*): la **Chambre basse** du Parlement russe, la Douma (*Lower Chamber/House*); l'instruction terminée, le dossier est transmis à la **chambre d'accusation** (*[Fr] court of criminal appeal*); devant la première **chambre pénale** du tribunal de Paris (*criminal division*)

chance (*nf*): des **chances égales** en matière d'emploi (*equal opportunity*); SEE ALSO **égalité**

chancelier, -ière (*nm,f*): le **chancelier de l'Echiquier**, le ministre anglais des Finances (*[Brit] Chancellor of the Exchequer*); lors d'une rencontre avec la **chancelière** allemande, Angela Merkel (*chancellor*)

chancellerie (*nf*): discorde entre la **Chancellerie** et Matignon (*[Fr] Ministry of Justice*); dans les **chancelleries** occidentales, on s'inquiète (*foreign ministry; chancellery*)

change (*nm*): SEE **agent, contrôle, réserve, taux**

changement (*nm*): mettre en place une politique de **changement** (*change*); la lutte contre le **changement climatique** (*climate change*); SEE ALSO **mobiliser, réticent**

chantier (*nm*): les **mises en chantier** s'élèvent à 310.000 logements cette année (*building start*); ce dossier sera un des **chantiers** prioritaires du gouvernement (*task [reform, project, legislation]*)

chapeauter (*vt*): participer à une opération militaire **chapeautée** par l'Allemagne (*led/overseen by Germany*)

chapelle (*nf*): PS: les vieilles **chapelles** n'ont plus la cote (*clique, coterie*); la nécessité d'en finir avec l'**esprit de chapelle** (*cliquishness*)

chapitre (*nm*): le rapport comporte neuf **chapitres** (*chapter; item*)

charbonnages (*nmpl*): l'opération entraînerait la fermeture de plusieurs **charbonnages** (*coal mine, colliery*)

charcutage (*nm*): procéder à un véritable **charcutage de la carte électorale** (*radical redrawing of electoral boundaries*)

charge (*nf*): un transfert de responsabilités et de **charges** (*responsibility*); aucune **charge** n'a été retenue contre lui (*charge, accusation*); l'ensemble des **charges sociales** qui pèsent sur les entreprises (*overheads [esp. social security contributions]*); pour une **prise en charge** plus efficace des délinquants sexuels (*taking responsibility [for]*); SEE ALSO **cahier**, **enfant**, **locatif**, **plan**, **témoin**

chargé, -e (*adj/nm,f*): quand celui-ci était ministre, **chargé de l'environnement** (*responsible for environmental affairs*); **chargé de mission** au cabinet du ministre de la Ville (*person holding special responsibility*)

charger (*vt*): les autorités ont **chargé** un comité d'experts d'enquêter sur cette affaire (*ask, instruct*)

chassé-croisé (*nm*): un **chassé-croisé** entre Londres et Paris (*to-ings and fro-ings*)

chaud, -e (*adj*): dans un quartier réputé **chaud** de la banlieue de Marseille (*dangerous*); SEE ALSO **annoncer**

chef (*nm*): les prérogatives d'un **chef d'Etat** (*head of state*); **chef de file** du principal parti de l'opposition (*leader*); malgré les réticences des **chefs d'entreprise** (*company director*); les **chefs d'établissement** dans les collèges et lycées (*head, principal*); parmi les **chefs d'inculpation**: association de malfaiteurs et trafic d'influence (*charge, count*); SEE ALSO **diplomatie**, **opposition**

chef-lieu *pl* **-x** (*nm*): les décisions sont prises au **chef-lieu du département** (*[Fr] administrative centre of the département*)

cheminot (*nm*): semaine agitée dans le secteur public: les **cheminots** en grève (*railway worker*)

chèque (*nm*): payer des achats au moyen de **chèques sans provision** (*bad/bounced cheque*); SEE ALSO **émission**, **opposition**

cher, chère (*adj*): SEE **vie**

cherté (*nf*): ils citent la **cherté de la vie**, et la difficulté d'acquérir un logement (*high cost of living*)

chevronné, -e (*adj*): parlementaire **chevronné** et plusieurs fois ministre (*experienced*)

chiffrage (*nm*): un **chiffrage** exact reste difficile à établir (*costing; figure*)

chiffre (*nm*): enregistrer une croissance **à deux chiffres** (*two-figure, in two figures*); un bénéfice de 3 millions d'euros pour un **chiffre d'affaires** de 22 millions (*turnover*)

chiffrer (*vt*): le parti a **chiffré** la plupart des mesures qu'il propose (*cost, estimate the cost [of]*); [**se**] (*vpr*): les morts **se chiffrent en milliers** (*number several thousand*)

choc (*nm*): le **choc** de deux nationalismes (*clash, conflict; collision*); depuis le premier **choc pétrolier** en 1973 (*oil crisis*)

chômage (*nm*): Renault décide des mesures de **chômage partiel** à Douai (*short-time working*); la grève risque de **mettre au chômage technique** de nombreux salariés (*lay off*); SEE ALSO **courbe, indemnisation, inscrit, montée, pointer, résorption, traitement**

chômé, -e (*adj*): une **journée chômée** par semaine dans l'usine d'Angers (*compulsory rest day; day off*)

chômer (*vi*): une partie du personnel devra **chômer** trois jours par mois (*be idle; be on reduced working hours*)

chômeur, -euse (*nm,f*): les **chômeurs de longue durée**, une catégorie exclue des allocations (*long-term unemployed*); SEE ALSO **embaucher, réinsertion**

chronique (*adj/nf*): le déséquilibre **chronique** des finances publiques (*chronic*); dans la **chronique financière** de l'hebdomadaire new-yorkais (*financial column/page*); SEE ALSO **défrayer**

chute (*nf*): la **chute** brutale du prix du pétrole (*fall, collapse*)

chuter (*vi*): les résultats semestriels ont **chuté** de 35% (*fall*)

ciblage (*nm*): le message doit être clair et son **ciblage** précis (*targeting*)

cibler (*vt*): l'annonce est **ciblée** sur les lecteurs du *Point* (*target; aim at*); des secteurs **bien ciblés** de l'économie (*[precisely] targeted*); SEE ALSO **frappe**

circonscription (*nf*): le député de la quatrième **circonscription** du Vaucluse (*electoral constituency/ward*)

circonstance (*nf*): deux **circonstances atténuantes** ont été retenues par le juge (*extenuating circumstances*); pour cette raison il **plaida les circonstances atténuantes** (*tendered a plea in mitigation*)

circulaire (*nf*): une **circulaire** qui porte sur les conditions de l'emploi obligatoire de la langue française (*circular; official instruction*)

circulation (*nf*): la **libre circulation des personnes** en Europe (*[person's] freedom of movement*)

circuler (*vi*): pour **le droit de circuler sans entrave** au sein de l'Union (*freedom of movement*)

citadin, -e (*adj/nm,f*): la France est de plus en plus **citadine** (*urban*); créer de nouvelles relations entre les **citadins** et les ruraux (*city/ town dweller*)

citation (*nf*): une sommation, ou **citation à comparaître** en justice (*court summons*); recevoir une **citation d'huissier** (*bailiff's summons*)

cité (*nf*): adjoint au maire de la **cité** de Bayonne (*municipality; city; town*); une **cité** de 200 logements répartis en huit bâtiments (*housing estate*); une **cité-dortoir** dans la banlieue parisienne (*dormitory town*); SEE ALSO **embraser, malaise**

citer (*vt*): il fut **cité comme témoin** (*call as witness*); toute personne trouvée en possession de drogue sera **citée devant les tribunaux** (*prosecute*)

citoyen, -enne (*nm,f*): elle était bosniaque et **citoyenne yougoslave** (*a Yugoslavian citizen*)

citoyenneté (*nf*): un test de **citoyenneté** pourrait être imposé aux immigrés (*citizenship*); mener une réflexion sur l'**éducation à la citoyenneté** (*teaching citizenship*)

civil, -e (*adj/nm*): la mort de deux **civils** après l'attentat à la bombe hier (*civilian*); le programme nucléaire aura un objectif purement **civil** (*civilian*); SEE ALSO **code, désobéissance, partenariat, partie, procédure, société, union**

civique (*adj*): SEE **droit**

civisme (*nm*): la conscription, considérée comme un outil d'intégration et de **civisme** (*sense of civic duty; public spiritedness*)

clandestin, -e (*adj/nm,f*): la répression du travail **clandestin** (*illegal; undeclared*); un [travailleur] **clandestin** en situation irrégulière (*illegal [immigrant] worker*); SEE ALSO **complaisance, expulsion, régularisation, rétention**

clandestinité (*nf*): le chef des rebelles, aujourd'hui **en clandestinité** (*in hiding*)

classe (*nf*): l'accès de 80% d'une **classe d'âge** au baccalauréat (*age group*); il fustige l'incompétence de la **classe politique** (*political community*)

classer (*vt*): le dossier sera-t-il **classé sans suite**, faute d'éléments? (*close a file on a case; decide there is no case to answer*)

clé, clef (*nf*): la consommation, la **clé** de la reprise tant attendue (*key*); la présence de femmes à des **postes-clés** (*key post*); avec **à la clé** une pression fiscale en hausse de 8% (*as a consequence*); la firme de Rennes **met la clé sous la porte** (*cease trading*)

client, -e (*nm,f*): Airbus: un premier **client** asiatique pour l'A340 (*customer, buyer*)

clientèle (*nf*): sa **clientèle électorale** se trouve dans les banlieues ouvrières (*electoral support*); SEE ALSO **fidéliser**

clientélisme (*nm*): le **clientélisme**, la corruption et la violence politique (*vote-catching gimmicks; populism*)

clignotant (*nm*): [*fig*] tous les **clignotants** sociaux sont au rouge (*warning light; key indicator*)

clivage (*nm*): accentuant le **clivage** entre les deux communautés (*rift; divide*); la décentralisation dépasse les **clivages politiques** (*political divisions*)

clocher (*nm*): [*fig*] stratégies industrielles et **esprit de clocher** (*parochialism*)

clore (*vt*): l'Assemblée **clôt** sa session en adoptant une loi sur la presse (*close, terminate*); la police a décidé de **clore l'enquête**, faute d'éléments (*close [a file]*); [**se**] (*vpr*): le sommet **s'est clos** sur des déclarations d'intention (*close/come to a close [with]*)

clos, -e (*adj*): l'instruction est **close** (*finished, complete*); SEE ALSO **huis clos**

clôture (*nf*): au lendemain de la **clôture** des négociations (*end, conclusion*); les cours de la Bourse **en clôture** (*at close of trading*)

clôturer (*vi*): l'indice CAC 40 **clôture** à 523,9 (*close; register at close of trading*); [**se**] (*vpr*): l'exercice qui vient de **se clôturer** (*come to an end, close*)

club (*nm*): l'Union des **clubs** pour le renouveau de la gauche (*political club*)

coalisé, -e (*adj/nm*): le rejet par les **coalisés** du plan de paix soviétique (*members of a coalition; allies*)

coalition (*nf*): SEE **gouvernement**

code (*nm*): selon le **code civil** (*civil code*); le **code pénal**, le recueil des lois définissant les infractions (*penal code*); SEE ALSO **contrevenant**

coercitif, -ive (*adj*): des mesures plus **coercitives** pour combattre la violence à l'école (*coercive, firm*)

coercition (*nf*): recourir à la **coercition** (*coercion; force*); s'exposer à des **mesures de coercition** par la force des armes (*coercive measures*)

cogestion (*nf*): dans la **cogestion**, les travailleurs participent aux prises de décisions (*joint management, co-management*)

cohabitation (*nf*): des jeunes qui prolongent la **cohabitation** avec leurs parents (*cohabitation*); la période de **cohabitation** qui s'ouvrit en 1986 (*[Fr] situation where the president and the prime minister are from different political parties*)

cohabiter (*vi*): le président socialiste, obligé de **cohabiter** avec une majorité parlementaire conservatrice (*cohabit [politically]*)

cohérence (*nf*): la candidate socialiste entend montrer **la cohérence de son projet** (*how coherent her programme is*)

cohérent, -e (*adj*): poursuivre une stratégie économique **cohérente** dans la durée (*coherent, consistent*)

cohésion (*nf*): le Premier ministre appelle la majorité à la **cohésion** (*solidarity; unity*); reconstituer la **cohésion sociale** dans les banlieues (*social harmony; good community relations*)

coiffer (*vt*): le même ministre **coiffe** à la fois l'aménagement du territoire et l'urbanisme (*head up, have overall responsibility for*)

col (*nm*): augmentation du nombre de **cols blancs** et des emplois féminins (*white-collar worker*)

colistier, -ière (*nm,f*): la tête de liste, mais aussi l'ensemble des **colistiers** (*candidate on same electoral list*)

collaborateur, -trice (*nm,f*): la firme recrute de nouveaux **collaborateurs** à l'étranger (*member of staff, staff*)

collaborer (*vi*): il **collabore** à plusieurs journaux, dont *Le Figaro* (*write [for]*)

collatéral, -e (*adj*): il y a déjà un **dégât collatéral** (*collateral damage*)

collecte (*nf*): des **collectes** pour venir en aide aux sinistrés (*collection*); la propagande et la **collecte de fonds** (*fund-raising*)

collecter (*vt*): les agences de presse **collectent** et diffusent les informations (*collect, assemble*)

collectif, -ive (*adj/nm*): les divers réseaux **collectifs** d'eau, d'électricité et de téléphone (*shared; public*); un **collectif** de soutien aux sans-abri (*action group*); SEE ALSO **convention, crèche, habitat**

collectivité (*nf*): son dévouement au service de la **collectivité** (*community; society as a whole*); la fusion du département et de la région en une seule **collectivité** (*local authority*); la région, élevée au statut de **collectivité territoriale** en 1982 (*[Fr] region enjoying a measure of autonomy*)

collège (*nm*): désigné par un **collège** de notables (*college; body of electors*); la composition du **collège électoral** des sénateurs a été fixée (*electoral college*); SEE ALSO **principal**

collimateur (*nm*): [*fig*] l'incinération **est dans le collimateur des écologistes** (*is under attack by the ecology movement*)

collusion (*nf*): la **collusion** entre classe politique et clans mafieux (*collusion*)

colombe (*nf*): [*fig*] une rare **colombe** parmi les faucons de Washington (*dove [pacifist]*)

colon (*nm*): Israël: l'armée expulse des **colons** à Hébron (*[Jewish] settler*)

colonie (*nf*): évacuer les **colonies de peuplement** en Cisjordanie (*settlement*)

colonne (*nf*): **sur quatre colonnes** à la une de l'édition dominicale (*across four newspaper columns*)

comité (*nm*): des discussions **en comité restreint** (*in a small group*); réunir un **comité d'experts** (*group of experts*); des projets de licenciements révélés au cours d'un **comité d'entreprise** (*works committee*); SEE ALSO **pilotage**

commande (*nf*): les **prises de commandes** ont été très flatteuses (*order*); [*fig*] être capable de **prendre les commandes** d'une entreprise (*take control*); SEE ALSO **annulation, carnet**

commanditaire (*nm*): les tueurs présumés et leurs **commanditaires** (*paymasters*)

commanditer (*vt*): soupçonné d'avoir **commandité** le meurtre (*be behind [crime]*)

commerçant, -e (*adj/nm,f*): le **petit commerçant** est-il condamné à disparaître? (*small shopkeeper*)

commerce (*nm*): malgré un mauvais résultat du **commerce extérieur** (*foreign trade*); un texte condamnant le **commerce des armes** (*arms trade*); les milieux criminels **faisant commerce de drogues dures** (*dealing in hard drugs*); SEE ALSO **détail, dominical, équitable, fonds, libéraliser, voyageur**

commercer (*vi*): les entreprises israéliennes qui **commercent** avec l'Irak (*trade*); la Suisse veut **davantage commercer** avec les Etats-Unis (*do more trade*)

commercial, -e *mpl* **-aux** (*adj/nm,f*): premier partenaire **commercial** de la Chine (*commercial, trading*); embaucher des **commerciaux** (*sales executive*); SEE ALSO **balance, négociation**

commercialisation (*nf*): Renault prévoit la **commercialisation** de ce modèle au Brésil (*marketing*)

commercialiser (*vt*): ses marques sont **commercialisées** dans 70 pays (*market; sell*)

commis (*nm*): plusieurs **grand commis de l'Etat** étaient présents (*senior civil servant*)

commissaire (*nm*): le **commissaire** européen à l'agriculture (*commissioner*); un **commissaire [de police]** a été mis en examen (*[police] superintendent*); le **commissaire aux comptes** présente son rapport aux actionnaires (*auditor*)

commissariat (*nm*): être conduit au **commissariat de police** (*police station*); le **haut commissariat** aux Réfugiés de l'ONU (*High Commission*)

commission (*nf*): la **commission** des affaires culturelles (*committee*); la **commission d'enquête** vient de publier son rapport (*committee of enquiry*); des investigations, sur **commission rogatoire** du juge d'instruction (*commission to take evidence*); le **versement de commissions douteuses** dans des marchés d'exportation (*paying illegal commission*); faire obstacle à la **commission d'un crime** (*committing of a crime*); SEE ALSO **réflexion, sénatorial**

commode (*adj*): l'absence de moyens de transport **commodes** (*convenient*)

commodité (*nf*): par souci d'efficacité et de **commodité** (*convenience*); (*pl*) une absence de **commodités** [voirie, eau potable, évacuation des eaux usées]; à louer, studio avec **commodités** (*services; facilities*)

commun, -e (*adj*): la **déclaration commune** de Londres et Dublin (*joint declaration*); SEE ALSO **droit, tronc**

communal, -e *mpl* **-aux** (*adj*): l'espace **communal** reste l'élément de base de la communauté (*communal, pertaining to the commune*)

communautaire (*adj*): l'Europe **communautaire** avait rendez-vous hier à Strasbourg (*pertaining to the European Community*); SEE ALSO **déroger**

communauté (*nf*): une charge sur la **communauté** (*general public, community*); l'ensemble des communes de la **communauté urbaine** de Bordeaux (*group of urban communes*); SEE ALSO **rapprocher**

commune (*nf*): une petite **commune** rurale du Doubs (*commune, administrative district*)

compagne (*nf*): expulsé de France avec sa **compagne** (*companion, partner [esp. common-law wife]*)

comparaître (*vi*): sept détenus ont **comparu** devant la chambre correctionnelle (*appear [in court]*); SEE ALSO **assignation, citation, délit, mandat**

comparution (*nf*): en attendant une **comparution** devant le conseil de discipline (*appearance [before a court]*); il pourrait **être jugé en comparution immédiate** (*be tried immediately*)

compétence (*nf*): les **compétences** professionnelles d'un candidat (*skill, competence*); on estimait que le ministre **sortait de sa compétence** (*went beyond his/her remit*)

compétent, -e (*adj*): l'absence de personnel formé et **compétent** (*competent, skilled*); les régions **sont compétentes** en matière d'urbanisme (*have authority to act*); s'adresser au **service compétent** (*responsible/appropriate department*)

compétitif, -ive (*adj*): supprimer des emplois pour rester **compétitifs** face à l'américain Boeing (*competitive*)

compétition (*nf*): l'entreprise, soumise à une **compétition accrue** (*increased competition*)

compétitivité (*nf*): améliorer la **compétitivité** de l'usine (*competitiveness*)

complaisance (*nf*): le gouvernement, accusé de **complaisance à l'égard de l'immigration clandestine** (*condoning illegal immigration*); SEE ALSO **pavillon**

complaisant, -e (*adj*): une attitude **complaisante** à l'égard du pouvoir (*indulgent*)

complément (*nm*): toucher le **complément familial** et une aide au logement (*means-tested family allowance*); le juge **demanda un complément d'information** (*asked for further information*)

complice (*adj/nmf*): d'éventuels **complices** susceptibles de commettre un nouvel attentat (*accomplice*)

complicité (*nf*): avec la **complicité** de la communauté internationale (*complicity; collusion*); inculpé de **complicité d'escroquerie** (*conspiracy to defraud*)

composante (*nf*): la **composante** d'extrême droite de la majorité (*element, component*)

composer (*vi*): il devra **composer** avec une Assemblée hostile à ses idées (*come to terms with*); (*vt*): les dix pays qui **composent** l'Afrique australe (*form, make up*)

compréhension (*nf*): Bonn compte sur la **compréhension** de Paris (*sympathy; understanding*)

compression (*nf*): le plan de restructuration conduira à **compression du personnel** (*staff cuts; redundancies*)

compromettre (*vt*): sa femme, également **compromise**, fut blanchie par la commission (*implicated, involved*); [**se**] (*vpr*): un diplomate qui **se compromet** dans une affaire d'espionnage (*compromise oneself*)

compromis (*nm*): un **compromis**, intervenu après treize heures de discussions (*compromise*)

compromission (*nf*): il avait perdu toute crédibilitè par ses **compromissions** avec l'ancien pouvoir (*compromise; [shady]deal; dishonourable behaviour*)

comptabiliser (*vt*): de nombreuses dépenses sont **comptabilisées** dans d'autres rubriques (*post, enter [in ledger]*)

comptabilité (*nf*): les enquêteurs ont épluché la **comptabilité** de la firme d'armements (*go through the accounts*)

comptable (*adj/nm*): compte tenu de l'**échéance comptable** de 1993 (*end of the accounting year*); les **experts-comptables** et les comptables agréés (*accountant*); SEE ALSO **expertise**

comptage (*nm*): des erreurs dans le **comptage des voix** (*counting of votes*)

comptant (*adj*): une remise accordée sur tout achat **comptant** (*cash*); (*adv*): une réduction de 10% pour **règlement au comptant** (*payment* in *cash*); SEE ALSO **payer**

compte (*nm*): approuver les **comptes** de l'exercice 2006 (*financial accounts*); retirer de l'argent d'un **compte de dépôt** (*deposit account*); il a démissionné pour **se mettre à son compte** (*set up his own business*); trois éléments doivent être **pris en compte** (*take into account*); la **prise en compte** du temps de service dans le calcul de la retraite (*taking into account*); la manière dont les médias **rendaient compte de l'affaire** (*reported the case*); SEE ALSO **commissaire, établir, règlement**

compte rendu (*nm*): le **compte rendu** de la réunion permettra de le savoir avec précision (*summary; minutes*)

compter (*vt*): la flotte **compte** 300 bâtiments (*comprise, number*); [**se**] (*vpr*): les morts et les blessés **se comptent par centaines** (*there are thousands of . . .*)

concentration (*nf*): une loi limitant les **concentrations** dans la presse (*merger*)

concertation (*nf*): une **concertation** franco-britannique sur la sécurité européenne (*discussions, dialogue*); la réforme sera précédée d'une **large concertation** (*extensive consultations*)

concerté, -e (*adj*): il faudra un **effort concerté** sur le plan international (*concerted effort*); l'Europe et l'OTAN: vers une **discussion concertée** (*joint discussions*)

concerter [**se**] (*vpr*): après **s'être concertés**, ils ont rejeté l'accord (*consult each other*)

conciliateur, -trice (*adj/nm,f*): nommé **conciliateur** par le ministre dans le conflit de la RATP (*mediator*)

conciliation (*nf*): une **conciliation** est prévue par des accords collectifs (*mediation, conciliation procedure*)

conclure (*vt*): le sommet israélo-palestinien devra **conclure un accord** sur Hébron (*reach an agreement*); le jury **a conclu au meurtre** (*returned a verdict of murder*)

conclusion (*nf*): la **conclusion d'un traité** sur l'interdiction des essais nucléaires (*signing of a treaty*)

concordant, -e (*adj*): des témoignages partiels, mais **tous concordants** (*all in agreement; which all tally*)

concours (*nm*): l'opération, organisée **avec le concours** de la Croix-Rouge (*with the help/support*); l'admission est **par voie de concours** (*by competitive examination*); SEE ALSO **avis, prêter, recruter**

concret, -ète (*adj*): aboutir rapidement à des résulats **concrets** (*concrete, tangible*); acquérir une **formation concrète** (*practical training*); SEE ALSO **mesure**

concrétisation (*nf*): l'emploi dépend de la **concrétisation** éventuelle de commandes en cours de négociation (*confirmation; coming into being*)

concrétiser (*vt*): sa visite permettra de **concrétiser** des projets de coopération entre les deux pays (*give practical effect to; bring to fruition*); **[se]** (*vpr*): un projet qui devrait **se concrétiser** d'ici à dix ans (*materialize; become a reality*)

concubin, -e (*nm,f*): **concubins** et mariés toujours inégaux face à l'impôt (*cohahitant, cohabitee*); SEE ALSO **couple**

concubinage (*nm*): un couple **vivant en concubinage notoire** (*[openly] cohabit, contract a common-law marriage*)

concurrence (*nf*): la **concurrence** en Europe se fait plus vive (*competition*); SEE ALSO **déloyal, face, fausser, jeu, libre, subir**

concurrencer (*vt*): le tunnel va **concurrencer** le trafic trans-Manche (*compete against*)

concurrent, -e (*adj/nm,f*): racheter un de ses principaux **concurrents** (*competitor*)

concurrentiel, -ielle (*adj*): demeurer **concurrentiel** sur un marché agressif (*competitive*)

concussion (*nf*): la **concussion** ou la perception illicite par un agent public de sommes qu'il sait ne pas être dues (*misappropriation of public funds*)

condamnation (*nf*): cette **condamnation** pourra faire jurisprudence (*conviction; sentence*)

condamné, -e (*nm,f*): un droit d'appel qui est ouvert au **condamné** comme au parquet (*sentenced person; convicted prisoner*)

condamner (*vt*): **être condamné** pour détournement de fonds (*be found guilty, be convicted*)

condition (*nf*): la somme de 1.000 euros, versée jusqu'à 16 ans **sous condition de ressources** (*subject to a means test*); SEE ALSO **carcéral, libérer, trêve**

conditionnel, -elle (*adj*): SEE **libération**

conduire (*vt*): c'est ce qu'ont confirmé des expériences **conduites** en Israël (*carry out; conduct*); il **conduisait le pays** pendant ces années difficiles (*govern the country*); SEE ALSO **ruine**

conduite (*nf*): la conception et la **conduite** de la politique étrangère (*conduct*)

confédération (*nf*): deux des grandes **confédérations syndicales** [CGT, CFDT] (*trade union confederation*)

confiance (*nf*): le manque de **confiance des consommateurs** (*consumer confidence*); l'Assemblée nationale a **voté la confiance** au gouvernement (*give a vote of confidence*); SEE ALSO **abus, capital**

confirmer (*vt*): la cour d'appel de Paris **confirme** le jugement du TGI (*uphold, confirm*); [**se**] (*vpr*): la reprise économique, si elle **se confirme** (*is confirmed*); SEE ALSO **ancrage**

confiscation (*nf*): la **confiscation** des terres palestiniennes (*seizure, confiscation*)

confisquer (*vt*): ni le Premier ministre ni le chef de l'Etat ne peut **confisquer la politique extérieure** (*take sole control of foreign policy*)

conflictuel, -elle (*adj*): les grévistes ont obtenu raison sur deux **sujets conflictuels** (*area of disagreement*)

conflit (*nm*): essayer d'empêcher de futurs **conflits sociaux**; mettre fin aux **conflits du travail** (*labour/industrial dispute*); SEE ALSO **enjeu, radicalisation, résoudre**

confondre (*vt*): les partis, **toutes tendances confondues**, sont d'accord là-dessus (*across the whole political spectrum*)

conforme (*adj*): ce qu'il a fait **est conforme à** la Constitution (*is in accordance with*); SEE ALSO **copie**

conformément (*adv*): **conformément** à la loi (*in accordance [with]*)

conformer [se] (*vpr*): le juge, **se conformant** aux réquisitions du parquet, fait arrêter le suspect (*follow, comply [with]*); **se conformer** aux conventions internationales (*abide [by]; conform [to]*)

conforter (*vt*): les entreprises soucieuses de **conforter** leurs parts de marché (*consolidate; increase*); une loi qui **conforte** le monopole gazier de Gazprom (*strengthen, reinforce*)

confusion (*nf*): un texte qui **prête à confusion** (*be open to misinterpretation*); le système de la **confusion des peines** permet de ne prendre en compte que la condamnation la plus lourde (*concurrent prison sentences*)

congé (*nm*): le plan social offre à tout licencié 24 mois de **congé-conversion**; se voir proposer des **congés-formation** (*paid retraining course*); le droit des salariés à des **congés payés** (*paid holiday*); sa décision: **se mettre en congé** du PS (*leave temporarily*); SEE ALSO **maladie, maternité, notifier, parental, sabbatique**

congédier (*vt*): le Premier ministre a **congédié** les commissions mises en place par son prédécesseur (*sack, dismiss*)

conjoint, -e (*adj/nm,f*): une offensive **conjointe** de patrons et de syndicats (*joint; combined*); le **conjoint** survivant se voit totalement exonéré de droits de succession (*spouse, partner*)

conjointement (*adv*): lancer **conjointement** un appel au calme (*jointly*)

conjoncture (*nf*): la **conjoncture** ou l'ensemble des variations à court terme de l'activité économique (*general economic climate*); SEE ALSO **retournement**

conjoncturel, -elle (*adj*): l'environnement **conjoncturel** était plutôt bon (*economic conditions*); cette spirale inflationniste est bien évidemment **conjoncturelle** (*short-term; cyclical*)

conjoncturiste (*nm*): les **conjoncturistes** prédisent une reprise de l'activité économique (*economic forecaster*)

conjugal, -e *mpl* **-aux** (*adj*): SEE **réintégrer**

conjugué, -e (*adj*): la chute **conjuguée** des prix du café et du cacao (*combined*)

conjuguer (*vt*): dans le domaine des transports, la Ville et l'Etat **conjuguent leurs efforts** (*collaborate, work together*)

conscience (*nf*): la **conscience** qu'on a de l'importance du nucléaire (*awareness*); **prendre conscience** de l'importance de l'engagement civique individuel (*realize, understand*); SEE ALSO **liberté, prisonnier**

conscription (*nf*): Allemagne: la **conscription**, longue de neuf mois, ne fait plus recette (*conscription*); SEE ALSO **dérober**

conscrit (*nm*): une armée allemande de **conscrits** (*conscript*)

consécutif, -ive (*adj*): hausse des carburants **consécutive** à celle du baril de pétrole (*following [upon]*)

conseil (*nm*): exercer la profession de **conseil juridique** (*legal adviser; [Brit] solicitor*); le projet sera discuté **en conseil des ministres** (*in Cabinet*); le projet fut accepté par le **conseil d'administration** (*board of directors*); SEE ALSO **société**

conseil général (*nm*): le **conseil général** est élu par tous les électeurs du canton (*[Fr] elected council of a* département)

conseiller, -ère (*nm,f*): un proche **conseiller** du président bosniaque (*adviser*); le maire, avec le **conseiller général** du canton (*councillor in French* département); les **conseillers municipaux** procèdent à l'élection du maire (*local/town councillor*)

conseil municipal (*nm*): lors du dernier **conseil municipal** de Colmar (*meeting of town/city council*)

conseil régional (*nm*): le **conseil régional**, l'administration locale qui se situe au niveau de la région (*regional council*)

consensuel, -elle (*adj*): un des thèmes les plus **consensuels** (*where there is a degree of consensus*)

consensus (*nm*): sur cette question **un consensus s'est dégagé** (*a consensus emerged*)

consentement (*nm*): le divorce **par consentement mutuel** (*by mutual consent*)

consentir (*vt*): on voit les commerçants **consentir d'énormes rabais** pour attirer la clientèle (*offer large discounts*); chez eux, **un effort important est consenti** pour la formation (*a considerable effort has been made*)

conservateur, -trice (*adj/nm,f*): un projet qui séduira la droite **conservatrice** (*conservative*); les **Conservateurs** remportent les élections (*Conservative [party]*)

consigne (*nf*): quelle sera la **consigne de vote** du Front national? (*voting recommendations*); la **consigne de grève** a été largement suivie (*strike call*)

consommateur, -trice (*nm,f*): où sont donc passés les **consommateurs**? (*consumer; customer*); SEE ALSO **défense, confiance**

consommation (*nf*): la **consommation** a augmenté d'environ 5% (*consumption*); le refus de la **société de consommation** (*consumer society*); SEE ALSO **bien, doper, inciter, sagesse**

consommer (*vt*): épargner plutôt que **consommer** (*spend [on consumer goods]*)

constat (*nm*): la commission dressa un **constat** très sévère (*report, conclusion, finding*); la police est venue **faire un constat** sur les lieux (*draw up a report*); faire procéder à un **constat d'huissier** (*bailiff's report*)

constatation (*nf*): deux **constatations** s'imposent (*observation, remark*); selon les **premières constatations** de la commission d'enquête (*preliminary findings*)

constater (*vt*): avec 275.000 crimes et délits **constatés** en 2005 (*record*); il est alors souhaitable de **constater un état des lieux** (*draw up an inventory*); SEE ALSO **avarie**

constituer [se] (*vpr*): il a décidé de **se constituer prisonnier** (*give oneself up, surrender*); SEE ALSO **partie**

constitution (*nf*): la **constitution** de la future équipe présidentielle (*setting-up, forming*); la **constitution** de ghettos ethniques (*formation*); SEE ALSO **non conforme**

consultance (*nf*): spécialiste dans la **consultance** économique (*consultancy*)

consultant, -e (*adj/nm,f*): **consultant** en stratégie d'entreprise dans un cabinet londonien (*consultant*)

consultatif, -e (*adj*): assister à une réunion **à titre consultatif** (*in an advisory capacity*)

consultation (*nf*): l'échec de la majorité lors des **consultations cantonales** de mars 2002 (*[Fr] departmental elections*)

contenir (*vt*): essayer de **contenir** le pouvoir d'achat (*rein in, control*)

contentieux, -ieuse (*adj/nm*): un épineux **contentieux territorial** (*territorial dispute*); s'adresser au **service des contentieux** (*legal department*); SEE ALSO **apurer, liquider, solder**

contenu (*nm*): on n'a pas de détails sur le **contenu** des conversations (*content, substance*)

contestataire (*adj/nm*): le **mouvement contestataire** semble s'essouffler (*protest movement*)

contestation (*nf*): la **contestation** prend de l'ampleur dans les ghettos noirs (*protest movement*); SEE ALSO **larvé**

contester (*vi*): vous pouvez **contester** (*appeal [against decision]*); (*vt*): l'avocat parisien qui avait **contesté le verdict** (*challenge the verdict*)

continent (*nm*): les fonctionnaires attirent l'attention du **continent** sur le malaise corse (*[mainland] France*)

contingent (*nm*): chaque formation reçoit un **contingent** strict d'invitations (*number, quota*); le **contingent** de 1.700 soldats français déployés au Liban (*contingent*); les **soldats du contingent** ont été envoyés pour rétablir la paix (*conscript troops*); SEE ALSO **appelé, recrue**

contingenter (*vt*): les exportations de fruits et légumes, longtemps **contingentées** (*subject to quotas*)

contournement (*nm*): enquête publique sur le **grand contournement** Ouest de Strasbourg (*bypass; ring road*); SEE ALSO **rocade**

contourner (*vt*): la Lituanie tente de **contourner** le blocus économique (*get round, circumvent*)

contracter (*vt*): **contracter un emprunt** pour acheter un bien immobilier (*arrange a loan*)

contractuel, -elle (*adj/nm,f*): avoir recours à des (agents) **contractuels**, non statutaires (*unestablished civil servant; contract staff*)

contraignant, -e (*adj*): des mesures très **contraignantes** pour le régime de Bagdad; notre législation du travail est plus **contraignante** que celle du Royaume-Uni (*restrictive*)

contraindre (*vt*): un troisième ministre **contraint à la démission** (*forced to resign*)

contrat (*nm*): signer un **contrat** (*deed, contract, agreement*); les **contrats à durée déterminée** ou CDD sont devenus la règle (*fixed-term contract*); SEE ALSO **décrocher, inexécution, juteux, remporter, résilier, union**

contravention (*nf*): les faits lui reprochés ne relèvent pas du délit mais de la **simple contravention** (*minor offence*)

contrecoup (*nm*): l'industrie **subit le contrecoup** d'un quasi-doublement de la TVA (*feel the effects*)

contrefaçon (*nf*): la **contrefaçon des marques**, assimilée dorénavant à la contrebande (*imitation of branded goods; pirating*)

contremaître (*nm*): suivre un apprentissage pour passer **contre-maître** (*foreman, supervisor*)

contre-performance (*nf*): une véritable **contre-performance** qui ne se reproduira plus (*bad result; poor performance*)

contre-pied (*nm*): il n'hésite pas à **prendre le contre-pied** de la politique définie par les Socialistes (*take the opposite course*)

contre-pouvoir (*nm*): la rue, seul véritable **contre-pouvoir** (*opposition force*)

contreseing (*nm*): le **contreseing** du Premier ministre est requis (*counter-signature*)

contresigner (*vt*): les actes du Président sont **contresignés** par un ministre (*countersign*)

contrevenant, -e (*nm,f*): aucune sanction n'est prévue contre les **contrevenants** (*offender*); les **contrevenants à la loi** de 1975 (*person in breach of a law*)

contrevenir (*vt*): les pays ayant **contrevenu** à l'embargo pétrolier (*contravene*)

contre-vérité (*nf*): dire des **contre-vérités**, sinon des mensonges (*untruth, falsehood*)

contribuable (*nm*): en 2005, l'ISF a fait fuir au total 649 **contribuables** (*taxpayer*); les **gros contribuables** bénéficieront autant que les cadres moyens des allégements fiscaux (*high taxpayer*)

contribution (*nf*): les **contributions indirectes** sont en France moins onéreuses (*indirect taxation*); travailler aux **contributions** (*[Fr] tax office*)

contrôle (*nm*): les **contrôles** de fin de trimestre (*[academic] test/ assessment*); instaurer des **contrôles à l'entrée dans le pays** (*immigration/customs checks*); procéder à un démantèlement des **contrôles des changes** (*exchange controls*); le juge le laisse libre, mais **sous contrôle judiciaire** (*under legal restrictions*); SEE ALSO **probatoire**

contrôler (*vt*): à la douane, on ne **contrôle** plus les passeports (*check, examine*)

controversé (*adj*): Merkel: une première année **controversée**; la **controversée** carte d'identité biométrique (*controversial*)

contumace (*nf*): condamné en 1997 **par contumace** à six mois de prison ferme (*in his absence*)

conurbation (*nf*): dans la **conurbation** londonienne (*conurbation*)

convaincre (*vt*): le nombre de sportifs **convaincus** d'avoir consommé du cannabis (*convicted/found guilty*)

convenir (*vi*): Paris et Tripoli ont **convenu** d'étudier la mise en place de projets communs (*agree*); (*v impers*): le **traitement qu'il conviendra d'appliquer** aux sociétés privatisées (*appropriate treatment*)

convention (*nf*): la nouvelle **convention** d'assurance-chômage (*agreement, contract*); patronat et syndicats représentatifs signent une **convention collective** (*collective labour agreement*); **tenir une convention** sur l'environnement (*hold a convention/ conference*); SEE ALSO **extradition**

conventionné, -e (*adj*): les **médecins conventionnés** ne sont pas concernés par ce train de mesures (*[Fr] state-approved doctor*)

conversion (*nf*): SEE **congé**, **zone**

convertir [**se**] (*vpr*): des paramilitaires colombiens **se convertissent dans le crime organisé** (*move into organized crime*)

convivial, -e *mpl* **-aux** (*adj*): un ordinateur muni d'un logiciel **convivial** (*user-friendly*)

convivialité (*nf*): les foyers socio-éducatifs et autres lieux de rencontre et de **convivialité** (*social interaction*)

convocation (*nf*): faire obstacle à la **convocation** d'une telle réunion (*convening; convoking*); en refusant de répondre à la **convocation** du juge (*summons*)

convoquer (*vt*): le chef de l'Etat **convoque des élections** pour l'automne (*call elections*); **convoquer** l'ambassadeur pour lui remettre une note de protestation (*send for, summon*)

coopérant (*nm*): travailler au Gabon en qualité de **coopérant** (*[Fr] young person doing national service in a non-military capacity in a developing country*)

coopération (*nf*): la **coopération** prend la forme d'aides financières et d'assistance technique (*[Fr] form of national service involving working abroad on aid project*)

coordination (*nf*): une **coordination** permet de revendiquer sans passer par les syndicats traditionnels (*joint action committee*)

coordonner (*vt*): pour **coordonner** la politique des deux pays (*co-ordinate*); [**se**] (*vpr*): Français et Américains semblent maintenant décidés à **se coordonner** (*co-ordinate their efforts, work together*)

copie (*nf*): l'original ou la **copie conforme** d'un document (*certified true copy*); des journalistes **en mal de copie** (*[who are] short of a story*)

coquille (*nf*): une version dactylographiée pleine de **coquilles** et de fautes de frappe (*misprint; typo*)

corbeille (*nf*): du côté de la **corbeille**, les actions grimpent en flèche (*[Fr] Paris Stock Exchange trading floor, Bourse*)

corps (*nm*): en attendant la décision du **corps électoral** (*electorate; the voters*); devant le **corps diplomatique** au grand complet (*diplomatic corps*); l'ensemble du **corps médical** est hostile au projet (*medical profession*); l'envoi d'un **corps expéditionnaire** (*task force*); SEE ALSO **séparation**, **supplétif**

correct, -e (*adj*): toucher un salaire **correct**, et bénéficier de bonnes conditions de travail (*reasonable, decent*); SEE ALSO **politiquement**

correctionnel, -elle (*adj*): le **tribunal correctionnel** statue sur les délits (*magistrate's court*)

cotation (*nf*): Danone : **cotation** suspendue (*listing, stock exchange quotation*)

cote (*nf*): le Premier ministre améliore sa **cote de popularité** (*approval rating*); [*fam*] le patriotisme économique à la française **n'a pas la cote** à Bruxelles (*is unpopular*); lorsque la **cote d'alerte** est dépassée (*danger point*)

coter (*vt*): la société vient d'**être cotée en Bourse** (*be listed/quoted on the Stock Exchange*)

cotisant, -e (*nm,f*): la population française passera à sept inactifs pour dix **cotisants** en 2008 (*person paying Social Security contributions*)

cotisation (*nf*): la **cotisation** des adhérents d'un syndicat (*membership due, contribution*); une augmentation de la seule **cotisation patronale** (*social security contribution paid by employer*)

cotiser (*vi*): tout assuré ayant **cotisé** à une caisse de retraite (*pay contributions*)

coulisse (*nf*): les consultations se poursuivent **en coulisse** (*behind the scenes*); un habitué des **coulisses du pouvoir** (*corridors of power*)

coup (*nm*): après des rumeurs de **coup de force** à Moscou (*coup*); à la faveur d'un **coup d'Etat** militaire sans effusion de sang (*coup, coup d'état*); **tomber sous le coup** de la nouvelle loi anti-fraude (*fall foul [of a law]*); le procureur les inculpe de **coups et blessures** (*aggravated assault*); SEE ALSO **filet**, **inculpation**

coupable (*adj/nmf*): il a été **jugé coupable** du meurtre de sa patronne (*find guilty, convict*); SEE ALSO **plaider**

coupe (*nf*): **faire des coupes claires** dans les effectifs de la fonction publique (*make drastic cuts/reductions*)

couple (*nm*): la disparition de l'avantage fiscal des **couples concubins** (*cohabiting couple*); les 4,8 millions de personnes **vivant en couple sans être mariées** (*living together; cohabiting*); SEE ALSO **pacsé**

coupure (*nf*): la **coupure** entre la base et la direction du parti (*gap; gulf*); plusieurs **coupures** de 200 euros ont disparu (*[bank]note, bill*)

cour (*nf*): la **cour d'assises** seule peut juger les crimes (*assize court; [Brit] Crown Court*); la Chambre des lords, **cour d'appel ultime** en Angleterre (*court of final appeal*)

courant, -e (*adj/nm*): le Parti socialiste, ses leaders et ses **courants** (*[political] clique*); SEE ALSO **expédier**, **franc**, **issu**

courbe (*nf*): les **courbes** de l'épargne et de la consommation (*curve; graph*)

courir (*vi*): un attentat dont les auteurs **courent encore** (*are still on the run*)

couronne (*nf*): une commune de la **couronne** parisienne (*outer suburbs of Paris*); dans les trois départements de la **petite couronne** (*[Fr] inner ring of* départements *within the Paris region*)

cours (*nm*): la faiblesse actuelle des **cours** (*share price*); le franc est près de son **cours plancher** (*floor, bottom rate*); l'euro est à son **cours plafond** (*ceiling rate*); **suivre des cours** à la faculté (*follow courses*); SEE ALSO **affaissement, envolée**

course (*nf*): la **course aux rendements** dans l'agriculture moderne (*maximizing yields*)

court, -e (*adj*): la **courte** expérience du pluralisme politique (*brief, short*); une **courte victoire** pour le président sortant (*narrow victory*); (*adv*): la gréve générale **prend de court** les dirigeants du pays (*take by surprise*); les négociations ont **tourné court** très rapidement (*be cut short; come to a premature end*); SEE ALSO **vue**

courtage (*nm*): à la Bourse de New York, le **courtage** est informatisé (*share brokerage*); les grandes **firmes de courtage** (*brokerage firm*)

courtier (*nm*): pour les **courtiers** et agents d'assurance (*broker*); **courtier en ligne**, un job qui attire une population jeune qui aime prendre les risques (*on-line broker*)

coût (*nm*): les entreprises essayent de réduire les **coûts salariaux** (*salary/wage costs*); loin de couvrir les **coûts de fabrication** (*production costs*); Continental engage une vaste **réduction de ses coûts** (*cost-cutting exercise*); SEE ALSO **bas, serrer**

coûteux, -euse (*adj*): rendant ces produits aussi **coûteux** que ceux produits en France (*dear, expensive*)

coutume (*nf*): le texte prévoit le maintien des **coutumes** islamiques (*custom, tradition*); SEE ALSO **us**

couverture (*nf*): obtenir une **couverture médicale gratuite** (*free medical cover*); des millions d'Américains sont privés de **couverture sociale** (*social security cover*)

couvre-feu (*nm*): lever le **couvre-feu** imposé il y a une semaine (*curfew*)

couvrir (*vt*): comparaître pour avoir **couvert** le versement de pots-de-vin (*cover up; accept after the fact*); **être couvert** par une assurance médicale personnelle (*have [insurance] cover*)

créance (*nf*): exiger le remboursement de ces **créances** (*money owed, debt*); avec 40 millions d'euros de **mauvaises créances** (*bad debt*); SEE ALSO **lettre**

créancier, -ière (*nm,f*): les **créanciers** de la Pologne commencent à serrer la vis (*creditor*)

crèche (*nf*): les enfants qui sont gardés dans des **crèches** collectives (*day nursery*); SEE ALSO **inexistant**

crédibilité (*nf*): le terrorisme avait **porté atteinte à la crédibilité** de l'OLP (*damage the credibility*); SEE ALSO **entamer**

crédible (*adj*): aucune dissuasion purement conventionnelle n'est **crédible** en Europe (*credible*); son projet est **peu crédible** aux yeux de la Gauche (*unconvincing*)

crédit (*nm*): un **crédit immobilier** se prend sur 20 ans (*mortgage loan*); tous les **crédits-formation** étaient épuisés pour 2005 (*training money*); SEE ALSO **débloquer, encadré, encadrement**

créditeur, -trice (*adj/nm,f*): son compte est **créditeur** de 2.300 euros (*in credit*); la centaine de banques **créditrices** (*creditor*)

créer (*vt*): **créer** de nouveaux postes (*create*); [**se**] (*vpr*): 3.000 nouvelles associations **se créent** chaque année (*are set up*); SEE **zizanie**

créneau *pl* **-x** (*nm*): leader sur certains **créneaux du marché** (*market sector*); [*fig*] le syndicat a l'air bien décidé à **monter au créneau** (*intervene; get involved*)

creusement (*nm*): **creusement du déficit** français des échanges de marchandises (*increasing deficit*)

creuser (*vt*): la France exporte plus mais **creuse son déficit** (*go further into the red*); [**se**] (*vpr*): **le fossé se creuse** entre les Etats-Unis et l'Europe (*the gap widens*)

creux, -euse (*adj/nm*): octobre à décembre, les **mois creux** de l'année (*slack months*); une bonne année, puis le **creux** de 1993 (*slack period*)

criant, -e (*adj*): les carences dans ce domaine apparaissent **criantes** (*glaring; flagrant*)

crime (*nm*): les **crimes** sont des infractions graves (*crime, [criminal] offence*); SEE ALSO **banalisation, commission, convertir, lieu**

criminalité (*nf*): le succès du gouvernement dans la lutte contre la **petite criminalité** (*petty crime; small crimes*); SEE ALSO **fléchissement, montant, répression**

criminel, -elle (*adj/nm,f*): un projet de loi introduisant un appel **en matière criminelle** (*in criminal cases*); lors du procès des **criminels de guerre** (*war criminals*); SEE ALSO **procès, réclusion**

crise (*nf*): chacun a ressenti les effets de la **crise** (*[economic] crisis, slump*); une des villes qui ont été les plus frappées par la **crise des banlieues** (*suburban decay and deprivation*); hausse des prix, **crise du logement** (*housing shortage*); SEE ALSO **cellule, endiguer, frais, réunion**

crispation (*nf*): malgré la **crispation** dogmatique de ce gouvernement (*inflexibility, unbending attitude*)

crisper [**se**] (*vpr*): ces dernières semaines, **les relations se sont crispées** (*tension has increased between them*)

croissance (*nf*): une très forte **croissance démographique** (*population growth*); dans un contexte de **croissance nulle** au troisième trimestre (*zero growth*); SEE ALSO **laissé-pour-compte, objectif, prévaloir, pronostic, soutenu, tirer**

croissant, -e (*adj*): l'écart **croissant** entre riches et pauvres (*growing, increasing*); à cause des **besoins croissants** en sources d'énergie (*growing needs/requirements*)

croître (*vi*): la dette extérieure de l'Asie ne cesse de **croître**; la production **croît** à un rythme soutenu (*grow, rise, go up*)

culpabilité (*nf*): une inculpation n'implique nullement la **culpabilité** de la personne inculpée (*guilt*)

culte (*nm*): un pays où tous les citoyens jouissent de la **liberté de culte** (*religious freedom*)

cumul (*nm*): grâce au **cumul des peines**, il passera 12 ans en prison (*adding together prison sentences*); le **cumul des mandats** locaux et nationaux (*multiple office-holding*)

cumuler (*vt*): il devient député, poste qu'il **cumule** avec la mairie de Châteauroux (*hold concurrently*); le nouveau P-DG va **cumuler les deux fonctions** (*hold both positions concurrently*)

cure (*nf*): la **cure d'austérité** se poursuit (*austerity policy/ measures*)

cursus (*nm*): l'école propose des **cursus** de trois ans (*academic course*); l'accompagnement des élèves tout au long de leur **cursus scolaire** (*school career, education*)

D

danger (*nm*): l'**enfance en danger** est devenue le domaine des départements (*children at risk*); SEE ALSO **non-assistance**

date (*nf*): se donner une **date limite** pour aboutir; la nouvelle **date butoir** est le 15 mai (*deadline; final date*)

débat (*nm*): cette délicate question **fait débat** parmi les experts (*be a subject of debate*); SEE ALSO **dépassionner**, **houleux**

débattre (*vt*): le sujet sera **débattu** lors d'un comité exécutif (*debate, discuss*)

débauchage (*nm*): le **débauchage** des quinze ouvriers alimente la chronique locale (*laying-off, making redundant*)

débaucher (*vt*): les entreprises ont tendance à **débaucher** (*lay off staff*)

débit (*nm*): réduire le **débit** du pétrole exporté par oléoduc (*flow, rate of flow*); un timbre fiscal peut se procurer dans n'importe quel **débit de tabac** (*tobacconist*)

débiter (*vt*): créditer son compte et **débiter** celui de son créancier (*debit*)

débiteur, -trice (*adj/nm,f*): les quinze Etats les plus fortement **débiteurs** (*in debt*); lorsque le **débiteur** ne respecte pas ses engagements (*debtor*)

déblocage (*nm*): le **déblocage** de 50.000 euros et la création de deux postes d'enseignement (*release [of funds]*); vers un **déblocage de la crise irakienne** (*end of the deadlock in Iraq*)

débloquer (*vt*): de part et d'autre, on veut **débloquer la négociation** (*get talks back on course, break the deadlock*); il promet de **débloquer des crédits** (*release funds*)

déboires (*nmpl*): les **déboires** industriels de l'avionneur Airbus continuent (*setbacks*)

débordement (*nm*): le gouvernement craint des **débordements** lors de la manifestation paysanne (*things getting out of hand*)

débouché (*nm*): un **débouché** pour les armes soviétiques (*outlet, market*); le marché du travail n'offre plus de nouveaux **débouchés** (*opening, job prospect*)

déboucher (*vi*): ces négociations pourraient **déboucher** sur des coopérations solides (*lead to, result in*)

débouter (*vt*): dans 50% des cas, **le plaignant est débouté** (*the plaintiff's case is dismissed*); les **déboutés** du droit d'asile (*person whose application/appeal has been rejected*)

débrayage (*nm*): un **débrayage** d'une heure à l'usine Peugeot (*stoppage*); en attendant, des **débrayages tournants** doivent toucher les sites français d'Alcatel (*stoppages by rota*)

débrayer (*vi*): les ouvriers **débrayent** pour protester contre l'agression (*stop work*)

débridé, -e (*adj*): la menace d'un interventionnisme **débridé** (*unbridled, unfettered*)

décalage (*nm*): il y a six heures de **décalage horaire** avec la France (*difference with local time; time gap*); Chirac et Prodi **en décalage** sur la Syrie (*out-of-step, in disagreement*)

décalé, -e (*adj*): être un peu **décalé par rapport à l'opinion** (*out of step with public opinion*)

décennie (*nf*): 4.500 emplois ont disparu en une **décennie** (*period of ten years, decade*)

décentralisation (*nf*): le débat sur la **décentralisation** (*devolution; decentralization of decision-taking responsibilities*)

décharge (*nf*): la fermeture prochaine de la **décharge** municipale (*dump, rubbish tip*); SEE ALSO **arguer, témoin**

décharger (*vt*): certaines firmes **sont déchargées** en partie de leurs impôts (*be exempt*); [**se**] (*vpr*): le département devra **se décharger** de certaines de ses fonctions sur les communes (*hand over, relinquish*)

déchet (*nm*): le ramassage des **déchets recyclables** (*recyclable waste*); le tri sélectif est un passage obligé pour **valoriser les déchets** (*recover waste [for recycling]*)

déchetterie (*nf*): une **déchetterie** où il est possible d'apporter tout ce qui est recyclable ou toxique (*waste collection centre*)

déchirer [**se**] (*vpr*): les Libanais **se déchirent** devant une opinion publique impuissante (*tear each other apart*)

déchoir (*vt*): la fiancée française d'un étranger est menacée d'**être déchue de ses droits civiques** (*be deprived of her civil rights*)

déchu, -e (*adj*): le président **déchu** a été conduit à l'aéroport militaire (*deposed*)

décider (*vt*): SEE **suite**

décideur (*nm*): organiser des rencontres avec les **décideurs** économiques de la région (*decision-taker*)

décision (*nf*): le tribunal rendra sa **décision** le 8 novembre (*verdict*); disposer d'un réel **pouvoir de décision** (*decision-taking powers*); SEE ALSO **révoquer, surseoir**

décisionnel, -elle (*adj*): il faut repenser le système **décisionnel** concernant l'économie du pays (*decision-making*); SEE ALSO **organe**

déclaration (*nf*): remplir un formulaire de **déclaration de sinistre** (*insurance claim notification*); le montant de ses **déclarations fiscales** (*declaration of income [for tax purposes]*); SEE ALSO **commun**

déclarer (*vt*): il n'avait pas à **déclarer ses revenus** en France (*declare one's income*); [**se**] (*vpr*): **un incendie s'est déclaré** hier en fin d'après-midi (*a fire broke out*); SEE ALSO **utilité**

déclenchement (*nm*): depuis le **déclenchement** de l'Intifafa en 2005 (*outbreak*)

déclencher (*vt*): ses propos ont **déclenché un véritable tollé** (*provoke an outcry of protest*)

décliner (*vt*): le président a **décliné** son invitation au sommet de Lyon (*refuse; decline, turn down*); refuser de **décliner son identité** (*give one's name*)

décollage (*nm*): [*fig*] le **décollage** de l'économie du Sud-Ouest (*take-off; getting off the ground*)

décoller (*vi*): sans apport massif de crédits, l'économie ne **décollera** pas (*get off the ground; take off*)

décommander (*vt*): la visite a été **décommandée** (*cancel*); [**se**] (*vpr*): un empêchement l'a obligé à **se décommander** (*cancel visit/appearance*)

décompte (*nm*): selon un **décompte** arrêté dimanche (*count; calculation*); en attendant l'ultime **décompte des voix** (*counting of votes*)

décompter (*vt*): déduire ou **décompter** les voix frauduleuses (*subtract, deduct*); on a **décompté** 1.800 morts à Bagdad en juillet (*count*)

déconcentration (*nf*): une plus grande **déconcentration** des services de l'emploi (*devolving, decentralizing*)

déconcentrer (*vt*): **déconcentrer** l'autorité gouvernementale (*devolve, decentralize*)

déconfiture (*nf*): la spectaculaire **déconfiture** du gouvernement (*defeat, rout*)

déconvenue (*nf*): une **déconvenue** pour le président socialiste (*disappointment; disaster*)

décote (*nf*): le titre étant coté à 3 euros, la **décote** atteint donc 12% (*fall in value/price*); le couple bénéficie d'une **décote de 20%** au titre de la résidence principale (*tax relief of 20%*)

découpage (*nm*): procéder à un nouveau **découpage électoral** (*drawing of constituency boundaries*)

découper (*vt*): **découper** un canton en trois circonscriptions électorales (*divide, cut up*)

décret (*nm*): selon le **décret** paru vendredi au *Journal officiel* (*decree, edict, order*)

décréter (*vt*): la décision de **décréter** un embargo sur les livraisons d'armes (*decree, order*); SEE ALSO **blocus**

décrispation (*nf*): un nouveau signe de la **décrispation Est-Ouest** (*easing of tension between East and West*)

décrisper (*vt*): leur libération va **décrisper la situation** (*ease/defuse the situation*)

décrochage (*nm*): le taux de **décrochage scolaire** (*doing badly at school; persistent truancy*); un **décrochage** international de l'industrie française (*falling behind; losing ground*)

décrocher (*vi*): certains étudiants **décrochent** en première année (*drop out [university]*); quand les salaires **décrochent de l'inflation** (*fail to keep up with inflation*); (*vt*): **décrocher un gros contrat** en Chine (*win a large order*)

décroître (*vi*): la ville de Paris a continué à voir sa population **décroître** (*decrease*)

décuplement (*nm*): le **décuplement** en dollars du prix du brut (*tenfold increase; large rise*)

décupler (*vi*): la population de Lagos a **décuplé** en 30 ans (*increase tenfold*); (*vt*): la crise eut pour effet de **décupler** le prix du brut (*increase tenfold*)

dédommagement (*nm*): les **dédommagements** versés aux familles des victimes (*compensation*)

dédommager (*vt*): **dédommager** partiellement les pieds-noirs de la perte de leurs biens (*compensate; indemnify*)

déduction (*nf*): la **déduction fiscale** d'une partie des cotisations syndicales (*deduction from taxable income*); SEE ALSO **bénéficier**

défaillance (*nf*): le nombre des **défaillances d'entreprises** a progressé de 10% (*company collapse; bankruptcy*)

défaillant, -e (*adj*): le nombre des **entreprises défaillantes** a progressé de 9% (*failed company/business*)

défalcation (*nf*): crédité de 1.000 voix d'avance, après **défalcation** des voix frauduleuses (*deduction*)

défalquer (*vt*): il a fallu **défalquer** les 2.000 voix suspectes (*deduct, subtract*)

défaut (*nm*): être arrêté par la police pour **défaut de port de casque** (*failure to wear a helmet*); les exportateurs, assurés contre les **défauts de paiement** (*default on payment*); l'innovation **fait défaut** dans ce pays (*be lacking, be in short supply*); SEE ALSO **jurisprudence**

défavorisé, -e (*adj/nm,f*): dans les zones urbaines et rurales **défavorisées** (*poor; disadvantaged*)

défection (*nf*): la **défection** d'une partie de son électorat (*defection; desertion*); **faire défection** et demander le droit d'exil (*defect*)

défendeur, -eresse (*nm,f*): le **défendeur**, la personne contre laquelle est engagé un procès civil (*defendant*)

défendre [se] (*vpr*): Bush **se défend** pied à pied sur l'Irak (*defends his policy*); **se défendre** d'être un néo-libéral (*deny*)

défense (*nf*): la **défense** a jusqu'au 19 novembre pour faire appel (*[counsel] for the defence*); une association de **défense des consommateurs** (*consumer protection/rights*); il est pour la **défense de fumer** dans les lieux publics (*ban on smoking*); SEE ALSO **capacité**, **légitime**

défenseur (*nm*): les **défenseurs** des inculpés demandent la relaxe (*defence counsel*)

déférer (*vt*): les parlementaires de l'opposition **défèrent** la nouvelle loi au Conseil constitutionnel (*submit; refer*); treize personnes ont été **déférées au parquet** (*refer for trial*)

défi (*nm*): l'Allemagne face au **défi** de l'Europe à vingt-sept (*challenge*); répondre aux **défis de la mondialisation** (*challenges of globalization*); SEE ALSO **relever**

défiance (*nf*): le Japon manifeste sa **défiance** à l'égard de la Chine (*mistrust, distrust*); le Sénat italien infirme le **vote de défiance** du 21 février (*vote of no confidence*)

déficit (*nm*): l'aggravation du **déficit extérieur** (*external trade deficit*); le **déficit d'exploitation** du groupe ne cesse de s'alourdir (*operating loss*); le problème du **déficit démocratique** (*absence of democracy*); SEE ALSO **creusement, creuser**

déficitaire (*adj*): les comptes lourdement **déficitaires** de la société (*showing a deficit*)

défier (*vt*): les dissidents continuent à **défier** la junte birmane (*defy*)

défilé (*nm*): en province, **défilés** spontanés et affrontements (*[protest] march*)

défiler (*vi*): lycéens et étudiants ont de nouveau **défilé** hier (*march [esp. in protest]*)

défiscalisation (*nf*): la **défiscalisation** totale est un attrait certain de ces propositions (*exemption from tax*)

défiscaliser (*vt*): des rémunérations en partie **défiscalisées** et dispensées de charges sociales (*exempt from tax*)

défrayer (*vt*): un incident qui a **défrayé la chronique** locale (*make the headlines*)

dégagement (*nm*): les conséquences du **dégagement** jordanien de Cisjordanie (*withdrawal, disengagement*)

dégager (*vt*): la firme a enfin **dégagé un bénéfice** (*make a profit*); [**se**] (*vpr*): deux tendances **se dégagent** de l'étude de l'OCDE (*emerge*); SEE ALSO **consensus**

dégât (*nm*): l'ampleur des **dégâts** (*damage, destruction*); la protection contre le **dégât des eaux** (*flooding; flood damage*)

dégel (*nm*): [*fig*] le **dégel** dans les relations sino-soviétiques (*thaw, détente*)

dégradation (*nf*): le nombre de vols et de **dégradations** (*damage [to property]; vandalism*); la **dégradation de la situation** en Algérie (*worsening situation*)

dégradé, -e (*adj*): la rénovation des quartiers **dégradés** (*run-down, dilapidated*)

dégrader (*vt*): les 35 heures **dégradent** la productivité des entreprises françaises (*damage, cause damage [to]*); [**se**] (*vpr*): la vie quotidienne des Parisiens **se dégrade** (*get worse, deteriorate*)

dégraissage (*nm*): procéder à un **dégraissage des effectifs** (*laying-off of staff*)

dégraisser (*vt*): la firme doit **dégraisse**r 1.000 postes supplémentaires (*cut back/shed [jobs]*); avec un appareil de production **dégraissé** (*leaner, slimmed down*)

dégrèvement (*nm*): des exonérations et des **dégrèvements fiscaux** (*tax relief*)

dégrever (*vt*): ces gains sont **dégrevés d'impôts** (*exempt from tax*)

dégringolade (*nf*): préoccupé par la **dégringolade** des cours du pétrole (*rapid fall; slump*)

dégringoler (*vi*): Villepin **dégringole** dans les sondages (*fall sharply, slump*); les prix **dégringolent** (*fall sharply, tumble*)

déjouer (*vt*): Londres **déjoue** un projet d'attentats terroristes (*foil*)

délabrement (*nm*): le **délabrement urbain** partout présent dans ces villes du nord du pays (*urban blight/decay*)

délai (*nm*): avant l'expiration des **délais** fixés par les ravisseurs (*deadline*); le **délai de résidence** requis pour acquérir la nationalité italienne (*period of residence*)

délégation (*nf*): envoyer une **délégation** auprès du ministre (*delegation*); **agir par délégation** pour le président (*act as proxy*); refuser toute **délégation de souveraineté** (*delegation of sovereignty*)

délégué, -e (*adj/nm,f*): le **délégué syndical** a communiqué la décision patronale aux travailleurs (*union representative; [Brit] shop steward*); SEE ALSO **ministre**

déléguer (*vt*): les Etats **délèguent** certains pouvoirs à Bruxelles (*delegate*)

délibéré (*nm*): lors du **délibéré**, il a surtout été question du premier des deux chefs d'inculpation (*deliberation by a court*); le tribunal a **mis son jugement en délibéré** au 26 juin (*adjourn for further deliberation*)

délicatesse (*nf*): Elf Aquitaine **en délicatesse** avec les autorités nigérianes (*in dispute*)

délictueux, -euse (*adj*): la vente et l'importation du hachisch restent **délictueuses** (*a criminal offence*); on les soupçonnait fortement d'autres **activités délictueuses** (*criminal activities*)

délinquance (*nf*): la **délinquance** quotidienne a doublé en dix ans (*crime*); la **grande délinquance** a beaucoup décru (*serious crime*); SEE ALSO **juvénile**

délinquant, -e (*adj/nm,f*): durcir la répression contre les **jeunes délinquants** (*juvenile delinquent; young offender*); SEE ALSO **enfance**

déliquescence (*nf*): tandis que l'URSS était **en pleine déliquescence** (*in a state of total decay*)

délit (*nm*): coupable du **délit** de recel (*offence*); dans le cas d'un **délit mineur** (*misdemeanour*); purger une peine de prison pour **délit de presse** (*violation of laws governing the press*); la COB enquête pour décider s'il y a eu **délit d'initié** (*insider dealing*); SEE ALSO **opinion**

délivrance (*nf*): la **délivrance** de plein droit d'une carte de séjour (*issue*)

délivrer (*vt*): le pouvoir de **délivrer** les permis de construire (*grant, issue*); le collège ne **délivre** aucun diplôme (*award*)

délocalisation (*nf*): la **délocalisation** des unités de production dans des pays à bas salaires (*relocation; transfer*)

délocaliser (*vt*): les industriels qui **délocalisent** leur production hors Hexagone (*relocate*); [**se**] (*vpr*): les entreprises qui désirent **se délocaliser en province** (*transfer operations to the provinces*)

déloyal, -e (*adj*): la **concurrence déloyale** des grandes surfaces vis-à-vis du petit commerce (*unfair competition*)

demande (*nf*): la **demande** est largement supérieure à l'offre (*demand*); le nombre de **demandes d'asile** déposées en 2006 en chute de 8% (*application for asylum*); SEE ALSO **approvisionner, gonflement**

demandeur, -eresse (*nm,f*): le **demandeur** a obtenu gain de cause (*plaintiff, complainant*)

demandeur, -euse (*nm,f*): les **demandeurs d'emploi** représentent 15% de la population active (*job-seeker*)

démantèlement (*nm*): le **démantèlement** de plusieurs réseaux internationaux (*breaking up*); procéder au **démantèlement des droits de douane** prévu par le traité (*removal of customs duties*)

démanteler (*vt*): Bruxelles: trafic de drogue **démantelé** (*break up*); il est question de **démanteler** le monopole public de l'électricité (*break up, dismantle*)

démarrage (*nm*): la campagne électorale a connu un **démarrage** hésitant (*start, beginning*)

démarrer (*vi*): les ventes **ont bien démarré** (*got off to a good start*); (*vt*): **démarrer** une affaire avec très peu d'argent (*start up*)

démenti (*nm*): **apporter un démenti** aux rumeurs de désunion (*deny*)

démentir (*vt*): il **dément** avoir eu des contacts avec les Iraniens (*deny*); [**se**] (*vpr*): un boom de la consommation **qui ne se dément pas** (*which continues unabated*)

démettre (*vt*): le roi a **démis** son ministre **de ses fonctions** (*dismiss, remove from office*); [**se**] (*vpr*): les élus **se sont démis** en bloc (*resign*)

demeure (*nf*): **mettre en demeure** les autorités de se prononcer sans délai (*instruct, order*); recevoir une **mise en demeure** d'un créancier (*notice to pay*)

démission (*nf*): il a **donné sa démission** au Président (*tender one's resignation*); la conséquence de la permissivité et de la **démission des parents** (*abdication of parental responsibility*); SEE ALSO **contraindre**, **lettre**, **remettre**

démissionnaire (*adj*): le premier ministre turc **démissionnaire** a sauvé sa coalition (*having tendered his resignation*)

démissionner (*vi*): l'impopulaire premier ministre nippon refuse de **démissionner** (*resign*); (*vt*): le ministre vient d'**être démissionné** par le Président (*be dismissed*)

démobiliser (*vt*): c'est un sale coup et qui va **démobiliser** le personnel (*demotivate*)

démuni, -e (*adj/nm*): la Grande-Bretagne **démunie** face aux défis sécuritaires (*powerless*); les femmes **démunies** et sans emploi (*impoverished, destitute*); dans un centre d'hébergement pour **les démunis** (*the destitute*)

dénégation (*nf*): en dépit des **dénégations** de Matignon (*denial*)

déni (*nm*): le **déni de justice** fait aux Palestiniens (*denial of justice, injustice*)

denier (*nm*): la population la plus déshéritée, habituée à **vivre des deniers publics** (*live off the state/on public funds*)

dénier (*vt*): la Russie **dénie** à l'OTAN le droit de décider des raids aériens (*refuse; deny*)

dénouement (*nm*): le **dénouement** sanglant de la prise d'otages (*outcome, conclusion*); le principal obstacle au **dénouement de la crise actuelle** (*resolution of the present crisis*)

dénouer (*vt*): réussir à **dénouer** un conflit (*resolve, end*); [**se**] (*vpr*): alors que la crise tarde à **se dénouer** (*come to an end; be resolved*)

denrée (*nf*): une **denrée** très recherchée (*commodity*); la montée de prix des **denrées alimentaires** et de l'immobilier (*foodstuffs*)

dénuement (*nm*): pour ceux qui vivent **dans le dénuement le plus total** (*in utter destitution*)

déontologie (*nf*): veiller au bon respect de la **déontologie** des médias (*code of professional ethics*)

déontologique (*adj*): cette solution poserait de graves problèmes **déontologiques** (*ethical, of professional ethics*)

départ (*nm*): il faudrait hâter les **départs à la retraite**, surtout en cas d'invalidité (*retirement*); une prime de 10.000 euros en cas de **départ volontaire** (*voluntary redundancy*); SEE ALSO **incitatif, indemnité, prime**

département (*nm*): la Corse est formée de deux **départements** (*[Fr] department: one of the main administrative divisions of France*)

dépassé, -e (*adj*): une vision **dépassée** de l'Europe (*outdated*)

dépassement (*nm*): le **dépassement** par rapport à la cible de Kyoto sera de 34% (*exceeding, overshooting*); le **dépassement budgétaire** est évalué à 10 milliards d'euros (*overspend*)

dépasser (*vt*): la demande a largement **dépassé** l'offre (*exceed*); le médecin peut **dépasser ces tarifs** pour certains soins (*charge higher fees*)

dépassionner (*vt*): son regard extérieur et neutre permet de **dépassionner le débat** (*take the heat out of [debate, discussions]*)

dépénalisation (*nf*): le débat sur la **dépénalisation** des drogues douces (*decriminalizing*)

dépénaliser (*vt*): devrait-on **dépénaliser** l'usage des drogues douces? (*decriminalize*)

dépendance (*nf*): le développement de la toxicomanie et la **dépendance à l'égard de l'aide sociale** (*dependency culture*)

dépendant, -e (*adj*): l'aide à domicile pour **personnes dépendantes** (*dependent persons*)

dépens (*nmpl*): acquitté, il a été **condamné aux dépens** (*order to pay costs of [court action]*)

dépense (*nf*): la maîtrise des **dépenses publiques** (*public expenditure*); le transfert aux collectivités locales de certaines **dépenses d'équipement** (*capital expenditure*); SEE ALSO **allouer**

dépensier, -ière (*adj*): nos concitoyens sont parmi les plus **dépensiers** pour leur santé (*spendthrift, extravagant*)

dépeuplement (*nm*): le **dépeuplement** dont souffre la Creuse (*depopulation*)

dépeupler [**se**] (*vpr*): le département de la Creuse **se dépeuple** progressivement (*become depopulated, lose its population*)

dépistage (*nm*): le **dépistage** du sida (*detection*)

dépister (*vt*): pour **dépister** le risque d'abus sexuel (*detect*)

déplacé, -e (*adj*): Liban: réintégration des **personnes déplacées** (*displaced person*)

déplacement (*nm*): le **déplacement** annoncé du Premier ministre en Chine (*journey, trip*); il y a eu des **déplacements de voix** considérables (*electoral swing*)

déplafonnement (*nm*): le **déplafonnement** des allocations familiales (*removal of ceiling*)

déplafonner (*vt*): en abaissant et en **déplafonnant** le taux des cotisations familiales (*remove ceiling/upper limit*)

déplaire (*vt*): ce contrat militaire avec la Chine **a déplu à Washington** (*displeased Washington*)

déploiement (*nm*): le Soudan accepte le **déploiement** d'une force 'hybride' au Darfour (*deployment*)

déployer (*vt*): le contingent italien **déployé** en Bosnie (*deployed*); [**se**] (*vpr*): l'immense activité qui **se déploie** actuellement en océan Indien (*be deployed*)

déposant (*nm*): un krach ne toucherait pas les **petits déposants** (*small investor/saver*)

déposer (*vi*): des témoins venus **déposer** devant le tribunal (*testify, give evidence*); (*vt*): 1989: invasion américaine pour **déposer** le dictateur (*depose, overturn*); 24.000 dossiers de régularisation ont été **déposés** (*submit [application]*); la société vient de **déposer son bilan** (*go into voluntary liquidation*); SEE ALSO **arme, plainte, pourvoi, préavis, recours**

déposition (*nf*): tout au long du procès, il a maintenu sa **déposition** (*statement, evidence*); au lendemain de la **déposition** du président (*deposing, deposition*)

dépôt (*nm*): avant la date limite de **dépôt des dossiers de candidature** (*submitting of applications*); beaucoup de PME sont **au bord du dépôt de bilan** (*facing bankruptcy*); en garde à vue **au dépôt** de la préfecture de police (*in a police cell*); SEE ALSO **banque, compte, mandat**

dépouillement (*nm*): après le **dépouillement des suffrages** (*counting of votes*)

dépouiller (*vt*): le temps requis pour **dépouiller un scrutin** (*count the votes*)

dépression (*nf*): la récession prend des allures de **dépression** (*depression, slump*)

déprime (*nf*): la Bourse a eu un nouvel accès de **déprime** mercredi (*gloom; depressed trading conditions*)

déprimé, -e (*adj*): une activité économique **déprimée** (*depressed*)

déprimer (*vi*): le yen s'effondre, la bourse **déprime** (*slump; be depressed*); (*vt*): le nouveau reflux du dollar a **déprimé** le franc (*depress, force down*)

députation (*nf*): **candidat à la députation** dans la 7ᵉ circonscription de Seine-et-Marne (*[Fr] parliamentary candidate*)

député, -e (*nm,f*): **député** socialiste et président du conseil général (*deputy, member of the French National Assembly*); membre de la SFIO, et **député-maire** de Marseille (*deputy and mayor*); SEE ALSO **fauteuil, non-inscrit, suppléance**

dérapage (*nm*): [*fig*] on s'inquiète des **dérapages** que pourrait entraîner l'application de ce décret (*abuse, excess*); il est vital qu'il n'y ait pas **dérapage de l'inflation** (*spiralling inflation*)

déraper (*vi*): [*fig*] les prix ont **dérapé** cette année (*rise sharply*); les comptes de l'assurance-maladie **dérapent** (*go out of control*)

déréglementation (*nf*): la **déréglementation** mondiale de la communication (*decontrolling, deregulation*)

dérégulation (*nm*): la **dérégulation** ou la suppression du monopole exercé par les entreprises publiques (*deregulation*)

déréguler (*vt*): il faut libéraliser la formation des prix, il faut **déréguler** (*deregulate*)

dérisoire (*adj*): les **dérisoires** retraites des agriculteurs (*derisory; absurdly low*)

dérive (*nf*): l'évolution des finances publiques, ou plutôt leur **dérive** (*drifting off course/out of control*); pour empêcher une **dérive terroriste** de l'islamisme (*drift towards terrorism*)

dérogation (*nf*): l'octroi d'une **dérogation** à la fermeture de dimanche (*dispensation*); les **dérogations** consenties aux Britanniques sont multiples (*exemption*)

déroger (*vi*): continuer à **déroger à la réglementation communautaire** (*go against Community rules*); ce serait **déroger à la règle établie** (*depart from established practice*)

déroulement (*nm*): le **déroulement** de l'enquête (*unfolding; progress*); la réforme leur assure un meilleur **déroulement de carrière** (*career development*)

dérouler [**se**] (*vpr*): les négociations de paix qui **se déroulent** à Genève (*take place*)

déroute (*nf*): une humiliante **déroute** pour le parti au pouvoir (*heavy defeat, rout*)

désaccord (*nm*): le PS et ses alliés **affichent leurs désaccords** sur presque tous les sujets (*display their disageements*); Ottawa et Washington toujours **en désaccord** sur la souveraineté arctique (*in disagreement*)

désaffection (*nf*): la **désaffection** qui menace les Conservateurs (*fall-off of support*)

désarmement (*nm*): accord sur le **désarmement** des rebelles (*disarming*); le **désarmement** dans le cadre d'un accord bilatéral (*disarmament*)

désarmer (*vi*): temps de travail: les professeurs **ne désarment pas** (*keep up the pressure; refuse to give in*)

désaveu *pl* -**x** (*nm*): un **désaveu** de sa politique en Irak (*rejection*); pour le Président, le **désaveu** est cinglant (*rebuff*)

désavouer (*vt*): désigné comme chef du parti, puis **désavoué** par les électeurs (*reject*)

désenclavement (*nm*): le **désenclavement** de la façade maritime, avec le projet autoroutier (*opening up*); une nouvelle étape dans le **désenclavement routier** du Massif central (*improved road access*)

désenclaver (*vt*): un projet susceptible de **désenclaver** le Gers, et donc de développer l'ouest du département (*open up, make less isolated*)

désendetter (*vt*): soucieux de **désendetter** l'Etat, le ministre maintient le cap choisi par son prédécesseur (*reduce the debt [of]*)

désengagement (*nm*): un **désengagement** total de Moscou sur la scène internationale (*disengagement*); l'Ethiopie poursuit son **désengagement** de Somali (*withdrawal*)

désengager [se] (*vpr*): le gouvernement a décidé de **se désengager** de l'opération (*pull out*)

désertification (*nf*): un département agricole **en voie de désertification** (*losing population*); des problèmes qui sont liés à la **désertification rurale** (*rural depopulation*)

désertifier [se] (*vpr*): l'espace rural continue à **se désertifier** (*become depopulated*)

désescalade (*nf*): Londres-Pékin: la **désescalade** (*reduction of tension*)

déshérité, -e (*adj/nm,f*): dans les quartiers les plus **déshérités** (*deprived*); les **déshérités**, les plus durement touchés par la crise (*underprivileged*)

désignation (*nf*): la **désignation** d'un successeur (*naming; choice; appointment*)

désigner (*vt*): **désigner** son dauphin (*name, appoint*)

désistement (*nm*): peu de **désistements**, beaucoup de candidats se maintiennent (*withdrawal [in favour of a better placed candidate]*)

désister [se] (*vpr*): le candidat socialiste **se désiste** en faveur du communiste (*withdraw, stand down*)

désobéissance (*nf*): l'opposition appelle à la **désobéissance civile** (*civil disobedience*)

désolidariser [se] (*vpr*): la classe politique **s'est désolidarisée** du président colombien (*dissociate o.s., withdraw one's support*)

dessaisir (*vt*): **dessaisir un juge** pour incompétence (*remove a judge from a case*); [se] (*vpr*): **se dessaisir** de ses fonctions d'adjoint au maire (*resign, relinquish office*)

dessaisissement (*nm*): son avocat demande et obtient le **dessaisissement du juge** (*removal of a judge [from a case]*)

desserte (*nf*): améliorer la **desserte** du site par les transports en commun (*service [esp. by public transport]*); le problème de la **desserte autoroutière** vers Paris (*motorway link*)

desservir (*vt*): le port de Dunkerque **dessert** tout le nord-ouest de l'Europe (*serve*); le Gers **n'est desservi par aucune voie de chemin de fer** (*possesses no railway connections*)

dessous (*nm*): admettre des **versements de dessous-de-table** à des partis politiques (*back-hander, under-the-counter payment*)

destituer (*vt*): les Républicains allemands **destituent** leur président (*dismiss*); le Congrès américain peut **destituer** le Président (*depose*)

destitution (*nf*): au lendemain du vote de **destitution** à l'endroit du président (*dismissal, removal from office*)

détaché, -e (*adj*): le personnel français **détaché** à l'étranger (*on secondment; on temporary assignment*)

détacher (*vt*): il a été **détaché** au ministère des Finances en 1997 (*second, assign temporarily [to]*)

détail (*nm*): dans le **commerce de détail** l'emploi reste un gros point noir (*retail sector; retailing*); SEE ALSO **prix**, **valeur**

détaillant, -e (*nm,f*): les **détaillants** vont répercuter cette hausse sur le consommateur (*retailer*)

détaxe (*nf*): une **détaxe** sur le prix imposé pour les livres scolaires (*reduction of tax*)

détaxer (*vt*): l'Etat peut **détaxer** la partie du revenu consacrée à l'épargne (*reduce tax on*)

détenir (*vt*): l'Etat **détient** 45% du capital de la firme (*hold, possess*); la police pourra **détenir** tout suspect pendant une durée de sept jours (*detain, hold in detention*)

détente (*nf*): la **détente** entre les deux super-puissances (*detente, improvement in relations*)

détenteur, -trice (*nm,f*): les **détenteurs** d'un passeport britannique (*holder*)

détention (*nf*): la **détention** de faux papiers (*being in possession of*); effectuer quatre ans de **détention provisoire** (*custody [pending trial]*); SEE ALSO **ordonnance**

détenu, -e (*adj/nm,f*): le nombre de **détenus** s'élevait à 50.000 personnes (*prisoner*)

déterminant, -e (*adj*): cette victoire, **déterminante** pour l'avenir du parti (*crucial, decisive*); un témoignage qui pourrait **s'avérer déterminant** (*prove decisive*)

détournement (*nm*): une affaire de **détournement** de subventions municipales (*misuse of funds*); inculpé de **détournement de mineur** (*abduction of a minor; corruption of a minor*)

détourner (*vt*): accusé d'avoir **détourné des fonds** qu'il avait fait voter en conseil municipal (*embezzle funds*)

dette (*nf*): la **dette extérieure** de l'Asie ne cesse de croître (*foreign debt*); la **dette des ménages** s'élève à 1.900 milliard d'euros (*household debt*); SEE ALSO **tiers-monde**

dévalorisation (*nf*): la progression du nombre des enseignants a facilité la **dévalorisation** de leur traitement (*devaluation; depreciation*)

dévaloriser [**se**] (*vpr*): le métier d'enseignant **se dévalorise** au fil des réformes (*lose prestige; be devalued*)

devancer (*vt*): **devancé** au premier tour, il se retira en faveur du socialiste (*head, lead*)

développement (*nm*): sur le thème de l'écologie et du **développement durable** (*sustainable development*)

déviance (*nf*): l'homosexualité était considérée comme une **déviance** (*deviant behaviour*)

déviant, -e (*adj*): réduire les comportements **déviants** (*deviant*)

déviation (*nf*): les travaux de la future **déviation** de Châteaudun ont débuté (*bypass*)

devise (*nf*): Patrie, Justice, Travail: la **devise** du parti unique (*motto, slogan*); la **devise** américaine est très demandée en ce moment (*currency*)

devoir (*nm*): invoquer un **devoir d'ingérence** au Darfour (*duty to intervene*)

dévolu, -e (*adj*): les nouvelles compétences **qui sont dévolues** à la région (*which have been allocated*)

dévolution (*nf*): des **dévolutions** successives de souveraineté au profit d'institutions internationales (*devolution, transfer*)

dialogue (*nm*): cette lettre poursuit le **dialogue de sourds** entamé avec le PS (*dialogue of the deaf*); SEE ALSO **approfondissement, renouer, volonté**

dialoguer (*vi*): Paris **dialogue** déjà avec l'Iran à propos du Liban (*talk, have talks*)

diffamation (*nf*): porter plainte pour **diffamation** (*slander; libel*); les **procès en diffamation** se multiplient en Grande-Bretagne (*libel action*)

diffamatoire (*adj*): des propos **diffamatoires** et mensongers (*defamatory; libellous*)

diffamer (*vt*): une personne qui s'estime **diffamée** peut attaquer la presse (*libel*)

différend (*nm*): des **différends** sur le futur statut du Kosovo persistent (*disagreement*); la Lettonie règle son **différend frontalier** avec la Russie (*border dispute*)

différer (*vt*): la Belgique **diffère** sa décision sur l'achat de l'avion français; chez les femmes désireuses de **différer** leur maternité (*defer, postpone*)

difficulté (*nf*): l'insertion des **jeunes en difficulté** ou victimes de l'exclusion (*children with learning/emotional difficulties*); SEE ALSO **sectoriel**

diffuser (*vt*): son portrait a été **diffusé** dans tous les aéroports (*distribute; circulate*); selon un nouveau bilan **diffusé** hier (*publish, put out*); SEE ALSO **tract**

diffusion (*nf*): après la **diffusion** du communiqué (*broadcast*); le magazine, qui subit une **baisse de sa diffusion** (*drop in circulation*)

dilapidation (*nf*): la lutte contre la **dilapidation** des fonds publics (*waste, squandering*)

dilapider (*vt*): les contribuables ont le sentiment que l'Etat **dilapide** leurs deniers (*fritter away, squander*)

diligenter (*vt*): l'ONU souhaite **diligenter une enquête** sur les massacres (*carry out an urgent enquiry*)

diminuer (*vi*): l'activité devra **diminuer** d'autant l'an prochain (*decrease*); (*vt*): on propose de **diminuer les effectifs** dans l'usine de Caen (*cut back on staff/numbers*)

diminution (*nf*): le temps partiel et la **diminution** du temps de travail; la **diminution** de l'impôt sur les fortunes (*reduction*)

diplomatie (*nf*): certains aspects de la **diplomatie américaine** (*American foreign policy*); première visite à Bagdad d'un **chef de la diplomatie française** (*French Foreign minister*)

diplomatique (*adj*): SEE **appui, corps, froid, incident, marchandage, rupture**

diplôme (*nm*): quitter l'école **sans diplôme** (*without qualifications*)

diplômé, -e (*adj/nm,f*): **diplômé** d'une école de commerce (*graduate*); les jeunes **diplômés** condamnés au chômage (*graduate; person with qualifications*)

directeur, -trice (*adj/nm,f*): le **directeur** du quotidien *Le Monde* (*editor-in-chief*); le président et le **directeur général** ont été renouvelés (*managing director*)

direction (*nf*): conserver la **direction** du parti (*leadership*); une rencontre entre **direction** et syndicats (*management*); avec le concours de la **direction** des affaires culturelles (*section, department*); SEE ALSO **assurer, douane, équipement, surveillance**

directive (*nf*): Bruxelles prépare une **directive** bien plus souple que la législation française (*directive, instruction*)

directoire (*nm*): l'établissement d'un **directoire** mondial en matière de sécurité (*directorate*); être nommé président du **directoire** (*directorate; board of directors*)

dirigeant, -e (*adj/nm*): les femmes sont peu représentées dans les **positions dirigeantes** (*senior or management positions/posts*); deux **dirigeants** de la société ont été arrêtés (*director*); les **dirigeants** socialistes s'y sont opposés en bloc (*leadership; leader*); SEE ALSO **instance**

diriger (*vt*): la première femme à **diriger** le parti (*lead*)

dirigisme (*nm*): le **dirigisme** de l'Etat français critiqué (*interventionism*)

dirigiste (*adj*): le choix entre une vision libérale et des solutions **dirigistes** (*interventionist*)

discours (*nm*): prononcer un **discours** devant l'ONU (*speech*); le **discours** d'extrême droite sur l'immigration (*rhetoric, discourse*); SEE ALSO **outrance**

discrimination (*nf*): lutter contre la **discrimination liée à l'âge** (*age discrimination*); l'absence de toute **discrimination fondée sur le sexe** (*sexual discrimination*)

discriminatoire (*adj*): des lois contre des **pratiques discriminatoires** (*discrimination, discriminatory practices*)

discriminer (*vt*): le système ne **discrimine** pas les petites entreprises (*discriminate against*)

disette (*nf*): passer d'une situation de **disette** à l'autosuffisance (*scarcity; food shortages*)

dispense (*nf*): bénéficier d'une **dispense** du service militaire (*exemption*); **accorder une dispense** pour des motifs graves (*grant a dispensation*)

dispenser (*vt*): des journées de formation **dispensées** par les cadres de l'INSEE (*give, dispense*); 6% des jeunes gens **sont dispensés** du service national (*be exempted*)

disponibilité (*nf*): de bonnes **disponibilités en logements** pour les employés (*availability of accommodation/housing*); la firme possède plus de 30 milliards de **disponibilités** (*liquid assets*); tenu pour responsable, il a été **mis en disponibilité** (*suspend from duty*)

disponible (*adj*): le **revenu disponible** par habitant, après impôts et cotisations sociales (*disposable income*)

disposer (*vt*): il affirme **le droit des peuples à disposer d'eux-mêmes** (*the right of nations to self-determination*)

dispositif (*nm*): un **dispositif** d'accueil et d'aide aux victimes (*scheme, operation*); au milieu d'un impressionnant **dispositif de sécurité** (*security operation*); le **dispositif policier** – plusieurs centaines d'hommes – se voulait discret (*police presence*)

disposition (*nf*): le Conseil constitutionnel annule deux **dispositions** de la loi des finances (*clause*); la police va **prendre les dispositions nécessaires** (*take all necessary measures*); dans un local **mis à disposition** par la mairie (*provide, supply*); la **mise à disposition** de 7.000 habitations à loyer plafonné (*provision [of]*)

disputer (*vt*): Strasbourg **dispute** à Bruxelles le titre de capitale européenne (*compete; vie for*); [**se**] (*vpr*): les deux partis **se disputent le centre** (*vie for the centre ground*)

dissension (*nf*): le projet suscite des **dissensions profondes** au sein du cabinet (*fundamental disagreement*)

dissidence (*nf*): l'Eglise américaine est au bord de la **dissidence** (*rebellion, breakaway*); deux sénateurs communistes ont **fait dissidence** (*break away, rebel*)

dissident, -e (*adj/nm,f*): le plus connu des **dissidents** chinois (*dissident*); le **groupe dissident** défie le parti (*dissident group*)

dissolution (*nf*): la **dissolution** de l'Assemblée nationale (*dissolving*); dans des situations de **dissolution de la cellule familiale** (*break-up of the family unit*)

dissoudre (*vt*): date à laquelle Londres doit **dissoudre** l'Assemblée (*dissolve*); le nouveau Président **dissoudra le Parlement** (*dissolve Parliament*)

dissuasif, -ive (*adj*): la peine de mort **est dissuasive** pour les terroristes (*is a deterrent*); en vente **à un prix dissuasif** (*at a prohibitive price*)

dissuasion (*nf*): la peine de mort peut **exercer un effet de dissuasion** (*deter*); le refus de la **dissuasion nucléaire** (*nuclear deterrent*)

divers, -e (*adj*): les listes **divers droite** et FN ont fusionné (*different right-wing*); SEE ALSO **fait divers**

diversification (*nf*): quelques initiatives de **diversification** industrielle ont été prises à temps (*diversification*)

diversifier (*vt*): la crise conduit la région Champagne-Ardennes à **diversifier ses activités** (*diversify*); [**se**] (*vpr*): Dell envisagerait de **se diversifier** dans la téléphonie mobile (*diversify, move [into]*)

dividende (*nm*): payer aux actionnaires un **dividende** confortable (*share dividend*)

doléance (*nf*): les **doléances** exprimées par les jeunes (*grievance*); SEE ALSO **cahier**

domicile (*nm*): l'emploi d'une **personne à domicile** donne droit à une réduction d'impôt (*domestic help*); le nombre de **sans domicile fixe** [SDF] s'accroît (*person of no fixed abode*); en 1992, il a **élu domicile** à Paris (*adopt as one's official address*); SEE ALSO **aide**, **inviolabilité**, **réintégrer**, **violation**

domicilier (*vi*): un ressortissant algérien **domicilié** à Londres (*living, residing*); les SDF peuvent **se faire domicilier** auprès d'un centre communal d'action sociale (*give as one's address [for official purposes]*)

dominical, -e *mpl* **-aux** (*adj*): ce quotidien, dans son **édition dominicale** (*Sunday edition*); autoriser le **commerce dominical** (*Sunday trading*); les commerces sont condamnés au **repos dominical** (*ban on Sunday trading; Sunday closing*); SEE ALSO **ouverture**

dommage (*nm*): l'indemnisation des **dommages** subis (*damage, prejudice*); il demande 10.000 euros de **dommages et intérêts** (*damages*)

dommageable (*adj*): ce blocage est **dommageable** à l'ensemble de l'économie mondiale (*prejudicial, harmful*)

don (*nm*): collecter des **dons** et des cotisations (*gift, donation*)

donation (*nf*): suppression des droits de **donation** et de succession (*settlement*)

donne (*nf*): la poussée des écologistes change la **donne politique** (*political balance of power*)

donnée (*nf*): ceci complique un peu plus les **données** du conflit israélo-arabe (*facts; situation*); le chômage a augmenté de 0,7%, **en données corrigées des variations saisonnières** (*according to seasonally adjusted figures*); SEE ALSO **banque, base**

donner (*vt*): **être donné largement battu** par tous les sondages (*be expected to lose heavily*); SEE ALSO **gain, lecture**

doper (*vt*): accroître les salaires pour **doper la consommation** (*stimulate consumption*)

dossier (*nm*): 2.000 **dossiers** ont été déposés par des demandeurs d'emploi (*application*); les syndicats restent divisés sur les **grands dossiers sociaux** (*major social questions*); autre **dossier sensible**: l'immigration (*difficult question*); SEE ALSO **brûlant, instruction, instruire, placard**

dotation (*nf*): la faiblesse de la **dotation** de la Comédie-Française (*grant, subsidy*)

doter (*vt*): les missiles **dotés** de charges conventionnelles (*equipped [with]*); [**se**] (*vpr*): l'Ecosse **se dote** d'un Parlement et de nouveaux pouvoirs (*acquire, obtain*); la Turquie **se dote** d'un gouvernement proeuropéen (*set up*)

douane (*nf*): abolition progressive des **droits de douane** (*customs duties*); SEE ALSO **passage**, **préposé**

douanier, -ière (*adj/nm,f*): SEE **barrière**, **tarif**

doublement (*nm*): Washington annonce le **doublement** de son aide à l'Ukraine (*doubling*)

doubler (*vi*): les exportations de produits finis ont **doublé** (*double*); (*vt*): un élève qui **double** sa classe de troisième (*repeat [a year]*)

doute (*nm*): ces révélations **mettent en doute** leurs affirmations (*cast doubts upon*); l'adoption du texte **ne semble pas faire de doute** (*seems assured*)

doyen, -enne (*nm,f*): le **doyen** de la nouvelle Assemblée (*oldest member*)

draconien, -ienne (*adj*): des **mesures draconiennes** de rétorsion furent prises (*draconian measures*)

drainage (*nm*): l'irrigation, le **drainage** et l'entretien des digues (*drainage*)

drainer (*vt*): élargir un ruiseau, **drainer** un marécage (*drain*); les collectivités locales **drainent** 12% des revenus fiscaux (*bring in [taxes]*)

drapeau *pl* **-x** (*nm*): le Nicaragua, avec plus de 100.000 hommes **sous les drapeaux** (*doing military service*)

droit (*nm*): l'Ecosse a un **droit** distinct du droit anglais (*legal system; system of law*); une infraction qui relève du **droit pénal** (*criminal law*); le mouvement pour les **droits civiques** aux Etats-Unis (*civil rights*); l'ivresse publique **relève du droit commun** (*is a common-law offence*); manifester pour les **droits des femmes** [avortement, contraception, emploi] (*women's rights*); empêcher l'exercice des **droits de la personne humaine** (*human rights*); le **droit du travail** anglais ne prévoit pas de période d'essai (*employment law*); leurs produits d'exportation sont frappés de **droits** anti-dumping (*duty, tax*); SEE ALSO **allocation**, **ayant droit**, **douane**, **égalité**, **Etat**, **plier**, **préemption**, **privation**, **règle**, **sang**, **sol**, **succession**, **valoir**, **veto**

droit, -e (*adj/nf*): quand **la Droite** est arrivée au pouvoir (*the Right*); flattant les sensibilités **de droite** (*right-wing*); SEE ALSO **basculement**, **divers**, **extrême**, **glissement**, **jeu**, **ultra**, **virer**

dumping (*nm*): estimant qu'il s'agissait de **dumping caractérisé** (*a clear case of dumping*); il faut appliquer les **règles anti-dumping** qui existent déjà (*anti-dumping laws*)

dur, -e (*adj/nm*): tous, sauf les **durs** du parti (*hardliner*); SEE ALSO **coup, ligne, noyau, pur, tendance**

durable (*adj*): Liban: l'ONU en quête d'une solution **durable** (*lasting*); SEE ALSO **aboutir, développement**

durcir (*vt*): la junte **durcit** sa politique de répression (*harden*); Paris presse l'ONU de **durcir le ton** avec l'Iran (*take a harder line*); [**se**] (*vpr*): la révolte **se durcit** au fil des jours (*intensify*)

durcissement (*nm*): un **durcissement** de l'attitude américaine (*hardening*); le **durcissement des sanctions** contre les mineurs (*stiffer penalties*)

durée (*nf*): la **durée** de la garantie (*duration, length*); la **durée de vie moyenne** de la femme (*life expectancy*); à la recherche d'un **poste salarié à temps plein et à durée indéterminée** (*full-time permanent position*); SEE ALSO **chômeur, contrat, hebdomadaire**

dysfonctionnement (*nm*): une table ronde sur le **dysfonctionnement** de l'économie corse (*dysfunction, malfunctioning*)

E

eau *pl* **-x** (*nf*): à la limite des **eaux territoriales françaises** (*French territorial waters*); les **eaux usées**, traitées dans des stations d'épuration (*waste water; effluent*); les **eaux ménagères** et les eaux d'origine industrielle (*waste [household] water*); SEE ALSO **adduction, dégât, voie**

ébranler (*vt*): une nouvelle affaire de corruption **ébranle** le pouvoir (*shake; weaken*); le parti **sort durement ébranlé** de ce scrutin (*emerge in a much weakened state*)

écart (*nm*): un accroissement de l'**écart des revenus** entre les riches et les pauvres (*income gap*); les deux hommes, **mis à l'écart** en 2004 (*sideline; sack*); des fautes sanctionnées par mutations ou **mises à l'écart** (*dismissal*)

écarter (*vt*): cette décision visait à **écarter** un homme jugé dangereux (*exclude, eliminate*); une coalition **écartée du pouvoir** au bout d'un an (*remove from power*); il **écarte** cependant toute augmentation du prix de l'essence (*rule out*)

échange (*nm*): la bonne tenue des **échanges** avec le Japon (*trade, commerce*); SEE ALSO **barrière, libéralisation**

échanger [**s'**] (*vpr*): plus de 10% des actions de la société **se sont échangées** hier (*change hands; be traded*)

échangeur (*nm*): un **échangeur** au cœur de l'agglomération lilloise (*road interchange*)

échantillon (*nm*): l'enquête portait sur un **échantillon** de 3699 personnes (*sample; specimen*)

écharpe (*nf*): l'**écharpe tricolore** que porte le maire (*[mayor's] sash*); le maire sortant a réussi à **garder son écharpe** (*be re-elected [as mayor]*)

échauffourée (*nf*): à Paris hier, **échauffourées** au cours d'une manifestation (*scuffle; skirmish*)

échéance (*nf*): cette **échéance** va obliger les deux antagonistes à s'entendre (*deadline*); incapable de rembourser les **échéances** de leurs crédits (*repayment*); les deux **échéances électorales** importantes de 2007 (*election*); son mandat **arrive à échéance** en février (*expire, come to an end*); SEE ALSO **comptable**, **indéterminé**

échéancier (*nm*): effectuer les remboursements selon l'**échéancier prévu** (*agreed schedule [of repayments]*)

échec (*nm*): censé **faire échec** à l'influence américaine dans la région (*thwart, foil*); le mouvement anti-avortement **mis en échec** (*thwarted, foiled*); l'objectif: détecter les enfants **en échec scolaire** (*performing poorly at school*)

échelle (*nf*): l'influence de la France est ressentie **à l'échelle du globe** (*worldwide; globally*); SEE ALSO **économie, fabriquer**

échelon (*nm*): on gravit les **échelon**s [hiérarchiques] largement à l'ancienneté (*grade, rung on the [promotion] ladder*)

échelonnement (*nm*): demander un **échelonnement de la dette** (*payment of a debt by instalments; spreading out of repayments; debt restructuring*)

échelonner (*vt*): avoir la faculté d'**échelonner les paiements** (*pay by instalments*); **[s']** (*vpr*): les versements peuvent **s'échelonner** sur plusieurs mois (*be spread over [a period of time]*)

échiquier (*nm*): une troisième force au centre de l'**échiquier politique** britannique (*political scene*); SEE ALSO **chancelier**

échoir (*vi*): le délai de livraison vient d'**échoir** (*expire*); la présidence de la commission **échoit à un Belge** (*fall to a Belgian*)

échouer (*vi*): une tentative de cessez-le-feu et de dialogue a **échoué** (*fail, come to nothing*); s'ils **échouent** à montrer leur engagement en faveur de la paix (*fail [to]*); Moscou **fait échouer** l'adoption d'un plan pour le Kosovo (*foil, prevent*); **[s']** (*vpr*): un bateau de croisière **s'échoue** en mer d'Egée (*run aground*)

éclabousser (*vt*): face aux scandales qui **éclaboussent** son gouvernement (*sully the good name of*)

éclaircir (*vt*): le procès n'a pas **éclairci le mystère** (*clear up/solve the mystery*); ses propos ont quelque peu **éclairci la situation** (*clarify the situation*)

éclaircissement (*nm*): l'**éclaircissement** du massacre se fait toujours attendre (*explanation*)

éclaté, -e (*adj*): un secteur très **éclaté** [81.000 salariés dans 350 entreprises] (*fragmented*)

éclatement (*nm*): au moment de l'**éclatement** de la fédération yougoslave (*break-up, split-up*); les conflits parents-enfants et l'**éclatement des familles** (*family breakdown*)

éclater (*vi*): avec la crise, de plus en plus de familles **éclatent** (*break up*); la coalition gouvernementale **menace d'éclater** (*is in danger of breaking down*); SEE ALSO **guerre**

école (*nf*): pour défendre l'**école libre** contre le gouvernement de gauche (*[Fr] private-sector school; denominational schooling*); les partisans de l'**école publique** (*state educational sector*); SEE ALSO **laïc, mixité**

économie (*nf*): partisan de l'**économie libérale** (*free-market economy*); dans l'ex-URSS, l'**économie parallèle** est florissante (*unofficial/black economy*); SEE ALSO **assistance, fructifier, relance, surchauffe**

économique (*adj*): SEE **éventuel, poumon, prépondérance, renouveau**

économiquement (*adv*): on ne fait rien pour les **économiquement faibles** (*lower-income groups*)

écoper (*vt*): il a **écopé de six mois de prison** avec sursis (*receive a six month prison sentence*)

écoulement (*nm*): pour assurer l'**écoulement** de ses produits manufacturés (*sale, selling*)

écouler (*vt*): **écouler** les invendus et les fins de série (*sell off; dispose of*)

écoute (*nf*): autoriser le recours aux **écoutes téléphoniques** (*phone-tapping*); on lui reproche d'**être trop à l'écoute des syndicats** (*listen too sympathetically to the unions*); SEE ALSO **indice**

écrasement (*nm*): depuis l'**écrasement** de l'insurrection communiste (*crushing*)

écraser (*vt*): la Commission européenne ne veut pas qu'on **écrase les prix** (*reduce prices drastically*); [**s'**] (*vpr*): un Mirage français **s'écrase** au Tchad (*crash*)

écritures (*nfpl*): SEE **faux**

écrouer (*vt*): un policier et ses complices **écroués** pour extorsion de fonds (*imprison*)

écroulement (*nm*): la fatalité d'un **écroulement** du totalitarisme (*collapse*)

écrouler [**s'**] (*vpr*): Albanie, le dernier régime communiste à **s'écrouler** (*collapse*)

édicter (*vt*): l'interdiction, **édictée** par Bruxelles, d'importer de la viande de bœuf (*decree*)

édulcorer (*vt*): [*fig*] il est vrai que le texte a été **édulcoré**, pour plaire à certains (*tone down*)

effectif, -ive (*adj/nm*): sont prises en compte les périodes de **travail effectif** (*actual work*); l'augmentation des **effectifs scolaires** (*pupil rolls*); SEE ALSO **dégraissage**, **diminuer**

effectuer (*vt*): la Corée du Nord a **effectué** sept essais de tirs de missiles (*carry out*); [**s'**] (*vpr*): la rentrée **s'est effectuée** dans le calme (*take place*); SEE ALSO **préavis**

effet (*nm*): SEE **néfaste**, **pervers**

effondrement (*nm*): l'**effondrement** de plusieurs bâtiments (*collapse*); l'**effondrement du marché** a surpris les spécialistes (*slump in the market*)

effondrer [**s'**] (*vpr*): c'est tout un pan de l'économie qui **s'effondre** (*collapse*); des sociétés bien cotées ont vu leurs cours **s'effondrer** (*collapse, plummet*)

effraction (*nf*): SEE **vol**

effritement (*nm*): l'**effritement** de nombreuses monnaies par rapport au dollar (*erosion*)

effriter [**s'**] (*vpr*): les monnaies européennes **se sont effritées** vis-à-vis du dollar (*lose value*)

effusion (*nf*): une prise de pouvoir **sans effusion de sang** (*without bloodshed*)

égal, -e *mpl* **-aux** (*adj*): une justice indépendante, **égale pour tous** (*the same for all*); SEE ALSO **chance**

égalitaire (*adj*): la Suède, royaume réputé si **égalitaire** (*egalitarian*)

égalité (*nf*): la justice sociale, et l'**égalité des chances** (*equal opportunity*); le combat pour l'**égalité des droits** (*equal rights*); les femmes demandent l'**égalité des salaires** (*equal pay*)

égide (*nf*): un cessez-le-feu **sous l'égide syrienne** (*under the aegis/ control of Syria*)

égratigner (*vt*): les administrateurs, dans leur rapport, **égratignent** les syndicats comme la direction (*criticize*)

élargi, -e (*adj*): Bercy pourrait disposer de **pouvoirs élargis** (*wider powers*)

élargir (*vt*): on **élargit** les catégories d'étrangers bénéficiant de la carte de résident (*extend, widen*); **élargir** un détenu (*discharge, release from prison*); **[s']** (*vpr*): dans une Europe appelée à **s'élargir** (*expand; become larger*); au cas où le conflit **s'élargirait encore** (*spread further*)

élargissement (*nm*): donner un coup de frein à l'**élargissement** de l'UE (*enlargement*); il récidiva, un mois à peine après son **élargissement** (*release, discharge*)

électeur, -trice (*nm,f*): dimanche l'**électeur** français se rend aux urnes (*voter*); les **électeurs** font confiance à leur député (*electorate*); SEE ALSO **indécis**

électif, -ive (*adj*): conquérir son premier **mandat électif** (*electoral mandate*); ceux qui se présentent à des **fonctions électives** (*elected office*)

élection (*nf*): on annonce des **élections anticipées** pour le 11 juillet (*early elections*); SEE ALSO **annulation, arbitrer, cantonal, convoquer, issu, partiel, pluraliste, présidentiel, primaire**

électoral, -e *mpl* **-aux** (*adj*): SEE **assise, clientèle, collège, corps, découpage, échéance, fichier, fief, fraude, participation, période, plate-forme, redécoupage**

électorat (*nm*): partir à la conquête de l'**électorat** (*electorate, voters*); ce sont les **électorats flottants** qui décident des élections (*floating voters*)

élément (*nm*): aucun **élément** n'a pu être retenu contre lui (*[piece of] evidence*); Scotland Yard dispose d'**éléments accablants** contre le suspect (*damning evidence*); SEE ALSO **incontournable**

élévation (*nf*): cette évolution, due à l'**élévation** des taux d'imposition (*raising*)

élevé, -e (*adj*): un chômage **élevé**, un marché de travail trop rigide (*high level [of]*); SEE ALSO **coût**

élever (*vt*): **élever** des barrières douanières (*erect, put up*); [**s'**] (*vpr*): le bilan **s'élevait** à 129 morts (*total; come to*); les autorités **s'élèvent** contre les accusations de torture (*protest [against]*)

éligibilité (*nf*): accorder le droit de vote et d'**éligibilité** aux femmes (*eligibility*)

éligible (*adj*): pour voter ou **être éligible** aux élections européennes (*be eligible for office*)

élire (*vt*): **élire** un député (*elect*); SEE ALSO **domicile**

élu,-e (*adj/nm,f*): une délégation d'**élus** lorrains (*elected represent-ative*); SEE ALSO **vacation**

élucider (*vt*): huit affaires ont été **élucidées** par les services de police (*solve*)

élyséen,-enne (*adj*): le Premier ministre porte ombrage aux desseins **élyséens** (*[Fr] presidential*)

emballement (*nm*): l'économie donne des signes d'**emballement** (*going out of control*); l'**emballement médiatique** est caractéristique de nos sociétés (*media hype*)

emballer [**s'**] (*vpr*): le crédit à la consommation risque de **s'em-baller** (*rise steeply; shoot up*)

embargo (*nm*): Paris assouplit l'**embargo pétrolier** vis-à-vis de Téhéran (*oil embargo*); le Soudan continue à enfreindre l'**embargo sur les armes** (*arms embargo*)

embauche (*nf*): le projet initial prévoit l'**embauche** de 50 salariés (*employment, taking on labour*); le nombre des **embauches fermes** augmente sensiblement (*firm offer of employment*); SEE ALSO **entretien, frilosité, monopole, salaire**

embaucher (*vt*): les firmes recommencent à investir et à **embaucher** (*take on/employ labour*)

embellie (*nf*): après la **courte embellie** des premiers mois de 2003 (*short-lived improvement*)

embrasement (*nm*): le risque d'un **embrasement** généralisé de la région (*unrest*)

embraser (*vt*): le crise de l'automne qui a **embrasé les cités** (*cause rioting in deprived housing estates*)

émettre (*vt*): la chaîne nationale, seule à encore **émettre** (*broadcast*); les Postes **émettent** une nouvelle série de timbres commémoratifs (*issue*); SEE ALSO **avis, réserve**

émeute (*nf*): lors des **émeutes urbaines** de l'été 2005 (*urban riots*)

émeutier, -ière (*nm,f*): le procès des **émeutiers** passionne l'opinion publique (*rioter*)

émission (*nf*): augmenter son capital par l'**émission de nouvelles actions** (*issue of new shares*); condamnés pour **émission frauduleuse de chèques** (*writing dud cheques*)

émoi (*nm*): alors que l'**émoi** suscité par sa défaite inattendue était encore vif (*surprise; confusion*); le retour de l'OLP **suscite l'émoi** en Israël (*cause concern; cause anger*)

émouvoir (*vt*): l'annulation de la visite a **ému** les Autrichiens (*upset; anger*); [**s'**] (*vpr*): le Président **s'est ému** des propos de son ministre (*express displeasure*)

emparer [**s'**] (*vpr*): SEE **mairie**

empiètement (*nm*): le chef de l'Etat met en garde contre tout **empiètement** sur la fonction présidentielle (*encroachment*)

empiéter (*vt*): le Premier ministre **empiète** sur le terrain présidentiel (*encroach*)

empirer (*vi*): les relations entre l'UE et la Russie ont tendance à **empirer** (*get worse*)

emploi (*nm*): l'**emploi** s'améliore, le chômage diminue (*employment/job situation*); continuer à chercher un **emploi fixe** (*permanent position*); SEE ALSO **atypique, axer, bassin, contrat, cumuler, familial, insécurité, offre, perspective, plein, précaire, précarité, sécurité, suppression, supprimer**

employé, -e (*nm,f*): des ménages qui prennent un **employé de maison** (*domestic help; servant*)

employer [**s'**] (*vpr*): Moscou **s'emploie à resserrer ses liens** avec Téhéran (*work to establish closer links*)

emporter (*vt*): la liste emmenée par l'ancien maire a **emporté** cette élection partielle (*win*); le conservateur **l'a emporté** au premier tour (*won, was victorious*)

emprise (*nf*): Moscou confirme son **emprise** sur les Etats indépendants (*hold, influence*)

énarque (*nm*): une direction composée de 200 fonctionnaires, la plupart **énarques** (*[Fr] graduate of the ENA*)

encadré, -e (*adj*): les HLM, très **encadrés** par l'Etat (*regulated, controlled*); à l'époque, **le crédit était encadré** (*credit restrictions were in force*)

encadrement (*nm*): l'**encadrement** est assuré par des officiers d'expérience (*training*); les femmes sont sous-représentées dans les **postes d'encadrement** (*managerial posts*); avec la levée de l'**encadrement du crédit** (*restriction on borrowing; credit controls*)

encadrer (*vt*): pour **encadrer** le travail des juges débutants (*train [and supervise]*); mais les syndicats ont du mal à **encadrer** ces mouvements spontanés (*control*)

encarté, -e (*adj/nm,f*): premier département en nombre d'adhérents, avec 4.000 **encartés** (*card-holding member*)

encarter [**s'**] (*vpr*): le refus de **s'encarter** dans un parti, un syndicat ou une association (*take out membership*)

enchère (*nf*): après une dernière **enchère** de 250 euros (*bid at auction*); SEE ALSO **adjuger**

enchérir (*vi*): les produits de première nécessité **enchérissent** au fil des semaines (*go up in price*); **enchérir** sur l'offre de vendredi (*make a higher bid*)

enchérissement (*nm*): par crainte d'un **enchérissement** des importations (*rise in cost*)

enclave (*nf*): l'**enclave** musulmane sécessionniste est tombée (*enclave*)

enclavement (*nm*): l'autoroute a mis fin à l'**enclavement** de la région (*isolation; inaccessibility*)

enclaver (*vt*): le Gers, totalement **enclavé**, contourné par de grands axes routiers (*landlocked*)

encombrement (*nm*): l'**encombrement des prisons** est un grand sujet de préoccupation (*prison overcrowding*)

encourir (*vt*): le principal prévenu **encourt** dix ans d'emprisonnement (*incur, be liable to*); lorsque la **peine encourue** n'excède pas cinq ans (*sentence incurred*)

endettement (*nm*): annuler l'**endettement des pays pauvres** (*third-world debt*)

endetter [**s'**] (*vpr*): **s'endetter** auprès d'établissements de crédit (*contract debts*); et les pauvres continuent à **s'endetter** (*go into debt*)

endiguer (*vt*): comment **endiguer** la violence dans les stades? (*curb, check*); dans le but d'**endiguer** la puissance chinoise (*check, arrest*); un plan destiné à **endiguer la crise** qui sévit dans ce pays (*contain the crisis*)

endosser (*vt*): **faire endosser par les Etats-Unis** son projet d'élections dans les territoires occupés (*get American endorsement*)

énergétique (*adj*): vers une alliance **énergétique** Moscou-Alger (*pertaining to energy supplies*); SEE ALSO **facture**

énergie (*nf*): le **prix de l'énergie** reste bas et a tendance à baisser (*energy prices*); SEE ALSO **renchérissement**

enfance (*nf*): une institution pour **enfance inadaptée** (*maladjusted children*); un service d'accueil téléphonique pour **enfance maltraitée** (*[cases of] child abuse*); l'ordonnance de 1945 relative à l'**enfance délinquante** (*juvenile crime/delinquency*)

enfant (*nmf*): la CGT réclame 30 euros par mois par **enfant à charge** (*dependent child*); SEE ALSO **abus**, **maltraitance**, **meurtrier**, **scolariser**, **traitement**, **tribunal**

enfreindre (*vt*): **enfreindre la loi** sur l'importation de l'ivoire (*be in breach of the law*)

engagé, -e (*adj/nm,f*): un journal **engagé**, mais non militant (*[politically] committed*); mobiliser davantage d'appelés pour remplacer les **engagés** (*enlisted soldier*)

engagement (*nm*): Barroso salue l'**engagement européen** du nouveau président français (*commitment to Europe*); le gouvernement **a pris des engagements** qui n'ont pas été tenus (*make promises*); SEE ALSO **accru**

engager (*vt*): il faudrait **engager un dialogue** avec Téhéran (*begin talks*); [**s'**] (*vpr*): la course pour la succession du leader **s'engage** (*start, get under way*); la Corée du Nord **s'engage** à cesser ses activités nucléaires (*promise, undertake [to]*); peu de femmes **s'engagent en politique** (*go into politics*); SEE ALSO **poursuite**

engin (*nm*): l'**engin** a explosé, faisant dix morts (*[explosive] device*); un bâtiment porteur d'**engins nucléaires** (*nuclear weapons*); SEE ALSO **fabrication**

engrenage (*nm*): la répression est responsable de l'**engrenage de la violence** (*the spiralling violence*); le Yémen **est entré dans l'engrenage de la guerre civile** (*is caught up in a vicious circle of civil war*)

enjeu *pl* **-x** (*nm*): se trouver face à un **enjeu** considérable (*challenge*); ne pas être d'accord sur l'**enjeu du conflit actuel** (*what is at stake in this conflict*)

enlever (*vt*): libération des journalistes **enlevés** par la guérilla (*kidnapped*); les Islamistes **enlèvent** 31 sièges (*win*); **enlever un marché** de 26 milliards d'euros (*win [a contract]*)

enlisement (*nm*): l'**enlisement** des Etats-Unis en Irak (*impasse*)

enliser [**s'**] (*vpr*): les négociations **s'enlisent**; les Américains **s'enlisent** en Irak (*get bogged down*); Gaza **s'enlise dans la violence** (*sinks further into violence*)

énoncé (*nm*): après l'**énoncé du verdict** (*pronouncement of the verdict*)

enquête (*nf*): la police a **ouvert une enquête** (*start an investigation*); lors d'une **enquête d'opinion** effectuée début mars (*survey; opinion poll*); le projet **sera soumis à enquête publique** (*will be the subject of a public enquiry*); SEE ALSO **azimut, clore, commission, diligenter, piétinement**

enquêter (*vi*): la commission qui **enquête** sur cette affaire (*investigate*)

enquêteur, -trice (*nm,f*): le meurtre laisse les **enquêteurs** perplexes (*investigator*)

enrayer (*vt*): tenter d'**enrayer** l'envolée des prix des produits laitiers (*check; curb*)

enregistrement (*nm*): l'**enregistrement** des gardes à vue dans les affaires criminelles (*recording [audio/video]*)

enregistrer (*vt*): 2006, l'année la plus chaude jamais **enregistrée** (*record; register*); le parti a **enregistré un revers** aux élections (*suffer a setback*)

ensanglanter (*vt*): le drame qui **ensanglante** l'ex-Yougoslavie (*bring bloodshed to*)

ensemble (*nm*): on a tendance à assimiler **grands ensembles** et délinquance (*high-density housing estate*)

entamer (*vt*): la grève de la faim qu'il avait **entamée** le 18 mars (*begin, start*); une défaite qui va largement **entamer sa crédibilité** (*damage one's credibility*)

entendre (*vt*): les auteurs présumés du vol **ont été entendus** par le juge (*have been questioned*); [**s'**] (*vpr*): Paris et Alger **s'entendent** sur le prix du gaz (*come to an agreement; agree*)

entente (*nf*): une amende infligée aux deux firmes pour **entente illicite** (*illicit [trade] agreement*); SEE ALSO **terrain**

entériner (*vt*): une réforme doit être **entérinée** par tous les Etats membres (*confirm, ratify*)

enterrement (*nm*): autre sujet de mécontentement: l'**enterrement de la réforme agraire** (*abandoning of agrarian reform*)

enterrer (*vt*): va-t-on **enterrer** le projet de gazoduc Algérie-Espagne? (*abandon*); le Canada **enterre le protocole de Kyoto** (*buries the Kyoto agreement*)

entourage (*nm*): selon l'**entourage du ministre** (*people close to the minister*); des malades dont l'**entourage** ne peut plus assumer la souffrance (*family; friends and relations*)

entraîner (*vt*): l'évolution technologique **entraîne** un besoin croissant de personnel qualifié (*cause; bring in its wake*)

entrave (*nf*): une action en justice pour **entrave** au droit syndical (*obstruction*); s'exprimer **sans entraves** (*freely*); SEE ALSO **circuler**

entraver (*vt*): la cherté du crédit **entrave** le commerce (*be a barrier [to]*); chercher par des chicanes à **entraver** la négociation (*hinder, impede*)

entremise (*nf*): amorcer un dialogue **par l'entremise des Etats-Unis** (*with the mediation of the United States*)

entreprendre (*vt*): avant d'**entreprendre** une importante réduction des forces armées (*undertake, carry out*)

entreprise (*nf*): dans cette **entreprise familiale** de Rouen (*family business*); SEE ALSO **chef, comité, défaillant, inadaptation, juriste, libre, moyen, public, rapprochement, stage**

entretenir (*vt*): l'illusion **entretenue** par la classe dominante (*foster, promote*); [**s'**] (*vpr*): il désire **s'entretenir** avec eux du rôle du Conseil constitutionnel (*have talks [about], discuss*)

entretien (*nm*): leur **entretien** est à la une de tous les quotidiens (*conversation; talks*); passer un **entretien d'embauche** (*job interview*); l'**entretien de la voirie** relève du maire (*highway repairs and maintenance*)

enveloppe (*nf*): fixer à 15 milliards d'euros l'**enveloppe d'allégements fiscaux** (*package of tax cuts*)

envenimer (*vt*): cela ne peut manquer d'**envenimer les rapports** entre les deux Etats (*poison relations*); [**s'**] (*vpr*): les relations sino-soviétiques **s'enveniment** (*grow more bitter/ acrimonious*)

envergure (*nf*): une **action d'envergure** est prévue par la RATP pour le 15 mai (*large-scale [industrial] action*); l'entreprise a **pris de l'envergure** (*expand, develop*)

environnement (*nm*): un tramway, considéré comme une **atteinte à l'environnement** (*environmentally harmful*); SEE ALSO **conjoncture, nuisance**

envol (*nm*): grâce à l'**envol de 30%** des prix du métal (*30% rise*)

envolée (*nf*): les gains réalisés grâce à l'**envolée des cours** (*surge in share prices*); l'**envolée des prix** inquiète le gouvernement (*soaring prices*)

envoler [**s'**] (*vpr*): les prix **se sont envolés** à Paris hier (*soar, rise steeply*)

envoyé, -e (*nm,f*): l'**envoyé spécial** belge est attendu dans les prochains jours (*special envoy*); reportage de notre **envoyé spécial** en Australie (*special correspondent*)

épargnant, -e (*nm,f*): une bonne partie des **petits épargnants** risque de vendre ses actions (*small saver/investor*)

épargne (*nm*): n'avoir aucune **épargne** et une retraite minimale (*savings*); accéder à la propriété grâce au **plan d'épargne logement** (*savings scheme offering low-interest mortgages*); SEE ALSO **livret, peser**

épargner (*vt*): il faut **épargner** davantage pour compenser la baisse des pensions (*save*)

épauler (*vt*): le ministre vient **épauler** le candidat dans sa campagne (*support, back*)

épingle (*nm*): cette affaire, **montée en épingle** par la presse (*blow up [out of all proportion]*); la firme a pu **tirer son épingle du jeu** (*emerge unscathed*)

épingler (*vt*): un rapport de la Cour des comptes **épingle** la gestion des hôpitaux (*single out for criticism*)

éplucher (*vt*): les experts **épluchent** les données économiques (*dissect, examine closely*); SEE ALSO **comptabilité**

épouvantail (*nm*): brandissant l'**épouvantail** de la natalité galopante (*bogy; scare*)

épreuve (*nf*): poursuite de l'**épreuve de force** entre le pouvoir et les rebelles (*confrontation; trial of strength*); une peine de prison avec sursis et **mise à l'épreuve pendant deux ans** (*a 2-year probationary period*); on doit passer des **épreuves facultatives** (*optional test/examination*)

épuration (*nf*): les travaux d'assainissement et d'**épuration** des collectivités locales (*water treatment*); l'**épuration ethnique** perpétrée par des escadrons de la mort (*ethnic cleansing*)

épurer (*vt*): **épurer** l'eau usée avant de la rendre au milieu naturel (*purify; treat*)

équilibre (*nm*): l'**équilibre des puissances**, et la sécurité collective (*balance of power [esp. military]*); le gouvernement **promet l'équilibre**, voire un excédent pour 2008 (*promises to balance the budget*)

équilibrer (*vt*): les PTT sont tenues d'**équilibrer** leurs recettes et leurs dépenses (*balance [budget]*)

équipe (*nf*): les **équipes** qui travaillent en 2 x 8 (*shift, shift workers, team*); le **personnel en équipe** travaillera 28 heures par semaine (*staff on shift work*)

équipement (*nm*): une meilleure utilisation des **équipements** (*plant, machinery*); les divers **équipements** culturels et sociaux (*[recreational] amenities*); 28.000 agents employés par la **direction de l'équipement** (*road maintenance department*); SEE ALSO **bien**, **dépense**

équiper [s'] (*vpr*): les entreprises prêtes à **s'équiper** (*invest in plant and machinery*)

équitable (*adj*): des produits issus du **commerce équitable** (*fair trade*)

équité (*nf*): on doit juger un impôt sur son **équité** et sur son efficacité (*fairness*)

équivoque (*nf*): une condamnation **sans équivoque** de la peine de mort (*unequivocal, unambiguous*); Tunisie: **lever les équivoques** entre Paris et le nouveau pouvoir (*remove misunderstandings*)

escalade (*nf*): marquant une nouvelle **escalade** dans la guerre (*escalation*)

escarmouche (*nf*): des **escarmouches** éclatèrent en fin de journée (*skirmish*)

escroc (*nm*): prison ferme pour l'**escroc** à la Sécu (*crook, swindler*)

escroquer (*vt*): accusé d'avoir voulu **escroquer** son assureur (*defraud, swindle*)

escroquerie (*nf*): être victime d'une **escroquerie** (*fraud, deception*); une peine de prison pour **escroquerie aux chèques volés** (*issuing stolen cheques*); SEE ALSO **complicité**

espèce (*nf*): exiger d'être payé **en espèces** (*in cash*); on peut effectuer des **retraits en espèces** dans toutes les agences de la banque (*cash withdrawals*)

espérance (*nf*): l'**espérance de vie** a nettement progressé en 2004 (*life expectancy*)

esprit (*nm*): SEE **chapelle, clocher**

essai (*nm*): nouvel **essai nucléaire** nord-coréen (*nuclear test*); SEE ALSO **ballon, periode**

essor (*nm*): les ventes d'ordinateurs connaissent un **essor** fulgurant (*boom, expansion*)

essoufflement (*nm*): des signes d'**essoufflement** de l'économie américaine (*running out of steam*)

essouffler [**s'**] (*vpr*): le miracle économique allemand **s'essouffle** (*run out of steam, lose momentum*)

essuyer (*vt*): le parti au pouvoir **essuya de lourds revers** lors des élections (*suffer heavy losses*); le fourgon **avait essuyé une rafale d'arme automatique** (*had come under automatic fire*); SEE ALSO **camouflet**

établir (*vt*): on a pu **établir** sa participation à l'attentat (*establish with certainty*); [**s'**] (*vpr*): 26% des demandeurs se sont vu accorder le droit de **s'établir** au Royaume-Uni (*settle*); son ambition: **s'établir à son compte** (*set up in business*)

établissement (*nm*): l'**établissement** d'un Etat palestinien (*setting up*); l'**établissement** normand, un des leaders des appareils ménagers (*company*); SEE ALSO **chef, zone**

étalage (*nm*): cet **étalage public** de griefs réciproques entre les deux pays (*public display*)

étalement (*nm*): l'**étalement des vacances** est loin d'être la règle en France (*staggering holiday periods*); le blocage de l'**étalement suburbain** (*suburban sprawl*)

étaler (*vt*): les pays arabes **étalent** leurs divisions face à Israël (*display, reveal*); [**s'**] (*vpr*): un programme économique **s'étalant sur trois ans** (*spread over three years*)

étape (*nf*): une nouvelle **étape** a été franchie (*stage*)

état (*nm*): des témoins **font état de massacres** (*report massacres*); le roi **fait état** de ses prérogatives constitutionnelles (*cite; put forward*); la fédération UMP de Paris **tient ses états-généraux** (*hold its convention*); SEE ALSO **remise, urgence**

Etat (*nm*): tenter de **rétablir l'Etat de droit** après les émeutes en Corse (*re-establish the rule of law*); le **tout-Etat** fabrique un peuple d'assistés (*excessive state control*); l'essor de l'**Etat-providence** et de la protection sociale (*Welfare State*); SEE ALSO **agent, appointer, chef, commis, sûreté**

état-civil (*nm*): le maire reste agent de l'Etat pour l'**état-civil** (*civil status; registry office dealing with civil status*)

étatique (*adj*): un système **étatique** de retraite (*state; of the state*)

étatisation (*nf*): l'**étatisation** du système de santé (*taking under state control*)

étatiser (*vt*): le gouvernement a **étatisé** les grandes entreprises (*bring under state control*)

étendre [s'] (*vpr*): l'agitation **s'étend** dans les Balkans (*spread*); la célèbre firme anglaise **s'étend** aux Etats-Unis (*expand its operations*)

étendu, -e (*adj*): le statut confère des pouvoirs **étendus** à l'exécutif (*wide, extensive*)

étiquette (*nf*): quoique peu connu, et **sans étiquette politique** (*without political affiliation*); SEE ALSO **valse**

étranger,-ère (*adj/nm,f*): 65% de la population active est **étrangère** (*foreign*); l'**étranger** ne comprend pas toujours nos réticences (*foreigners; foreign countries*); SEE ALSO **irrégulier, mainmise, provenance**

étrennes (*nfpl*): sombres **étrennes** pour des milliers de licenciés en puissance (*Christmas box; New Year's present*)

étude (*nf*): l'**étude sur le terrain** révèle l'ampleur du problème (*on-site study*); le lancement d'une **étude d'impact** (*impact study*); SEE ALSO **faisabilité, sanction**

euphorie (*nf*): finie l'**euphorie** des années de plein emploi (*euphoria*)

euphorique (*adj*): la conjoncture **euphorique** de cette fin d'année (*bullish, buoyant*)

évacuer (*vt*): il n'est pas question d'**évacuer** la zone de sécurité (*withdraw from*); le ministre a **évacué** deux questions importantes (*evade; shrug off*)

évasion (*nf*): l'Italie veut s'attaquer à l'**évasion fiscale** (*tax avoidance*); SEE ALSO **tentative**

éventail (*nm*): des personnes d'un large **éventail** socio-économique (*range, spectrum*); l'**éventail des salaires** s'est élargi aussi en Suède (*salary range*)

éventualité (*nf*): l'**éventualité** d'élections anticipées (*possibility*)

éventuel, -elle (*adj*): afin de déjouer d'**éventuels complots terroristes** (*any future terrorist plots*)

éventuellement (*adv*): la région parisienne et **éventuellement** la province (*possibly; perhaps*)

éviction (*nf*): deux heures après son **éviction du pouvoir** (*removal from power*)

évincement (*nm*): des élections aboutissant à l'**évincement** des communistes (*ousting*)

évincer (*vt*): il a été **évincé** de la direction (*oust*)

évoluer (*vi*): 35 heures, retraites: des sujets sur lesquels le PS commence à **évoluer** (*evolve, change*); à l'époque **il évoluait dans les milieux d'extrême droite** (*he moved in far right-wing circles*)

évolutif, -ive (*adj*): un poste passionnant et **évolutif** (*with good promotion prospects*)

évolution (*nf*): favoriser une **meilleure évolution de carrière** pour les ouvriers (*improved career development*)

exacerbé, -e (*adj*): un mouvement au nationalisme **exacerbé** et à l'antisémitisme avoué (*extreme*)

exacerber [s'] (*vpr*): la situation risque de **s'exacerber** (*get worse, deteriorate*)

exactions (*nfpl*): de nombreuses **exactions**, commises par des militaires (*atrocities*)

examen (*nm*): le juge chargé de l'**examen** de la plainte (*investigation*); détenir des suspects sans les **mettre en examen** (*indict, charge with an offence*); cinq **mises en examen** ont été prononcées dans cette affaire (*charge, indictment*); SEE ALSO **lecture**

excédent (*nm*): l'**excédent commercial** du prêt-à-porter français (*trade surplus*); à son départ, il laisse la Sécurité sociale **en excédent** (*in the black; in surplus*)

excédentaire (*adj*): le commerce extérieur de la France est **excédentaire** (*in surplus*)

excéder (*vt*): la production **excédait** nettement la demande (*exceed*)

exclu, -e (*adj/nm,f*): défenseur du prolétariat et des **exclus** (*the marginalized; social outcasts*)

exclure (*vt*): le gouvernement **exclut** toute négociation avec les chefs indépendantistes (*rule out*); une nouvelle flambée de violence **n'est pas à exclure** (*cannot be ruled out*)

exclusif, -ive (*adj/nf*): éviter toute **exclusive**, tout esprit de chapelle (*exclusion; debarment*)

exclusion (*nf*): après l'**exclusion** des jeunes musulmanes voilées (*expulsion [from school]*); la lutte contre la misère et l'**exclusion** (*marginalization; alienation*); SEE ALSO **zone**

exclusivité (*nf*): British Telecom n'a plus l'**exclusivité du téléphone** (*monopoly of telephone services*)

exécutant, -e (*nm,f*): un des **exécutants** présumés de l'attentat (*person carrying out a deed*)

exécuter (*vt*): l'entreprise chargée d'**exécuter les travaux** (*carry out the work*)

exécutif, -ive (*adj/nm*): le maire est l'**agent exécutif** de la commune (*executive officer*); Premier ministre et Président partagent le **pouvoir exécutif** (*executive power*); SEE ALSO **bureau**

exécution (*nf*): une conférence internationale chargée de l'**exécution** des accords (*implementation*); un projet qu'on n'a jamais **mis à exécution** (*carry out, implement*)

exempt, -e (*adj*): ces importations sont **exemptes de taxe** (*duty-free*)

exempter (*vt*): cette loi **exempte** les fermiers de taxes et d'impôts pendant cinq ans (*exempt*)

exemption (*nf*): les **exemptions** au service national (*exemption*); l'**exemption de TVA** serait souhaitable (*exemption from value-added tax*)

exercer (*vi*): un avocat **exerçant** dans un cabinet privé (*practise, be in practice*); (*vt*): perdre un pouvoir qu'il **exerçait** depuis 16 ans (*exercise [authority, power]*); SEE ALSO **pression**

exercice (*nm*): l'**exercice** du droit syndical (*exercising [right, power]*); les actionnaires ont approuvé les comptes de l'**exercice fiscal** (*financial year; accounting period*); ministre **de plein exercice** un an plus tard (*fully-fledged*); SEE ALSO **avocat**

exigence (*nf*): le nouveau traité européen, un grand défi et une grande **exigence** (*demand, requirement*); Hongkong: l'**exigence démocratique** reste intacte (*desire for democracy*)

exonération (*nf*): l'**exonération des charges sociales** accordée aux entreprises embauchant des jeunes (*exemption from paying social security contributions*)

exonérer (*vt*): sont **exonérés d'impôts** les intérêts du livret de Caisse d'épargne; quant à l'ISF, la résidence principale en serait **exonérée** (*exempted from tax*)

exorbitant, -e (*adj*): le pouvoir **exorbitant** de quelques responsables (*inordinate, exorbitant*); une revendication jugée **exorbitante** (*excessive*)

expédier (*vt*): le gouvernement en fin de mandat se contente d'**expédier les affaires courantes** (*deal with day-to-day business*)

expérience (*nf*): l'**expérience** d'ouverture hebdomadaire en nocturne (*experiment*); il s'agit d'une **expérience-pilote** de lutte contre le chômage féminin (*experimental scheme*)

expérimental, -e *mpl* **-aux** (*adj*): un service mis en place **à titre expérimental** (*as an experiment*)

expérimenté, e (*adj*): les deux candidats **sont peu expérimentés** en politique étrangère (*are inexperienced, have little experience*)

expérimenter (*vt*): quinze villes vont **expérimenter** de nouveaux rythmes scolaires (*try out*)

expertise (*nf*): procéder à des **expertises** (*expert evaluation; appraisal*); une **expertise comptable** fait découvrir un détournement de fonds important (*financial audit*)

expiration (*nf*): lors de l'**expiration** de la période d'essai (*expiry*); son mandat ne **vient à expiration** qu'au mois d'août (*expire, come to an end*)

expirer (*vi*): un nouvel ultimatum **expire** lundi (*expire*)

exploitant, -e (*nm,f*): les **exploitants** des salles de cinéma (*owner, manager*); 2.000 **petits exploitants** font le siège du ministère de l'Agriculture (*small farmer, smallholder*)

exploitation (*nf*): une autorisation d'**exploitation** de salles de jeux (*operating, running*); il déplorait l'**exploitation médiatique** de l'affaire (*media exploitation/hype*); les **grandes exploitations** dominent dans la Beauce (*large farming unit*); SEE ALSO **déficit, équilibre, frais, résultat**

exploiter (*vt*): ils **exploitent** quelques hectares dans le Gers (*farm [land]*); **exploiter un petit commerce** dans le centre ville (*run a small business*)

exportateur, -trice (*adj/nm,f*): la Chine sera le premier **exportateur** mondial d'ici 2010 (*exporter, exporting nation*); SEE ALSO **brut**

exportation (*nf*): en dépit des faibles **aides à l'exportation** (*export subsidies*); SEE ALSO **marché**

exporter (*vt*): **exporter** le surplus de la production (*export*)

exposé (*nm*): après l'**exposé** du ministre sur ce sujet (*presentation; talk*); la réforme est justifiée par l'**exposé des motifs** suivant (*preamble [to bill] explaining grounds for its adoption*)

expression (*nf*): SEE **liberté**

exprimer (*vt*): les réticences **exprimées** par le ministre (*voice*); [**s'**] (*vpr*): le ministre, invité à **s'exprimer** devant la commission (*speak*)

expulser (*vt*): Khartoum **expulse** deux diplomates occidentaux (*expel*); la décision d'**expulser** les squatters (*evict*)

expulsion (*nf*): partisan de l'**expulsion des clandestins** (*expulsion/ deportation of illegal immigrants*); SEE ALSO **arrêté**, **attente**

extension (*nf*): **extension** de l'agitation sociale en Algérie (*spread; growth*); SEE ALSO **projet**

extérieur, -e (*adj/nm*): la dépendance de l'économie vis-à-vis de l'**extérieur** (*the outside world*); en cas d'événements graves **à l'extérieur** (*abroad*); SEE ALSO **aide**, **commerce**, **déficit**, **dette**

extorquer (*vt*): avoir recours à la torture pour **leur extorquer des aveux** (*get them to confess*)

extorsion (*nf*): ils accusent le commissaire d'**extorsion de fonds** (*extortion*)

extrader (*vt*): un ressortissant turc **extradé** des Pays-Bas (*extradite*)

extradition (*nf*): la France et l'Argentine ne sont pas tenues par une **convention d'extradition** (*extradition agreement*)

extrait (*nm*): un **extrait de compte** est envoyé à la fin du mois (*bank statement*); le bulletin de naissance est remplacé par l'**extrait d'acte de naissance** (*birth certificate*)

extrême (*adj*): les militants d'**extrême droite** (*of the extreme/far right*)

extrémisme (*nm*): la montée de l'**extrémisme islamiste** (*Islamic fundamentalism*)

extrémiste (*adj/nmf*): il faudra choisir entre lui et les **extrémistes** palestiniens (*extremist*)

F

fabricant (*nm*): des contrats mirobolants en perspective pour les **fabricants d'armes** (*arms manufacturer*)

fabrication (*nf*): après avoir informatisé la **ligne de fabrication** (*production line*); une forte explosion produite par un **engin de fabrication artisanale** (*home-made bomb/explosive device*); SEE ALSO **coût, procédé**

fabriquer (*vt*): **fabriquer** des meubles (*manufacture, produce*); la décision de les **fabriquer en série** (*mass-produce*)

face (*nf*): **faire face** à la concurrence des hypermarchés (*face the competition of, compete with*); ne plus pouvoir **faire face à ses remboursements** (*keep up one's repayments*)

face-à-face (*nm*): lors de leur récent **face-à-face** télévisé (*one-to-one debate; confrontation*)

facilité (*nf*): nous pouvons consentir des **facilités de paiement** (*easy repayment terms*)

faction (*nf*): les diverses **factions** qui composent l'opposition au régime en place (*faction, group*); les policiers **en faction** devant la porte du ministère (*on [guard] duty*)

facturation (*nf*): exiger une **facturation** en dollars (*billing; invoicing*)

facture (*nf*): notre **facture énergétique** a quintuplé depuis 1998 (*energy bill*); faire transiter des fonds sous couvert de **fausses factures** (*false accounting/invoicing*)

facturer (*vt*): les barils de pétrole étant **facturés** en dollars (*invoice, bill*)

facultatif, -ive (*adj*): l'heure de religion **facultative** (*optional*); SEE ALSO **épreuve**

faible (*adj*): s'inquiéter du **faible niveau de la production** (*low production levels*); des crédits accordés aux **ménages à faible revenu** (*low-income household*); SEE ALSO **économiquement, rapport**

faiblement (*adv*): le commerce extérieur a **faiblement** augmenté en volume (*very slightly*)

faiblesse (*nf*): la **faiblesse de l'euro** représente une occasion à saisir pour les exportateurs (*weakness of the euro*); la **faiblesse des moyens** consacrés à l'Université (*inadequate funding*); SEE ALSO **force**

faiblir (*vi*): demande et production **faiblissent**, mais on continue à embaucher (*fall*)

faille (*nf*): les **failles** du système anti-piratage de Sony Music (*flaw, weakness*)

faillite (*nf*): le fabricant belge est au bord de la **faillite** (*bankruptcy*); la ville, sinistrée par la **faillite** de ses industries lourdes (*collapse*)

faisabilité (*nf*): la Banque mondiale va financer une **étude de faisabilité** (*feasibility study*)

fait (*nm*): l'homme était en état d'ébriété **au moment des faits** (*when the event took place*); il conteste l'ensemble des **faits qui lui sont reprochés** (*charges, accusations*); la mesure **entrait dans les faits**, malgré la contestation des syndicats (*was implemented, came into effect*); les Américains **prennent fait et cause** pour les rebelles (*give total backing*); SEE ALSO **avouer, nier, reconnaître**

fait divers (*nm*): un entrefilet **dans la rubrique des faits divers** (*in the 'news in brief' column*)

familial, -e *mpl* **-aux** (*adj*): les **emplois familiaux** [garde d'enfants, assistance aux personnes âgées] (*domestic employment*); SEE ALSO **allocation, cellule, entreprise, planification, planning, quotient, regroupement, rupture**

famille (*nf*): les aides sont réservées aux **familles nombreuses** (*family with more than two children*); deux garçons de **familles désunies** des faubourgs de la ville (*broken home*); la **famille d'accueil** chez qui l'enfant avait été placé (*host family*); SEE ALSO **éclatement, salaire**

fantoche (*adj/nm*): il s'en prend au **régime fantoche** de Kaboul (*puppet regime*)

fantôme (*adj/nm*): véritable **ville-fantôme** depuis la fermeture de la mine (*ghost town*); des milliers d'étudiants **fantômes** inscrits dans les universités (*bogus*); SEE ALSO **cabinet**

farouche (*adj*): l'enjeu d'une **farouche** bataille commerciale (*fierce, bitter*); **farouche partisan** de cette réforme (*staunch advocate*)

farouchement (*adv*): le Japon, un pays **farouchement** antinucléaire (*fiercely*); il était **farouchement opposé** à l'entrée de son pays dans le Marché commun (*bitterly opposed*)

faste (*adj*): depuis lors, le parti vit une période **faste** (*successful*); une **année faste** pour les Postes et Télécommunications (*good/ profitable year*)

faucon (*nm*): [*fig*] le déclin des **faucons** néo-conservateurs (*hawk, hard-liner*)

fausser (*vt*): pour éviter de **fausser la concurrence** (*distort competition*)

faute (*nf*): être licencié pour **faute professionnelle** (*professional misconduct*); SEE ALSO **licenciement**

fauteuil (*nm*): il faudra choisir entre sa mairie et son **fauteuil de député** (*parliamentary seat*)

fauteur, -trice (*nm,f*): ils ont arrêté des **fauteurs de troubles** (*troublemaker; rabble-rouser*); il dénonce les **fauteurs de guerre** dans le camp occidental (*warmonger*)

fautif, -ive (*adj/nm,f*): l'automobiliste **fautif** se voit confisquer son véhicule (*at fault, guilty*)

faux, fausse (*adj/nm*): en possession d'un **faux passeport** (*false/ forged passport*); sous le coup d'une inculpation pour **faux et usage de faux** (*forgery and use of forged documents*); inculpé pour **faux en écritures** (*false accounting*); SEE ALSO **facture, inscrire, témoignage**

fédéral, -e *mpl* **-aux** (*adj*): secrétaire **fédéral** du PC de Seine-Saint-Denis (*federal*)

fédération (*nf*): lors de la constitution de la **fédération** de Russie (*federation [of states]*); la **fédération** départementale de la métallurgie (*[Fr] local federation of trade unions representing a single trade*)

fédérer (*vt*): cet impôt qui divise la gauche et **fédère** l'opposition (*unite, bring together*)

féliciter [**se**] (*vpr*): les syndicats **se félicitent** de la décision; les Etats-Unis **se félicitent** de la visite du ministre français à Bagdad (*be very pleased [at]*)

féminin, -e (*adj*): la population active **féminine** (*female*); SEE ALSO **activité**

femme (*nf*): le code civil ne connaît que la **femme mariée** (*married woman*); **femme au foyer** depuis son mariage (*[unemployed] housewife*); venir en aide aux **femmes isolées** [veuves, divorcées, séparées] (*woman living alone*); SEE ALSO **droit**, **policier**

féodalité (*nf*): empêcher la constitution de **féodalités** et restaurer l'autorité de l'Etat (*powerful [semi-autonomous] group*)

férié, -e (*adj*): les **jours fériés**, y compris le dimanche (*[public] holiday*)

ferme (*adj*): des peines de deux à six ans de **prison ferme** (*prison sentence without remission*); SEE ALSO **embauche**

fermer (*vt*): l'usine vient de **fermer ses portes** (*close down, go out of business*)

fermeté (*nf*): une plus grande **fermeté** de Tokyo à l'égard de Pékin (*firmness*); encouragé par la **fermeté** de la place new-yorkaise hier (*firmness [market, prices]*)

fermeture (*nf*): de nouvelles **fermetures de sites** sont annoncées (*plant/factory closure*)

feuille (*nf*): recevoir sa **feuille d'impôts locaux** (*[Brit] council tax demand*); rédiger sa **feuille d'imposition** (*income tax return*); fournir sa dernière **feuille de paie** (*pay slip*)

fiabilité (*nf*): la publicité met en avant la **fiabilité** du produit; un taux de **fiabilité** de 95% (*reliability, dependability*)

fiable (*adj*): des statistiques jugées **peu fiables** par les experts occidentaux (*unreliable*)

fichage (*nm*): la réglementation relative au **fichage informatique** (*putting on computer file*)

fiche (*nf*): retourner la **fiche d'inscription**, dûment remplie (*enrolment form*); les retenues sont portées sur la **fiche de paie** (*pay slip*)

ficher (*vt*): ces personnes, **fichées** en France au grand banditisme (*on police files*)

fichier (*nm*): avoir accès aux **fichiers** des services de l'Etat (*files; records*); en l'absence de tout **fichier électoral** (*electoral register*); SEE ALSO **informatisé**

fidèle (*adj/nmf*): **fidèle** et ami de toujours du président (*loyal supporter*)

fidéliser (*vt*): conserver un service peu rentable pour **fidéliser la clientèle** (*retain one's customers*)

fief (*nm*): fils d'un parlementaire dont il hérite le **fief électoral** (*electoral stronghold*)

filet (*nm*): important **coup de filet** anti-ETA à Cahors (*[police] raid*)

filiale (*nf*): le groupe, qui a des **filiales** à Genève et à Bruxelles (*subsidiary [company]*)

filialiser (*vt*): Sandoz France **filialise** ses activités chimie et agrochimie (*hive off into subsidiary companies*)

filière (*nf*): de nouvelles **filières** ont été mises en place dans les lycées (*pathway, course of study*); la police a pu **remonter toute une filière** d'immigration clandestine (*trace a whole network [drugs, crime]*)

finance (*nf*): le monde de la **finance** (*finance*); une réforme des **finances publiques** s'avère urgente (*public finances*); SEE ALSO **loi**

financement (*nm*): la loi sur le **financement** des partis politiques (*financing*); avec l'aide de **financements publics** (*public funds/funding*)

financer (*vt*): comment **financer** un tel investissement? (*finance, fund*)

financier, -ière (*adj*): SEE **chronique, liquider, malversation**

fisc (*nm*): le **fisc** estime le bénéfice qu'il a pu faire sur son chiffre d'affaires; les concubins sont mal vus par le **fisc** (*tax authorities*)

fiscal, -e *mpl* **-aux** (*adj*): SEE **abattement, déclaration, déduction, évasion, foyer, fraude, incitation, paquet, paradis, ponction, pression, recette, redressement**

fiscalité (*nf*): la **fiscalité** y est plus lourde qu'en France (*taxation, taxes*); SEE ALSO **peser**

fixe (*adj/nm*): avec un **salaire fixe**, assorti de commissions (*basic salary*); SEE ALSO **domicile, emploi, idée, poste**

flambée (*nf*): en raison de la **flambée** des prix de l'immobilier (*steep rise*); cette **flambée de violence** n'a donné lieu à aucune interpellation (*outbreak of violence*)

flamber (*vi*): les prix des produits agricoles **flambent** (*rise sharply, soar*); spéculation qui risque de **faire flamber le titre** (*make a share price rise sharply*)

fléau pl -x (*nm*): lutter contre le **fléau** de la corruption (*blight*); la violence au foyer, devenue un véritable **fléau social** (*blight on society*)

flèche (*nf*): les cours du pétrole avaient **monté en flèche** (*rise sharply*)

fléchir (*vi*): le nombre des sans-travail a **fléchi** cette année (*fall, come down*); les Européens tentent de **faire fléchir** le leader bosniaque (*sway, influence*)

fléchissement (*nm*): le **fléchissement** de la demande de logements (*fall, reduction*); le net **fléchissement de la criminalité** enregistré en 2004 (*fall in crime*)

florissant, -e (*adj*): grâce à une activité touristique **florissante** (*flourishing, thriving*)

flottant, -e (*adj*): SEE **électorat**

flou, -e (*adj/nm*): profitant d'un **flou juridique** total (*absence of a clear legal precedent*)

flux (*nm*): pour une meilleure maîtrise des **flux migratoires** (*immigration*)

focaliser (*vt*): en **focalisant l'attention** sur les problèmes (*focus attention*); [**se**] (*vpr*): ne pas **se focaliser** exclusivement sur le volet sécuritaire (*focus, concentrate*)

foi (*nf*): selon certaines sources **dignes de foi** (*reliable, trustworthy*); son avocat **plaida la bonne foi** (*claimed that his client acted in good faith*)

foncier, -ière (*adj/nm*): une nouvelle politique **foncière** est nécessaire (*relating to land ownership*); le coût du **foncier** est un lourd handicap pour les jeunes qui veulent s'installer (*real estate, land*); SEE ALSO **bâti, propriétaire**

fonction (*nf*): il a pris ses **fonctions** fin août (*position, post*); les **hautes fonctions** auxquelles il aspire (*high office*); après la **prise de fonctions** du Premier ministre (*taking office*); la **fonction publique** représente 21% de l'emploi salarié (*civil service*); SEE ALSO **cumuler, électif, logement, quitter, reconduire, relever, titulariser, valorisant**

fonctionnaire (*nm*): il n'est pas normal que 24% de la population soit **fonctionnaire** (*civil servant*); **haut fonctionnaire** au ministère de la Défense (*senior civil servant*)

fond (*nm*): des **désaccords de fond** divisent les deux hommes (*fundamental differences of opinion*); SEE ALSO **article**

fondamentalisme (*nm*): le **fondamentalisme** islamique menace les sociétés occidentales (*[religious] extremism; fundamentalism*)

fondamentaliste (*adj/nmf*): les **fondamentalistes** hindouistes l'emporteraient si l'on votait aujourd'hui (*fundamentalist*)

fondateur, -trice (*adj/nm,f*): la France, **membre fondateur** de l'Union (*founder member*)

fondation (*nf*): lors de la **fondation** de l'Etat d'Israël en 1948 (*founding, setting-up*)

fondé de pouvoirs (*nm*): envoyer un **fondé de pouvoirs** pour traiter avec la délégation chinoise (*authorized representative*)

fondement (*nm*): les accusations sont **sans fondement** (*groundless*)

fonder (*vt*): la société, **fondée** en 1958 (*founded, set up*); le désir de **fonder un foyer** (*start a home and family*); [**se**] (*vpr*): le juge **se fonde** sur une loi de 1990 (*base his judgment*)

fonds (*nm*): **récolter des fonds** en faveur des familles des grévistes (*collect funds*); on a prétendu que des **fonds publics** serviront à financer la campagne électorale (*public money/funds*); les sept milliards de **fonds propres** qu'apportera l'Etat (*capital, funding*); conserver le **fonds de commerce**, mais céder les locaux (*business*); SEE ALSO **bailleur, blanchiment, collecte, commerce, détourner, extorsion, retrait**

force (*nf*): heurts entre manifestants et **forces de l'ordre** (*police*); la **force de frappe** nucléaire française (*strike force*); les **forces et les faiblesses** de notre système judiciaire (*strengths and weaknesses*); SEE ALSO **coup, épreuve, interposition, usage**

forfait (*nm*): l'instauration en 2008 d'un **forfait** de 0,50 euro sur les médicaments (*fixed charge*); le **forfait hébergement** reste à la charge du patient (*[standard] accommodation fee*)

forfaitaire (*adj*): payer une cotisation **forfaitaire** (*fixed-rate*)

forfaiture (*nf*): la **forfaiture** ou un manquement grave dans l'exercice de ses fonctions (*abuse of authority; malfeasance*)

formation (*nf*): la **formation** d'écoles pour immigrés islamiques (*founding, setting up*); les autres **formations de l'opposition** préféraient s'abstenir (*opposition party*); consacrer 1,2% de la masse salariale à la **formation continue** (*in-service training*); SEE ALSO **alternance, congé, crédit**

former (*vt*): un animater social **formé sur le tas** (*trained on the job/in the field*); [**se**] (*vpr*): **se former** pendant son temps de loisir (*undergo training*)

formulaire (*nm*): le **formulaire d'inscription** dûment rempli (*registration form*); SEE ALSO **viser**

fort, -e (*adj*): **forte augmentation** des loyers à Paris (*big rise*); SEE ALSO **franc, homme, perte**

fortune (*nf*): **faire fortune** dans l'immobilier (*make a fortune, get rich*); SEE ALSO **impôt, soumis**

foudres (*nfpl*): la Syrie **encourt les foudres de Ryad** (*incurs the wrath of Ryad*)

fouet (*nm*): la pêche française **touchée de plein fouet** par la baisse des cours (*hard-hit*); le système des primes **donne un coup de fouet** à la production (*stimulate, boost*)

fouille (*nf*): la police pratique des **fouilles** impromptues sur des individus qu'elle suspecte (*searching, frisking*)

fourchette (*nf*): le taux de syndicalisation se situe **dans une fourchette** comprise entre 12 et 16% (*within a range*); la **fourchette des rémunérations** a été jusqu'ici très étroite (*wage differential*)

fournir (*vt*): les pays qui **fournissent en armes** les rebelles (*arm, supply with arms*)

fournisseur (*nm*): principal pays **fournisseur**: la Chine (*supplier; dealer*); le **fournisseur d'accès** à l'Internet, Neuf Cegetel (*[Internet] service provider*)

fourniture (*nf*): la France a signé un contrat pour la **fourniture** d'une usine de retraitement nucléaire (*supply*); la **fourniture** de services sociaux et éducatifs (*provision*)

foyer (*nm*): des centaines de **foyers** privés d'électricité (*household*); la construction d'un **foyer** pour personnes âgées (*hostel; [residential] home*); la taxe sera perçue par **foyer fiscal** et non plus par résidence (*household [for tax purposes]*); SEE ALSO **femme, fonder, monoparental, violence**

fracassant, -e (*adj*): les déclarations **fracassantes** d'un porte-parole (*sensational*)

fracture (*nf*): sensible à son discours sur la **fracture sociale** en France (*profound division within society*)

fragile (*adj*): des PME **fragiles**, touchées de plein fouet par la crise (*vulnerable*); les populations les plus **fragiles** (*at risk; vulnerable*)

fragiliser (*vt*): la société française est aujourd'hui **fragilisée** (*weaken, make vulnerable*)

fraîchement (*adv*): la proposition a été **fraîchement** accueillie (*coolly; without enthusiasm*)

frais (*nm*): les marges ont baissé et les **frais généraux** sont très lourds (*overheads*); les **frais d'exploitation** sont très élevés (*operating costs*); devoir régler intégralement les **frais de procédure** (*[court/legal] costs*); SEE ALSO **menu, note**

français, -e (*adj/nm,f*): SEE **franco-français, nationalité, préférence**

franchise (*nf*): les correspondances avec les services publics bénéficient de la **franchise postale** (*exemption from postal charges*); un achat **en franchise d'impôt** (*tax-free*); instituer une **franchise médicale** avec un plafond annuel par personne (*patient contribution towards cost of medical treatment*)

franco-français, -e (*adj*): le problème est moins une affaire Est-Ouest qu'**une affaire franco-française** (*a specifically French matter*)

francophone (*adj/nmf*): une école **francophone** de droit (*French-language*); la population **francophone** de Bruxelles (*French-speaking*)

francophonie (*nf*): la **francophonie** ou la communauté de langue des pays francophones (*the French-speaking world*); la vivacité de la **francophonie** en Roumanie (*French as a world language*)

frappe (*nf*): des **frappes ciblées** contre les camps d'entraînement des rebelles (*targeted strikes*); Paris réclame des **frappes aériennes** (*air strikes*); SEE ALSO **force**

frapper (*vt*): l'ensemble de la fiscalité qui **frappe** le patrimoine des Français (*be a charge upon [esp. tax]*)

fraude (*nf*): des accusations de **fraude électorale** (*electoral fraud*); la persistance d'une forte **fraude fiscale** (*tax evasion*); SEE ALSO **arguer**

frauder (*vt*): les contribuables salariés ne pourront plus **frauder** (*defraud [the taxman]*)

fraudeur, -euse (*nm,f*): la chasse aux **fraudeurs** s'intensifie (*swindler, defrauder*)

frauduleux, -euse (*adj*): la **gestion frauduleuse** de l'ancien maire (*corrupt administration*); SEE ALSO **agissement, émission**

freiner (*vi*): les Britanniques **freinent** sur le futur mini traité européen (*try to impede progress*); (*vt*): le souci aussi de **freiner** la hausse des prix (*curb; put a brake on*)

fréquentation (*nf*): la **fréquentation** des transports en commun est en baisse (*number of people using a [public] facility*)

fréquenter (*vt*): les élèves qui **fréquentent** les écoles primaires publiques (*attend [esp. school]*); les touristes **fréquentant la capitale** (*visiting the capital*)

friche (*nf*): la **mise en friche** d'une partie des terres agricoles en France (*leaving fallow*); transformer les **friches industrielles** en zone d'activité (*industrial waste land*)

frileux, -euse (*adj*): l'**attitude frileuse** de la Grande-Bretagne vis-à-vis les institutions européennes (*cautious or chilly attitude*)

frilosité (*nf*): critiqué pour sa **frilosité** en politique étrangère (*over-cautiousness*)

froid, -e (*adj/nm*): sa visite met fin à une période de **froid diplomatique** entre la France et la Syrie (*strained diplomatic relations*); SEE ALSO **guerre**

froisser (*vt*): sa réaction semble avoir **froissé** les autorités algériennnes (*offend*)

fronde (*nf*): la **fronde** des eurosceptiques conservateurs (*revolt, rebellion*)

fronder (*vi*): certains députés de la majorité **frondent** (*are in revolt; rebel*)

frondeur, -euse (*adj/nm,f*): ces initiatives **frondeuses** sont réprouvées par les inconditionnels du parti (*rebellious; insubordinate*); grossissant le rang des **frondeurs** au sein de son parti (*rebels*)

frontalier, -ière (*adj/nm*): un **incident frontalier** fait dix morts (*border incident*); 30.000 **frontaliers** vont travailler en Allemagne (*person working across the border*); SEE ALSO **différend**

frontière (*nf*): s'infiltrant à travers la **frontière septentrionale** du pays (*northern border*); SEE ALSO **reconduite, verrouiller**

fructueux, -euse (*adj*): les entretiens ont été plus **fructueux** que prévu (*fruitful, useful*)

fuir (*vt*): il avait **fui** la répression en 2003 (*flee [from]*); ceux qui tentaient de **fuir le pays** (*flee the country*)

fuite (*nf*): selon des **fuites** émanant de son entourage (*leak; indiscretion*); 10.000 **fuites de cerveaux** par an vers les Etats-Unis (*brain drain*); une **fuite en avant** qui reporte à plus tard la solution des problèmes (*reluctance to take necessary action*); SEE ALSO **délai**

fuseau (*nm*): Londres, dont le **fuseau horaire** permet de traiter dans la journée avec New York et Tokyo (*time zone*)

fusion (*nf*): leur opposition à la **fusion** des deux entreprises (*merger*); SEE ALSO **monopole**

fusionner (*vi*): contraindre les entreprises à **fusionner** ou à se rapprocher (*amalgamate; merge*); (*vt*): le groupe français va **fusionner** les activités de sa filiale avec celles du constructeur américain (*merge*)

fustiger (*vt*): la presse américaine **fustige** la France pour sa pusillanimité (*censure, denounce*)

G

gabegie (*nf*): Bruxelles dénonce la **gabegie** de l'aide au tiers-monde (*waste [due to bad management]*)

gadget (*nm*): un **gadget** pour retrouver les suffrages des jeunes? (*gimmick; token measure*)

gage (*nm*): Londres réclame des **gages** supplémentaires à Dublin; la monnaie unique, un **gage** de croissance et de création d'emplois (*guarantee*)

gain (*nm*): le **gain** de quatre sièges (*winning, gaining*); négocier avec les syndicats des **gains de productivité** (*productivity increases*); la cour **donne gain de cause** à la société Peugeot (*find in favour of*); SEE ALSO **boursier**

galère (*nf*): la **galère** des jeunes peu diplômés (*hard grind; struggle*)

galérer (*vi*): **galérer** toute une journée, sans résultat tangible (*have a hard time; have a lot of hassle*)

garant, -e (*adj/nm,f*): le créancier peut alors réclamer au **garant** l'intégralité de la dette (*guarantor*); **se porter garant** n'est pas un acte anodin (*stand guarantor [for sb]*)

garantie (*nf*): pour un chômeur de plus de 60 ans, on applique la **garantie de ressources** (*top-up of social security benefit for the out-of-work*)

garantir (*vt*): la marque NF **garantit** la conformité des produits à des normes de qualité (*guarantee, ensure*); SEE ALSO **viser**

garde (*nm*): le **garde des Sceaux** fait le bilan de ses années à la tête du ministère de la Justice (*French Minister of Justice*); (*nf*): obtenir la **garde** de ses enfants (*custody*); la présence d'un avocat pendant les **gardes à vue** (*period of police custody*); les syndicats **adressent une mise en garde** au gouvernement (*issue a warning*)

garde-fou (*nm*): les députés ont mis quelques **garde-fous** au projet de loi (*safeguard*)

garder (*vt*): les aides pour **faire garder** son enfant (*have [child/ sick/elderly person] looked after*); [**se**] (*vpr*): mais il **s'est bien gardé** de tout triomphalisme (*carefully avoided*); SEE ALSO **anonymat, écharpe**

garderie (*nf*): la mise en place de **garderies** et de jardins d'enfant (*child-minding facilities*); SEE ALSO **halte-garderie**

gardien, -ienne (*nm,f*): des **gardiens de la paix** du commissariat voisin (*police officer, policeman*); emmener ses enfants en bas âge chez la **gardienne** [d'enfants] (*childminder*)

gauche (*adj/nf*): **la** Gauche a des chances de l'emporter (*the Left*); SEE ALSO **ancrage, glisser**

gel (*nm*): un long **gel** des relations avec Paris (*suspension*); le **gel des salaires** a conduit directement à la chute du gouvernement (*wage freeze*)

geler (*vt*): Bruxelles veut **geler** les prix agricoles (*freeze*); la France **gèle** ses relations avec Pékin (*suspend*)

gendarme (*nm*): le cafouillage de l'enquête, la concurrence entre **gendarmes** et policiers (*policeman; [Fr] gendarme*)

gendarmerie (*nf*): une vive tension entre la **gendarmerie** et la police est à craindre (*police force; [Fr] Gendarmerie*); la mission de la **gendarmerie mobile**: le maintien et le rétablissement de l'ordre (*[Fr] riot police*); SEE ALSO **relever**

gêne (*nf*): la **gêne des usagers** du métro devrait être limitée (*inconvenience [to travellers]*)

général, -e *mpl* **-aux** (*adj*): SEE **assemblée, avocat, conseil général, conseiller, frais**

généralisé, -e (*adj*): les scandales et la corruption **généralisée** (*widespread*)

généraliser (*vt*): le CNPF et les patrons cherchent à **généraliser** le travail précaire (*bring into widespread use*); [**se**] (*vpr*): le mouvement de mécontentement **se généralise** (*spread; become widespread*)

généraliste (*adj/nmf*): en France, on a une chaîne de télévision **généraliste** de trop (*general; general interest*); les [médecins] **généralistes** sont les parents pauvres de la profession (*doctor in general practice*)

gérance (*nf*): pendant leur **gérance**, l'affaire a périclité (*[period of] management*)

gérant, -e (*nm,f*): **gérant** d'un complexe touristique en Corse (*manager*)

gérer (*vt*): une situation délicate à **gérer** pour la Maison Blanche (*deal with, control*); 30% des citoyens estiment que leur ville est **bien gérée** (*well administered*)

gestion (*nf*): confier la **gestion** à un entrepreneur du privé (*management, administration*); certains médias **critiquent sa gestion de la crise nucléaire** (*criticize his handling of the nuclear issue*); SEE ALSO **frauduleux, paritaire, quotidien, trésorerie**

glissade (*nf*): la **glissade** du dollar devient inquiétante (*slide*)

glissement (*nm*): le **glissement** constaté vers la répression (*shift*); en dépit d'un **glissement à droite** aux élections municipales (*swing to the right*)

glisser (*vi*): les sondages indiquent que l'électorat **glisse à gauche** (*shift to the left*)

global, -e *mpl* **-aux** (*adj*): le **résultat global** est satisfaisant (*overall result*); 70% du **montant global du contrat** (*total contract price*); SEE ALSO **dotation**

gonflement (*nm*): le **gonflement de la demande** suivra obligatoirement (*increase in demand*)

gonfler (*vt*): le taux de participation a été largement **gonflé** (*inflate; exaggerate*)

gouvernant, -e (*adj/nm,f*): l'incapacité des **gouvernants** à réduire des inégalités criantes (*government; those in power*)

gouvernement (*nm*): la démission du **gouvernement** ne saurait tarder (*government*); le **gouvernement de coalition** nippon mis en échec (*coalition government*); SEE ALSO **tomber**

grâce (*nf*): bénéficier d'une **grâce** présidentielle (*pardon; reprieve*)

gracier (*vt*): un gouverneur texan **gracie** un condamné à mort (*grant a pardon [to], reprieve*)

grandeur (*nf*): la Chine, puissance économique **de première grandeur** (*of the first order/magnitude*)

gratuité (*nf*): la **gratuité des transports** pour RMIstes rejetée (*free travel on public transport*); un local mis à leur disposition **avec la gratuité du loyer** (*rent-free*)

gré (*nm*): les cours du baril fluctuent **au gré des événements** au Moyen-Orient (*as the situation dictates*); **au gré des votes**, sa majorité s'est évanouie (*as vote followed vote*)

greffe (*nm*): extrait des minutes du **greffe** de la Cour d'appel de Paris (*registry; Office of Clerk to the Court*)

greffier, -ière (*nm,f*): les notes d'audience prises par le **greffier** (*clerk to the court*)

grève (*nf*): le syndicat **appelle à la grève** (*call for a strike*); les transports paralysés par une **grève illimitée** (*indefinite strike*); la grogne y a pris la forme de **grèves perlées** (*go-slow tactics*); la seule arme de la direction: la **grève patronale** (*lockout*); faire pression sur l'employeur au moyen de **grèves sauvages** (*wildcat strike*); des **grèves sur le tas** ont arrêté la production (*sitdown strike*); la **grève du zèle** a contraint le patron à fermer l'usine (*work-to-rule*); SEE ALSO **consigne, mot d'ordre, mouvement, piquet, préavis, rythmer**

grever (*vt*): de lourdes charges sociales **grèvent** les PME en France (*place a heavy burden on*); les virements **sont grevés de frais de transfert** (*incur high transfer costs*)

grief (*nm*): répondre aux **griefs** formulés par le syndicat (*complaint; grievance*)

griffe (*nf*): articles et vêtements portant la **griffe** Cardin (*maker's label*); des méthodes terroristes **portant la griffe d'al-Qaida** (*bearing the hallmark of al-Qaida*)

grille (*nf*): l'émission a été supprimée de la **grille des programmes** (*programme schedule*); les salaires de base s'alignent sur la **grille de salaires** de la Banque de France (*salary structure, pay scale*)

grogne (*nf*): devant la montée de la **grogne syndicale** en France (*simmering union discontent*); SEE ALSO **venir**

grogner (*vi*): les Allemands **grognent** contre l'effort fiscal qui leur est demandé (*complain*)

gros, grosse (*adj/nm*): **le gros des manifestants** s'est regroupé plus loin (*the main body of protesters*); **les gros** semblent à l'abri de la crise (*the wealthy, the rich*); SEE ALSO **contribuable, négociant, polémique, prix, rapporter**

grossir (*vi*): et le chiffre pourrait **grossir** encore (*rise*); (*vt*): ils ne veulent pas **grossir** les deux millions de chômeurs (*increase, swell*)

grossiste (*nm*): le **grossiste** ou intermédiaire achète au producteur (*wholesaler*)

groupe (*nm*): une filiale française d'un **groupe** américain (*group, conglomerate*); mettre en place un **groupe de travail** sur la toxicomanie (*working party*); les interventions des divers **groupes d'intérêt** (*interest group*); les **groupes de pression**, comme le lobby noir américain (*pressure group, lobby*); SEE ALSO **appartenance**

groupuscule (*nm*): un **groupuscule** d'extrême droite (*small group; faction*)

guérilla (*nf*): les massacres de civils perpétrés par la **guérilla** (*guerrilla group*); SEE ALSO **recrudescence**

guerre (*nf*): la **guerre éclata** entre le Tchad et la Libye (*war broke out*); dans la **guerre des prix** engagée sur les vols transatlantiques (*price war*); SEE ALSO **butin**, **criminel**, **exacerbation**, **fauteur**, **larvé**, **sanglant**

guichet (*nm*): les **guichets** du réseau Barclays (*service point; counter [esp. of bank]*)

H

habilitation (*nf*): la **loi d'habilitation** autorisant le gouvernement à prendre par ordonnances des mesures économiques (*law empowering government [to legislate by decree]*)

habiliter (*vt*): les lois **habilitent** le gouvernement à recourir aux ordonnances (*empower, entitle*)

habitat (*nm*): l'aménagement de l'**habitat ancien** (*older housing*); les **habitats collectifs** et notamment les logements sociaux (*apartment block*); SEE ALSO **marché**

habitation (*nf*): la distance entre le **lieu d'habitation** et le lieu de travail (*place of residence, home*); vivre en HLM [**habitation à loyer modéré**] (*[Fr] cheap council housing*); SEE ALSO **immeuble, taxe**

halte-garderie (*nf*): la **halte-garderie** accueille les enfants de moins de six ans (*short-stay child-care facility; day nursery*)

handicapé,-e (*adj/nm,f*): des aides aux personnes dépendantes âgées ou **handicapées** (*handicapped, disabled*); une maison d'accueil pour **handicapés adultes** (*disabled adult*)

harcèlement (*nm*): victime de **harcèlement sexuel**, elle porta plainte (*sexual harassment*)

harki (*nm*): hommage aux **harkis** soldats de la France (*Algerian soldier who fought on the French side during the Algerian war*)

hausse (*nf*): la **hausse des impôts** ne dépassera pas 2,9% (*tax increases*); subir de plein fouet les **hausses de loyer** (*rent rises*); la **tendance est à la hausse** sur les marchés des changes (*upward trend; 'bullish' conditions*); SEE ALSO **moduler, réévaluation, revoir, vertigineux**

hausser (*vt*): il propose de **hausser** le plafond à 150.000 euros (*raise, increase*)

haussier,-ière (*adj*): la place de Shanghaï est à nouveau **haussière** (*rising, bullish*)

haut, -e (*adj*): il dénonce la corruption **en haut lieu** (*in high places*); (*adv*): les prix du pétrole **au plus haut** depuis 13 ans (*at their highest [level]*); SEE ALSO **chambre, commissariat, fonction, fonctionnaire, gamme, niveau, niveler, rang**

hebdomadaire (*adj/nm*): fixer la **durée hebdomadaire de travail** à 36 heures (*length of the working week*); *Unité*, **hebdomadaire** du Parti socialiste (*weekly newspaper*); SEE ALSO **presse**

hébergement (*nm*): renforcer le dispositif d'**hébergement** des sans abri (*housing, shelter*); un **centre d'hébergement** pour les SDF (*hostel*); SEE ALSO **forfait**

héberger (*vt*): **héberger** des vieux qui ne sont plus capables de vivre seuls chez eux (*house, accommodate*)

hégémonie (*nf*): la double **hégémonie** de la France et de la Grande-Bretagne au Proche-Orient (*hegemony*)

hémicycle (*nm*): dans l'**hémicycle du palais Bourbon**, les parlementaires sont répartis en groupes (*[Fr] benches of the National Assembly*)

hémorragie (*nf*): taxe qui lui fait craindre une **hémorragie des capitaux** hors d'Europe (*outflow of capital*)

héritage (*nm*): le partage des biens mobiliers lors d'un **héritage** (*inheritance*)

hériter (*vi*): la question de savoir qui va **hériter** (*inherit, come into an inheritance*); (*vt*): **hériter** d'une grande fortune (*inherit*)

héritier, -ière (*nm,f*): les **héritiers** en ligne directe (*heir*)

heure (*nf*): l'Espagne **à l'heure de la mondialisation** (*in the age of globalization*); **l'heure est venue** de faire jouer à plein la diplomatie (*the time has come/it is time [to]*); les **heures supplémentaires** sont rémunérées au même taux (*overtime*)

heurt (*nm*): des **heurts** ont éclaté pendant un meeting électoral (*clash, fighting*); la transition s'est faite **sans heurts** (*smoothly*)

heurter (*vt*): une décision qui a vivement **heurté** l'opinion publique en Allemagne (*offend, upset*); [**se**] (*vpr*): la foule **se heurtait à l'armée** (*clashed with the army*)

hexagonal, -e *mpl* **-aux** (*adj*): enfin sorti d'un gaullisme trop **hexagonal** (*[Fr] chauvinistic*); l'Autriche, très critique vis-à-vis du **laxisme hexagonal** (*French laxity*)

hexagone (*nm*): l'ambiguïté des rapports entre la Corse et l'**Hexagone** (*metropolitan France*)

hiérarchie (*nf*): se conformer aux instructions de la **hiérarchie** (*top brass; higher echelons*); l'ensemble de la **hiérarchie des salaires** (*wage scales*)

hiérarchique (*adj*): l'enseignante avait déjà eu maille à partir avec sa **hiérarchie** (*superiors*); il est fortement conseillé de **suivre la voie hiérarchique** (*go through the correct channels*)

homicide (*nm*): condamné à deux ans de prison pour **homicide involontaire** (*manslaughter*); inculpé d'**homicide volontaire** et écroué (*murder*)

homme (*nm*): le nouvel **homme fort** du pays depuis le coup de force (*strong man*); des **hommes de main** qui manipulent en réalité leurs commanditaires (*collaborator; agent*)

homologue (*adj/nmf*): le Premier ministre, comme son **homologue** espagnol (*opposite number; counterpart*)

homologuer (*vt*): les nouveaux tarifs ont été **homologués** et seront appliqués dès janvier (*ratify, approve*)

horaire (*adj/nm*): le Smic **horaire** sera porté à 10 euros (*hourly, per hour*); choisir entre un système d'**horaires modulables** et un temps partiel; les **horaires à la carte** sont également pratiqués à la Société générale (*flexible working hours; flexitime*); SEE ALSO **décalage**, **non respect**, **plage**

hors (*prep*): **hors pétrole**, la hausse des prix à la consommation n'accélère pas (*excluding oil products*); SEE ALSO **cause**, **loi**

hôte (*nmf*): l'**hôte** actuel de la Maison Blanche (*incumbent, occupant*)

hôtel de ville (*nm*): ses chances de reconquérir l'**hôtel de ville** sont minces (*town hall; mayoral office*)

houille (*nf*): le charbon britannique revient plus cher que la **houille importée** (*imported coal*)

houiller, -ère (*adj/nf*): compressions de personnel dans l'**industrie houillère** (*coal industry*); la fermeture récente des **houillères** de Provence (*colliery, coal mine*)

houleux, -euse (*adj*): **débat houleux** hier à l'Assemblée (*stormy/ rowdy debate*)

huée (*nf*): il est reparti **sous les huées du public** (*to the boos of the audience*)

huer (*vt*): d'autres ont **hué** certains de ses propos (*boo, deride*)

huis clos (*nm*): on pourrait **demander le huis clos** (*ask for proceedings to be held in camera*); (*adv*): l'audience a eu lieu **à huis clos** (*in camera, behind closed doors*)

huissier (*nm*): un **huissier** posté à l'entrée de l'hémicycle (*usher*); l'**huissier [de justice]** est venu saisir les biens et expulser les locataires (*bailiff*); SEE ALSO **citation**, **constat**

humanitaire (*adj*): les **organisations humanitaires** s'inquiètent (*aid organization*); SEE ALSO **ingérence**

hygiène (*nf*): s'adresser aux **services d'hygiène** départementaux (*public health department*)

hypothèse (*nf*): l'**hypothèse** de sa candidature aux élections semble assez fantaisiste (*hypothesis*); les parents **excluent l'hypothèse d'une fugue** (*rule out the idea that [the child] ran away from home*); SEE ALSO **écarter**

hypothétique (*adj*): attendre un **hypothétique** redressement (*hypothetical*)

idée (*nf*): retenons-en quelques **idées-forces** (*key idea; central theme*); la sécurité est une **idée fixe** de la droite (*obsession*); SEE ALSO **prévaloir**

identitaire (*adj*): ranimer le **sentiment identitaire** de la communauté (*sense of identity*); SEE ALSO **revendication**

identité (*nf*): SEE **décliner, pièce, vérification**

illégal, -e *mpl* **-aux** (*adj*): le financement **illégal** des partis politiques (*illegal*); SEE ALSO **détention, immigrant**

illégalité (*nf*): les nouvelles centrales syndicales **agissent dans l'illégalité** (*be in breach of the law*)

illicite (*adj*): le lock-out préventif est **illicite** (*unlawful*); le travail **illicite** ou clandestin (*illegal*); SEE ALSO **entente, trafic**

îlot (*nm*): dans certains **îlots** frappés par la délinquance (*[housing] block*)

îlotage (*nm*): dans les quartiers chauds, l'**îlotage** sera mis en place (*area surveillance; community policing*)

îlotier (*nm*): 300 **îlotiers** se partagent le terrain (*community policeman*)

image de marque (*nf*): la nécessité de redorer son **image de marque** (*brand image; corporate identity*)

immatriculation (*nf*): les **immatriculations** devraient peu diminuer l'an prochain (*registration [esp. of new vehicle]*); SEE ALSO **plaque**

immatriculer (*vt*): une voiture **immatriculée** dans l'Aude (*register*)

immeuble (*nm*): la construction de huit **immeubles de bureaux** (*office block*); un **immeuble [d'habitation]** de la rue du Dragon (*apartment block*); SEE ALSO **bien**

immigrant, -e (*adj/nm,f*): la plupart sont des **immigrants illégaux** (*illegal immigrant*)

immigration (*nf*): une famille étrangère ou **issue de l'immigration** (*of immigrant stock*); SEE ALSO **complaisance**

immiscer [**s'**] (*vpr*): Amman n'a pas l'intention de **s'immiscer** dans les affaires intérieures de Bagdad (*interfere, meddle*)

immixtion (*nf*): l'**immixtion** croissante de la justice dans la vie politique italienne (*interference; meddling*)

immobilier, -ière (*adj/nm*): avec l'envolée spectaculaire des prix de l'**immobilier** (*property, real estate*); SEE ALSO **arnaque, boom, crédit, prêt**

immobilisme (*nm*): il dénonce l'**immobilisme** des partis traditionnels (*reluctance to change*); l'**immobilisme** coupable de la communauté internationale (*failure to act*)

impasse (*nf*): l'**impasse politique** à Bagdad (*political deadlock*); SEE ALSO **débloquer**

impayé, -e (*adj/nmpl*): les heures supplémentaires sont souvent **impayées** (*unpaid*); la saisie, la procédure extrême en cas d'**impayés de loyer** (*arrears of rent*)

impératif, -ive (*adj/nm*): des besoins **impératifs** (*vital, urgent*); insister sur l'**impératif** d'économies budgétaires (*urgency; necessity*)

impéritie (*nf*): la corruption générale et l'**impéritie** de l'Etat (*incompetence*)

implantation (*nf*): la société poursuit sa stratégie d'**implantations** en Asie (*setting up [business/factory]*)

implanter (*vt*): l'entreprise japonaise décide d'y **implanter** un site de production (*set up, locate*); [**s'**] (*vpr*): le premier hôtelier occidental à **s'implanter** à Moscou (*set up business*); beaucoup d'immigrants polonais **s'implantèrent** dans le Nord (*settle*)

implication (*nf*): condamné pour son **implication** dans l'assassinat de l'ancien ministre (*involvement*)

impliquer (*vt*): les éléments manquent pour **impliquer** les Etats-Unis dans le kidnapping (*implicate*); [**s'**] (*vpr*): **s'impliquer** dans le comité de gestion (*get involved*)

importance (*nf*): en raison de leur **importance** stratégique (*importance*); l'**importance** des effectifs envoyés indique la gravité de la situation (*size, number*)

important, -e (*adj*): l'**importante** minorité hongroise en Roumanie (*sizeable*); un pays confronté à d'**importants** problèmes politiques et sociaux (*major; serious*)

imposable (*adj*): à condition que le **revenu imposable** ne dépasse pas 20.000 euros (*taxable income*)

imposer (*vt*): en aucune manière la religion ne serait **imposée** (*impose, make obligatory*); le nouveau système **impose** chaque adulte d'un montant égal (*tax, assess for tax*); [**s'**] (*vpr*): la difficulté pour les femmes de **s'imposer** dans un secteur peu féminisé (*make an impact*); la vigilance **s'impose** plus que jamais (*be necessary*); SEE ALSO **plat**

imposition (*nf*): l'**imposition** du vote à bulletin secret avant chaque grève (*imposing*); les plus-values réalisées ne font l'objet d'aucune **imposition** (*tax, taxation*); SEE ALSO **feuille, seuil, tranche**

impôt (*nm*): les Britanniques payent un fort **impôt sur le revenu** (*income tax*); l'**impôt sur les grandes fortunes** [IGF] fut supprimé en 1986 (*wealth tax*); l'**impôt sur les sociétés** doit descendre à 40% (*corporation tax*); SEE ALSO **allégement, alourdir, arriéré, assiette, assujettissement, dégrever, exonérer, feuille, franchise, hausse, recette, réduction, réforme, soumis**

imprévu, -e (*adj/nm*): une visite **imprévue** par le député de la circonscription (*unexpected; surprise*); **sauf imprévu**, il assistera à la réunion (*barring unforeseen circumstances*)

impulsion (*nf*): il faudrait **donner une impulsion nouvelle** à la construction européenne (*give fresh impetus*)

impunité (*nf*): les auteurs de l'attentat ont **obtenu l'impunité** (*go unpunished*)

inactif, -ive (*adj/nm,f*): familles défavorisées, parents **inactifs**, échec scolaire (*out-of-work, unemployed*)

inaction (*nf*): la famille de l'otage français dénonce l'**inaction** de Paris (*failure to act; lack of initiative*)

inactivité (*nf*): retourner à l'**inactivité** ou au chômage (*inactivity; unemployment*)

inadaptation (*nf*): cette **inadaptation** à la demande mondiale (*failure to adjust*); il explique le chômage par l'**inadaptation de l'éducation nationale à l'entreprise** (*failure of the educational system to prepare the young for the world of work*)

inadapté, -e (*adj*): le Bac, examen **inadapté** aux besoins contemporains (*ill-suited*); SEE ALSO **enfance**

inadéquation (*nf*): une **inadéquation** entre l'offre et la demande (*discrepancy*); lutter contre l'**inadéquation** de notre système de formation (*shortcomings*)

inamical, -e *mpl* **-aux** (*adj*): une tentative de prise de contrôle **inamicale** du groupe textile (*unwelcome, hostile*); SEE ALSO **offre**

inapte (*adj*): l'héritier est considéré comme **inapte** à devenir roi (*unfit, unsuited*); ceux qui sont **inaptes au travail** (*unfit for work*)

incapacité (*nf*): profitant de l'**incapacité** de notre vieille Europe à se réformer (*inability*); sa maladie lui vaut trois mois d'**incapacité de travail** (*unfitness for work*)

incarcération (*nf*): une mesure alternative à l'**incarcération** (*prison sentence*)

incarcérer (*vt*): inculpé et **incarcéré** à la maison d'arrêt (*imprison, lock up*)

incidence (*nf*): avoir de lourdes **incidences** sur la rentabilité de l'opération (*effect, repercussion*)

incident (*nm*): ceci avait manqué de déclencher un **incident diplomatique** (*diplomatic incident*)

incitatif, -ive (*adj*): Air France proposerait au personnel des **mesures incitatives de départ** (*early retirement incentives*)

incitation (*nf*): les **incitations à la haine raciale** sont passibles de lourdes sanctions (*incitement to racial hatred*); des **incitations fiscales** qui comprennent des abattements de 100% pour dépenses d'équipement (*tax incentive*)

inciter (*vt*): **inciter** les jeunes à prendre part à la vie politique (*encourage, prompt*)

incivilité (*nf*): la délinquance, les **incivilités** et les actes de violence (*general lawlessness*)

incohérence (*nf*): le président du Conseil italien est handicapé par les **incohérences** de sa coalition (*disunity*)

incompressible (*adj*): le parquet demande une **peine incompressible** de 30 ans (*sentence without remission, minimum sentence*)

incontesté, -e (*adj*): il devient en 1978 le maître **incontesté** du pays (*unchallenged*)

incontournable (*adj*): la guérilla des Khmers rouges en fait un **élément incontournable** de tout règlement (*key element*); l'Iran s'affirme comme une puissance régionale **incontournable** (*which cannot be ignored*)

incorporation (*nf*): l'étudiant peut repousser son **incorporation** à 24 ans (*military draft, call-up*); SEE ALSO **report, sursis**

incriminer (*vt*): les personnes **incriminées** dans ce dossier (*incriminated; implicated*)

inculpation (*nf*): la libération de prisonniers détenus sans la moindre **inculpation** (*formal charge*); **être sous le coup d'une inculpation** pour proxénétisme aggravé (*face criminal charges*); SEE ALSO **chef**

inculpé, -e (*adj/nm,f*): le seul **inculpé** toujours détenu (*person charged with an offence*)

inculper (*vt*): mort d'un manifestant: un policier **inculpé** (*charge, indict*); un suspect pourra être détenu **sans être inculpé** (*without being charged*)

incurie (*nf*): l'opposition dénonce l'**incurie** des gestionnaires travaillistes (*negligence; inefficiency*); l'**incurie budgétaire** dans le secteur privé (*lack of thrift*)

indécis, -e (*adj/nm,f*): rarement les **électeurs indécis** ont été aussi nombreux (*floating voter, 'don't know'*)

indéfectible (*adj*): allié **indéfectible** de Damas (*loyal, unswerving*)

indélicat, -e (*adj*): des fonds détournés par des intermédiaires **indélicats** (*dishonest, unscrupulous*)

indélicatesse (*nf*): accusé d'**indélicatesse**, il fut démis de ses fonctions (*dishonesty*)

indemnisation (*nf*): vers une réforme de l'**indemnisation du chômage** (*unemployment benefit*)

indemniser (*vt*): l'Etat refuse d'**indemniser** les victimes (*indemnify, compensate*)

indemnité (*nf*): l'**indemnité de logement** versée aux instituteurs (*housing allowance*); toucher des **indemnités d'arrêt-maladie** égales à 80% du salaire brut (*sick pay*); une **indemnité de départ** égale à un mois de salaire par année d'ancienneté (*severance pay*)

indépendance (*nf*): les Albanais du Kosovo réclament l'**indépendance** dans les plus brefs délais (*independence*); SEE ALSO **accéder, accession**

indépendantiste (*adj/nmf*): comment contenir la fièvre **indépendantiste** des républiques soviétiques? (*separatist*); les **indépendantistes** veulent négocier en position de force (*separatist; member of independence movement*)

indéterminé, -e (*adj*): un projet proposé en juin puis **remis à une échéance indéterminée** (*postponed indefinitely*); SEE **durée**

indexation (*nf*): mettre fin à l'**indexation** des salaires sur les prix (*indexing*)

indexer (*vt*): les pensions seront **indexées sur les prix** (*index-linked to prices*)

indice (*nm*): la police ne dispose d'aucun **indice** sérieux (*clue*); l'**indice de l'INSEE** permet de constater l'évolution des prix pendant une période donnée (*[Fr] retail price index*); l'**indice d'écoute** a baissé (*TV/radio audience rating*); SEE ALSO **accabler**

indigent, -e (*adj/nm,f*): même les **indigents** seront tenus de s'acquitter du nouvel impôt (*destitute; poor*)

indiscuté, -e (*adj*): un monopole longtemps **indiscuté** (*undisputed, unchallenged*)

indu, -e (*adj*): cette société aurait perçu des commissions **indues** (*unjustified, unwarranted*)

indûment (*adv*): occuper **indûment** un lit hospitalier (*without due cause*); on lui reproche d'avoir **indûment** touché plus de 13.000 euros (*wrongfully; fraudulently*)

inédit, -e (*adj*): selon un sondage **inédit** de la Sofres (*unpublished*); des élections pluralistes, **inédites** dans l'histoire du pays (*unprecedented*)

inégalité (*nf*): une politique de redressement des **inégalités** (*inequality; disparity*); il y dénonçait les **inégalités sociales** (*social inequality*); SEE ALSO **aggraver**

inemploi (*nm*): un statut qui garantit un revenu minimum en cas d'**inemploi** (*unemployment, being out of work*)

inexécution (*nf*): réclamer des dommages et intérêts en cas d'**inexécution du contrat** (*failure to honour a contract*)

inexistant, -e (*adj*): le chômage, **inexistant** sous les régimes communistes (*non-existent*)

inexistence (*nf*): l'**inexistence** d'une véritable opposition politique (*lack; absence*); des problèmes réels, comme l'**inexistence d'une politique de la jeunesse** (*absence of a youth policy*)

inféoder [s'] (*vpr*): une radio totalement **inféodée au pouvoir** (*in government hands*)

infirmer (*vt*): **infirmer** un jugement; la chambre d'accusation **infirme** les ordonnances prises par le juge d'instruction (*overturn, quash*)

infléchir (*vt*): il a **infléchi** la position de son parti sur l'IVG (*modify [slightly]*); [**s'**] (*vpr*): la production décline, les exportations **s'infléchissent** (*slump, fall*)

infléchissement (*nm*): nouvel **infléchissement** de la position de Washington (*adjustment, shift; reorientation*)

inflexion (*nf*): Bruxelles salue l'**inflexion** de Nicolas Sarkozy sur la Turquie (*change [of policy]*)

influence (*nf*): SEE **trafic**

influent, -e (*adj*): un journal **influent** en raison de son lectorat (*influential*)

infondé, -e (*adj*): des critiques totalement **infondées** (*unjustified, groundless*)

information (*nf*): cette **information** n'a pas encore été confirmée (*report; news*); après la fin de l'enquête de la police, le parquet **ouvre une information** (*start a preliminary investigation*); SEE ALSO **complément**, **presse**

informatique (*adj/nf*): SEE **fichage**, **piratage**, **saisie**

informatisé, -e (*adj*): un système **informatisé** d'enregistrement du cheptel (*computerized*); les informations sont collectées sur des **fichiers informatisés** (*data files*)

infraction (*nf*): il conteste les **infractions** qui lui sont imputées (*offence*); des **infractions à la législation** sur les stupéfiants (*breach of the law*); SEE ALSO **pluralité**

infrastructure (*nf*): le groupe brésilien renforce ainsi son **infrastructure** européenne (*base; organization*)

infructueux, -euse (*adj*): après des mois de discussions **infructueuses** (*fruitless*)

ingérence (*nf*): Irak: Washington dénonce l'**ingérence** d'agents iraniens (*interference*); les limites de l'**ingérence humanitaire** (*interference on humanitarian grounds*); SEE ALSO **devoir**, **non-ingérence**

ingérer [**s'**] (*vpr*): ne pas **s'ingérer** dans les affaires intérieures d'autres pays (*interfere, meddle*)

initié, -e (*nm,f*): lors du rachat de la société, des **initiés** ont gagné des millions de dollars (*insider trader/dealer*); SEE ALSO **délit**

injure (*nf*): les textes de loi qui répriment l'**injure raciale** (*racial abuse*); des propos qui lui ont valu une mise en examen pour **injures à caractère raciste** (*racist remarks*)

innocence (*nf*): démontrer l'**innocence** de son client (*innocence*); SEE ALSO **présomption**

innocent, -e (*adj*): **innocent** du meurtre (*innocent, not guilty*)

innocenter (*vt*): **innocenté** du meurtre, grâce à l'ADN (*clear, find innocent*)

inobservation (*nf*): l'**inobservation** des normes de sécurité (*failure to observe; non-compliance with*)

inopérant, -e (*adj*): les remèdes s'avèrent **inopérants** (*ineffective*)

inopiné, -e (*adj*): à moins d'un retournement de situation **inopiné** (*unexpected, surprise*); des contrôles sont faits, à grande échelle et **de façon inopinée** (*in a random manner*)

inopinément (*adv*): il a dû démissionner **inopinément** la semaine dernière (*unexpectedly*)

inquiéter [s'] (*vpr*): les syndicats de magistrats unanimes à **s'inquiéter** (*express concern*)

inquiétude (*nf*): l'OCDE manifeste sur ce point de réelles **inquiétudes** (*anxiety, concern*)

insalubre (*adj*): la démolition de **logements insalubres** (*slum housing*)

insatisfaction (*nf*): leur **insatisfaction** vis-à-vis du président sortant (*dissatisfaction*)

inscription (*nf*): le directeur d'une école refuse l'**inscription** de sept enfants marocains (*[school] registration*); SEE ALSO **dossier, fiche, formulaire**

inscrire [s'] (*vpr*): **s'inscrire** à la faculté des Lettres (*register/enrol [for educational course]*); il tenait à **s'inscrire en faux** contre ces allégations (*strongly deny, refute*); SEE ALSO **liste**

inscrit, -e (*adj/nm,f*): le nombre d'**inscrits au chômage** a augmenté de 12% (*registered jobless*); SEE ALSO **non-inscrit**

insécurité (*nf*): le sentiment d'**insécurité**, un nouveau phénomène social (*feeling unsafe*); la lutte contre l'**insécurité urbaine** (*urban violence*); le manque d'enseignants et l'**insécurité des locaux** (*unsafe condition of the [school] buildings*)

insérer (*vt*): un programme qui vise à **insérer** 15.000 jeunes dans les entreprises (*find employment [for]*); [**s'**] (*vpr*): des jeunes qui ne sont pas parvenus à **s'insérer socialement** (*become socially integrated*)

insertion (*nf*): l'**insertion sociale** des migrants polonais en France (*social integration*); pour faciliter l'**insertion professionnelle des jeunes** (*integration of the young into a work environment*); SEE ALSO **revenu**, **stage**

insolvabilité (*nf*): en état d'**insolvabilité** notoire, la procédure de redressement judiciaire a été ouverte à leur égard (*insolvency*)

insolvable (*adj*): une forte augmentation du nombre de foyers **insolvables** (*insolvent*)

inspecteur, -trice (*nm,f*): l'**inspecteur d'Académie** au niveau départemental (*education officer; inspector of schools*)

inspection (*nf*): la nomination d'un instituteur par l'**inspection académique** (*[Fr] schools inspectorate*); l'**inspection du Travail**, sise au chef-lieu du département (*[Fr] factory inspectorate*)

installation (*nf*): optimiser les nouvelles **installations** (*equipment, plant*)

installer [**s'**] (*vpr*): les jeunes ménages qui cherchent à **s'installer** (*set up home*); plus de 12.000 Polonais **se sont installés** à Paris depuis deux ans (*settle*); son ambition: **s'installer à son compte** (*set up in his own business*)

instance (*nf*): les plus hautes **instances** irakiennes (*authority, body*); condamné **en première instance**, puis en appel (*in a court of first instance*); des dossiers **en instance** (*awaiting a decision, pending*); SEE ALSO **régulation**, **tribunal**,

instauration (*nf*): partisan de l'**instauration de quotas** (*setting of quotas*); malgré l'**instauration de l'état d'urgence** (*declaration of a state of emergency*)

instaurer (*vt*): avoir l'intention d'**instaurer** une démocratie réelle (*set up, establish*); [**s'**] (*vpr*): l'ordre nouveau qui **s'instaure** en Afrique australe (*come about; be set up*)

instituer (*vt*): le Smic, **institué** en 1968; faut-il **instituer** un service civil obligatoire? (*set up, establish*)

instituteur, -trice (*nm,f*): l'indemnité de logement versée aux **instituteurs** (*primary school teacher*)

institution (*nf*): l'**institution** d'un pouvoir dominé par l'armée (*establishment*); les **institutions politiques** de la nouvelle République (*political institutions*); SEE ALSO **doter**

instruction (*nf*): l'**instruction du dossier** a été confiée au juge Dupont (*preliminary examination of the case*); une centaine d'arrêtés, circulaires et **instructions** ont été publiés (*directive*); SEE ALSO **juge**

instruire (*vt*): le juge chargé d'**instruire la plainte** (*investigate a complaint*); un juge d'instruction de Rennes va **instruire le dossier** (*conduct an investigation; prepare a case for judgment*)

insuffisance (*nf*): dénoncer les **insuffisances** du système de santé (*shortcomings; defects*); l'**insuffisance du budget** consacré à la justice (*inadequate level of spending*); SEE ALSO **provision**

insurgé, -e (*nm,f*): Damas, accusé de soutenir des groupes d'**insurgés** irakiens (*insurgent, rebel*)

insurger [s'] (*vpr*): l'association **s'est insurgée** contre cette attitude (*protest against; condemn*)

insurrection (*nf*): Sri-Lanka, ravagée par les **insurrections** depuis 1983 (*uprising*)

intangibilité (*nf*): insister sur l'**intangibilité** des frontières (*inviolability*)

intégral, -e *mpl* **-aux** (*adj*): le texte **intégral** de son discours (*whole, complete*)

intégralité (*nf*): Téhéran exporte l'**intégralité de son brut** via le Golfe (*all her oil production*)

intégrant, -e (*adj*): SEE **partie**

intégration (*nf*): l'**intégration** de la Bulgarie dans l'UE (*entry; admission*); le nouveau ministre de l'**intégration** et de la lutte contre l'exclusion (*social integration*)

intégrer (*vt*): **intégrer** la fonction publique (*join; enter*); le Premier ministre voulait l'**intégrer** dans son cabinet (*include, appoint*); **[s']** (*vpr*): la volonté de **s'intégrer** en milieu rural (*integrate; settle*)

intégrisme (*nm*): la montée de l'**intégrisme** dans ce pays en majorité musulman (*fundamentalism*)

intégriste (*adj/nm*): les **intégristes**, partisans de la stricte application des dogmes et des pratiques musulmanes (*fundamentalist*)

intégrité (*nf*): restaurer l'**intégrité territoriale** du Liban (*territorial integrity*)

intempestif, -ive (*adj*): les remarques **intempestives** du ministre (*untimely; ill-timed, inopportune*)

intenable (*adj*): la position française était **intenable** (*untenable*)

intenter (*vt*): il **intenta un procès** contre les autorités françaises (*institute proceedings*)

intention (*nf*): un sondage lui donne 52% des **intentions de vote** (*promised/intended vote*)

interdiction (*nf*): depuis l'**interdiction** de la publicité pour le tabac (*ban [on]*); la **levée de l'interdiction** des activités politiques (*lifting of the ban*)

interdire (*vt*): le seul quotidien indépendant du pays a été **interdit de publication** (*be banned [esp. newspaper]*); l'étranger risque d'**être interdit de séjour** (*be refused a residence permit*); [**s'**] (*vpr*): Paris **s'interdit** d'apporter une aide logistique au dictateur (*refuse*)

interdit (*nm*): la levée des **interdits** concernant la consommation d'alcool (*ban, restriction*)

intéressant, -e (*adj*): proposer des conditions très **intéressantes** (*attractive*)

intéressé, -e (*adj/nm,f*): l'idée fut bien accueillie par les **intéressés** (*interested party*)

intéressement (*nm*): une réduction des salaires avec **intéressement aux résultats de la société** (*profit-sharing; profit-related pay scheme*); SEE ALSO **prime**

intéresser (*vt*): la réforme **intéressera** 1,5 million de familles (*concern*); il faut les **intéresser directement aux résultats de l'entreprise** (*give a share [esp. of profits]*)

intérêt (*nm*): Péchiney cède ses **intérêts** aux Japonais (*stake; operation*); SEE ALSO **abaisser, groupe, taux, travail**

intérieur, -e (*adj*): SEE **affaire, politique**

intérim (*nm*): les deux millions de salariés du secteur de l'**intérim** (*temporary work*); s'adresser à une **société d'intérim** (*temping agency*); **assurer l'intérim** de la direction financière (*deputize for; cover for*); SEE ALSO **mission**

intérimaire (*adj/nmf*): la composition d'un gouvernement **intérimaire** (*interim, caretaker*); embaucher des **[travailleurs] intérimaires** (*temporary worker*)

interjeter (*vt*): leurs avocats vont **interjeter appel** de la décision (*lodge an appeal*)

interlocuteur, -trice (*nm,f*): les Russes, seuls **interlocuteurs** des Serbes (*negotiating partner*)

intermédiaire (*adj/nm*): trouver une **solution intermédiaire** (*compromise*); les ventes d'armes dégagent des commissions énormes pour les **intermédiaires** (*middleman*); se proposer pour **servir d'intermédiaire** (*mediate*); négocier **sans intermédiaire** (*directly*)

intermittent, -e (*adj/nm,f*): les dockers mensualisés et les **intermittents** (*contract worker; casual labour*); **intermittents du spectacle**: vers plus de précarités? (*worker in the entertainment industry, without regular employment*)

interne (*adj*): une coalition en proie à des dissensions **internes** (*internal*); SEE ALSO **promotion**

interpellation (*nf*): **il y a eu dix interpellations** lors des manifestations (*ten people were detained for questioning*)

interpeller (*vt*): **interpeller** directement le ministre sur un dossier (*question; challenge*); six jeunes ont été **interpellés** et placés en garde à vue (*stop for questioning [by police]*)

interposer [**s'**] (*vpr*): les Casques bleus **s'interposent** aux quatre coins du monde; **s'interposer** dans le déchirement yougoslave (*intervene [to keep the peace]*)

interposition (*nf*): il propose une **force d'interposition** entre le Tchad et le Soudan (*intervention force*)

interprète (*nm*): **se faire l'interprète** de l'ensemble des travailleurs (*represent, speak for*)

interrogatoire (*nf*): subir douze heures d'**interrogatoires** (*questioning*)

interroger (*vt*): après avoir été **interrogé**, il a été écroué (*question*); [**s'**] (*vpr*): l'Angola **s'interroge** sur les véritables intentions de Pretoria (*wonder [about]*)

intersyndicale (*nf*): l'**intersyndicale** justice, regroupant magistrats, avocats et fonctionnaires (*inter-union committee*)

intervenant, -e (*nm,f*): les discours des divers **intervenants** (*speaker [in debate]*)

intervenir (*vi*): la décision d'**intervenir** militairement au Burundi (*intervene*); **intervenant** devant les assises du parti (*speak [in debate/discussion]*); **faire intervenir** les comités d'entreprise (*bring/call in, involve*); ces mesures **interviennent** dix jours après la promulgation de la loi (*come into effect*)

intervention (*nf*): à la veille de l'**intervention** militaire en Tchétchénie (*intervention*); consacrant son **intervention** aux questions européennes (*speech; contribution [to a debate]*)

intimité (*nf*): inculpé pour atteinte à l'**intimité de la vie privée** (*privacy of the individual*)

intoxication (*nf*): le mensonge et l'**intoxication**; dénoncer une campagne d'**intox[ication]** (*disinformation; propaganda*)

intraitable (*adj*): la base demeure **intraitable** sur sa revendication principale (*uncompromising; inflexible*); le ministre **est resté intraitable sur ce point** (*remained adamant on this point*)

intransigeant, -e (*adj*): la Pologne, **intransigeante** face à la Russie (*uncompromising, unyielding*)

introduction (*nf*): remettre à plus tard son **introduction en bourse** (*going public; listing on the stock exchange*)

invalider (*vt*): la Cour suprême a **invalidé** hier cette décision (*quash*)

inverser (*vt*): ne rien faire qui pourrait **inverser la tendance** (*reverse the trend*)

investir (*vt*): le candidat **investi** par l'UDF (*appoint, select*); des sans-papiers **investissent** une église parisienne (*occupy, take over [building]*); persuader les entreprises à **investir** et les ménages à consommer (*invest*); **[s']** (*vpr*): **il s'est beaucoup investi** dans le règlement de la crise libanaise (*put in a lot of effort; involve oneself fully*)

investissement (*nm*): un gros effort d'**investissement** sera fait (*investment*); SEE ALSO **amortir**

investiture (*nf*): briguer l'**investiture** du parti (*nomination [as candidate]; investiture*)

inviolabilité (*nf*): quant à l'**inviolabilité** des frontières (*intangibility, inviolability*); la protection de la vie privée, notamment l'**inviolabilité du domicile** (*right to privacy in one's own home*)

irréductible (*adj/nmf*): l'opposition **irréductible** de plusieurs députés libéraux (*out-and-out, implacable*); les **irréductibles** refusent tout compromis (*diehard, hardliner*)

irrégularité (*nf*): des élections tachées d'**irrégularité** (*irregularity*)

irrégulier, -ière (*adj*): l'Etat continue à combattre le séjour **irrégulier** des étrangers (*illegal; unauthorized*); la prolifération d'**étrangers en situation irrégulière** (*illegal immigrants*)

irresponsabilité (*nf*): son **irresponsabilité** lui évite toute poursuite judiciaire (*unimpeachability*); l'**irresponsabilité politique** du parlement européen (*[political] non-accountability*)

irresponsable (*adj*): le Président était **irresponsable** (*not accountable for his actions before a higher authority*)

isolé, -e (*adj*): le PCF se retrouve **isolé** sur cette question (*isolated*); SEE ALSO **femme, parent**

isolement (*nm*): l'aggravation de l'**isolement économique** du pays (*economic isolation*)

isoloir (*nm*): les électeurs ne se bousculent pas dans les **isoloirs** (*voting booth*)

issu, -e (*adj*): le premier président turc **issu du courant islamiste** (*with Islamic political roots*); un gouvernement **issu d'élections libres** (*democratically elected*); SEE ALSO **immigration**

issue (*nf*): quelle que soit l'**issue** du scrutin (*result*)

J

jachère (*nf*): imposer la **jachère**, et casser la course aux rendements (*taking land out of cultivation; leaving land fallow*)

jacobin, -e (*adj/nm,f*): l'Etat centralisateur et **jacobin** renforce son emprise sur la société (*Jacobinic, centralizing*)

jacobinisme (*nm*): purs produits du **jacobinisme** centralisateur (*state centralism*)

jacquerie (*nf*): face à la **jacquerie** des paysans en colère (*uprising; revolt*)

jaune (*adj/nm*): le **métal jaune**, et la pierre: deux valeurs refuges (*gold*); on les traitait de **jaunes** et de vendus (*blackleg, strike breaker*)

jet (*nm*): **jets de pierres** sporadiques et charges de CRS (*stone-throwing [esp. by demonstrators]*)

jeu *pl* **-x** (*nm*): être en faveur du **libre jeu de la concurrence** (*free/ unrestricted competition*); Autriche: la crise **fait le jeu de l'extrême droite** (*play into the hands of the far right*); aucun intérêt matériel n'**est en jeu** (*be at stake*); SEE ALSO **épingle**

jeune (*adj/nmf*): SEE **cas, difficulté**

jour (*nm*): les atrocités commises en Bosnie sont peu à peu **mises au jour** (*reveal, uncover, bring to light*); la **mise à jour** de la programmation réclamerait 20 millions d'euros (*bringing up to date*); SEE ALSO **chômé, férié, ouvrable, ouvré**

journal *pl* **-aux** (*nm*): dans une ordonnance publiée dans le **Journal officiel** du 21 mars (*[Fr] government publication containing details of new acts, laws etc*); les images du **journal télévisé** (*television news bulletin*); SEE ALSO **un**

journée (*nf*): une **journée ouvrée** par semaine (*working day*); la mise en place de la **journée continue** (*remaining open over lunch hour [office, shop]*); les syndicats se mobilisent et organisent des **journées d'action** (*day of action*); SEE ALSO **chômé**

judiciaire (*adj*): le **[pouvoir] judiciaire**, en vertu du principe de la séparation des pouvoirs, est indépendant (*judiciary*); SEE ALSO **administrateur, administration, antécédent, casier, contrôle, liquidateur, police, poursuite, procédure, redressement**

juge (*nm*): les **juges** appartiennent à la magistrature assise (*judges; [Brit] the Bench*); le **juge d'instruction**, à la fois juge et enquêteur (*[Fr] examining magistrate*); SEE ALSO **suppléant**

jugement (*nm*): le **jugement** sera rendu le 4 juin (*verdict, judgment*); SEE ALSO **délibéré, prévenu**

juger (*vt*): le tribunal d'instance **juge** les délits peu graves (*judge/ try [a case]*); quatre ans de détention **sans être jugé** (*without being brought to trial*); SEE ALSO **coupable**

juguler (*vt*): comment **juguler** l'inflation? (*halt*); un plan pour **juguler la violence** dans les stades (*bring an end to violence*)

junte (*nf*): la **junte militaire** qui est au pouvoir (*military junta*)

juré (*nm*): pour être **juré d'assises**, il faut être citoyen français (*juror*); **les jurés** ont conclu à une mort naturelle (*the jury*)

juridiction (*nf*): une **juridiction** créée pour statuer sur des affaires d'espionnage (*court, tribunal*); SEE ALSO **assise**

juridique (*adj*): la femme et la **profession juridique** (*legal profession*); SEE ALSO **conseil, flou, vide**

jurisprudence (*nf*): le verdict de l'affaire Fatima peut **faire jurisprudence** (*set a precedent*); dans cette situation, **la jurisprudence fait défaut** (*there is no legal precedent*)

juriste (*nm*): un **juriste** spécialisé en droit du travail (*jurist, legal expert*); un poste de **juriste d'entreprise** (*company lawyer*)

jury (*nm*): une seule femme dans le **jury**?; après délibération, le **jury** a rendu son verdict (*jury*)

jusqu'au-boutisme (*nm*): il risque de payer cher son **jusqu'au-boutisme** (*hardline stance*)

jusqu'au-boutiste (*adj/nm*): une position **jusqu'au-boutiste** contre toute réforme des institutions (*hardline*)

justice (*nf*): transmettre un dossier à la **justice** (*the law*); les associations de consommateurs peuvent **aller en justice** (*go to court*); il menaçait de les **attaquer en justice** (*take sb to court*); SEE ALSO **action, déni, palais, plainte, poursuite, repris, saisir, témoigner, traduire**

justiciable (*adj/nmf*): un délit **justiciable** d'une peine de prison (*punishable*)

justificatif, -ive (*adj/nm*): fournir un **justificatif** (*documentary evidence*)

justification (*nf*): une **justification** de son nouveau domicile, par exemple une quittance de loyer (*[documentary] evidence; proof*)

justifier (*vt*): **justifier** d'un domicile et de ressources suffisantes (*furnish proof*)

juteux, -euse (*adj*): **juteux contrats d'armement** pour Washington dans le Golfe (*lucrative arms contracts*)

juvénile (*adj*): la **délinquance juvénile** ne fait que s'aggraver (*juvenile crime*)

K

kiosque (*nm*): disponible dans tous les **kiosques à journaux** (*news-stand, newspaper kiosk*); l'hebdomadaire **a retrouvé les kiosques** ce matin (*is back on the news-stands*)

krach (*nm*): depuis le **krach boursier** d'octobre dernier (*stock market crash*)

kyrielle (*nf*): l'annonce de toute une **kyrielle de mesures** (*a whole string of measures*)

L

Labour (*nm*): le **Labour** se pose en alternative aux conservateurs (*[Brit] Labour Party*)

lâche (*adj*): une conception **plus lâche** du fédéralisme (*looser, more loose*)

lâcher (*vt*): les Républicains commencent à **lâcher** le président sur la guerre en Irak (*abandon*)

laïc, -ïque (*adj/nm,f*): pays **laïc** et ouvert à l'Occident (*secular*); l'affaire du foulard islamique à l'**école laïque** (*secular [state] school*)

laïcité (*nf*): la **laïcité de l'enseignement** est toujours son crédo (*secular education*)

laissé-pour-compte (*nm*): pour venir en aide aux **laissés-pour-compte de la croissance** (*casualties of economic growth*); que faire pour les jeunes **laissés-pour-compte du système d'enseignement**? (*those who are failed by the educational system*)

laminer (*vt*): la concurrence a **laminé les marges** (*erode/squeeze profit margins*); elle **lamine** ses concurrents dans les sondages d'opinion (*wipe out, crush*)

langue (*nf*): il possède à merveille la **langue de bois** des politiciens (*cliché-ridden language; [political] cant*)

larcin (*nm*): quinze jours de préventive pour un **larcin** de 15 euros (*petty theft*); SEE ALSO **menu**

larvé, -e (*adj*): la **guerre civile larvée** qui ravage ce pays centre-américain (*state of undeclared civil war*)

laxisme (*nm*): accusé de **laxisme** dans la lutte contre la mafia (*being soft; permissiveness*); SEE ALSO **hexagonal**

laxiste (*adj*): une politique **laxiste** en matière de délinquance juvénile (*permissive*)

leader (*nm*): le **leader** extrémiste allemand lavé d'une accusation de racisme (*leader*)

lecteur, -trice (*nm,f*): les **lecteurs** de la presse people (*readers*)

lectorat (*nm*): compter sur la fidélité d'un **lectorat** important (*readers; readership*)

lecture (*nf*): adopter un texte **en première lecture** (*on a first reading [parliamentary bill]*); **donner lecture** d'un communiqué (*read [out]*)

légaliser (*vt*): **légaliser** ou dépénaliser les drogues aurait des conséquences graves (*legalize*)

légalité (*nf*): agir tout en **restant dans la légalité** (*keep within the law*)

légiférer (*vi*): comment **légiférer** sur une question si personnelle? (*legislate; lay down the law*)

législateur, -trice (*nm,f*): le **législateur** a fait preuve de bon sens (*lawmaker; the law*)

législatif, -ive (*adj/nm*): dans les [élections] **législatives** de mars, la droite est revenue au pouvoir (*general election*); le **législatif** jadis avait trop de pouvoir face à l'exécutif (*legislature, legislative body*)

législation (*nf*): la mise en œuvre de **législations** écologiques (*laws, legislation*); SEE ALSO **infraction**, **trust**

législature (*nf*): la durée d'une **législature** est de cinq ans (*term of office [parliament]*)

légitime (*adj*): le magistrat **a retenu la légitime défense** (*accepted a plea of self-defence*)

légitimité (*nf*): le gouvernement de transition, **sans légitimité populaire** (*without a mandate from the people*)

legs (*nm*): un **legs** qui est contesté par les héritiers (*legacy; bequest*)

léguer (*vt*): avoir un patrimoine à **léguer** (*hand down; pass on*); **léguer par testament** sa fortune à une organisation caritative (*bequeath*)

lettre (*nf*): l'ambassadeur présente ses **lettres de créance** (*credentials*); envoyer une **lettre de démission** (*letter of resignation*); des **lettres de licenciement** envoyées aux salariés (*letter of dismissal; redundancy notice*); SEE ALSO **revendicateur**

levée (*nf*): la **levée des sanctions** imposées par le Conseil de sécurité (*lifting of sanctions*); la première phase du financement prévoit la **levée** de 75 milliards en capital (*raising [esp. of capital]*); l'accord a déclenché une **levée de boucliers** du côté protestant (*strong opposition; outcry*)

lever (*vt*): l'état d'urgence sera bientôt **levé** (*lift, end*); EDF s'apprête à **lever** plus de cinq milliards d'euros (*raise [capital]*); SEE ALSO **équivoque**

liaison (*nf*): les **liaisons routières** trans-Pyrénées (*road link*)

libellé (*nm*): le **libellé** du texte de révision de la Constitution (*wording*)

libeller (*vt*): acheter des avoirs **libellés en dollars** (*payable in dollars*)

libéral, -e *mpl* **-aux** (*adj/nm,f*): la politique économique est d'orientation **libérale** (*non-interventionist*); les **libéraux** préconisent la liberté des changes (*free-marketeer, liberal economist*); SEE ALSO **économie, projet**

libéralisation (*nf*): ouvrir les frontières, et multiplier la **libéralisation des échanges** dans tous les domaines (*easing of restrictions*)

libéraliser (*vt*): **libéraliser le commerce** et diminuer l'intervention de l'Etat (*ease/lift restrictions on trade*)

libéralisme (*nm*): le **libéralisme** anglais s'oppose à l'interventionnisme français (*free-market system; liberalism*)

libération (*nf*): il s'est vu refuser une **libération conditionnelle** (*release on parole*); la prison à perpétuité sans possibilité de **libération anticipée** (*early release*); la loi sur la **libération des loyers** (*removal of rent controls*)

libérer (*vt*): le prix des carburants a été entièrement **libéré** (*decontrol, deregulate*); la décision du juge de le **libérer sous caution** dans l'attente de son procès (*free/release on bail*)

liberté (*nf*): une charte des **libertés** fondamentales (*freedom*); l'auteur présumé du crime a été **mis en liberté provisoire** (*[release on] parole*); une période de **liberté surveillée** sous le contrôle d'un éducateur (*[release on] probation*); revenir à la **liberté des prix** et laisser jouer la concurrence (*freedom from price controls*); prôner la **liberté de réunion** et d'association (*freedom of assembly*); la **liberté de presse** ne sera pas remise en cause (*freedom of the press*); la **liberté de conscience** est garantie par la constitution (*freedom of conscience*); la **liberté d'expression**, ce pilier de la démocratie (*freedom of speech*); SEE ALSO **caution, culte**

libre (*adj*): une entorse à la règle générale de la **libre concurrence** (*free competition*); des contraintes qui entravent la **libre entreprise** (*free-market economy*); SEE ALSO **accès, école, jeu**

libre-échange (*nm*): le **libre-échange** avec les Etats-Unis créera 20.000 emplois (*[policy of] free trade*)

libre-échangiste (*adj*): il dénonça la dérive **libre-échangiste** de l'Europe (*free-market, free-trade*)

licence (*nf*): se voir octroyer une **licence exclusive** de production et de distribution (*exclusive licence*)

licencié, -e (*adj/nm,f*): **licencié** en droit privé de la faculté d'Alger (*graduate*); un club qui a démarré avec une vingtaine de **licenciés** (*person registered [with sports federation]*); aux **licenciés [économiques]** sera versée une allocation spéciale (*worker made redundant*)

licenciement (*nm*): les demandeurs d'emploi qui s'inscrivent à l'ANPE pour **licenciement [économique]** (*redundancy; lay-off*); une protection contre les **licenciements injustifiés** (*unfair dismissal*); SEE ALSO **lettre, prime**

licencier (*vt*): on parle de **licencier** 150 employés (*make redundant, lay off*)

licite (*adj*): le lock-out consécutif à une grève est **licite** (*lawful, within the law*)

lieu *pl* **-x** (*nm*): enquêter **sur les lieux du crime** (*at the site of the crime*); le développement de la démocratie **sur le lieu de travail** (*in the workplace*); SEE ALSO **état, haut, occuper**

lieu-dit (*nm*): le hameau a été ravalé au rang de **lieu-dit** (*[named] place, locality*)

ligne (*nf*): suivant aveuglément la **ligne du parti** (*party line*); il est partisan d'une **ligne dure** vis-à-vis de la Corée du nord (*hard-line [policy]*); Hamas et Hezbollah **dans la ligne de mire d'Israël** (*in the sights [of]; targeted [by]*); SEE ALSO **courtier, fabrication**

limitrophe (*adj*): la situation humanitaire dans le Darfour et dans les **régions limitrophes** (*neighbouring regions*)

limogeage (*nm*): le **limogeage** d'un directeur de journal (*dismissal, sacking*)

limoger (*vt*): le président **limogea** le chef d'état-major de l'armée (*sack, dismiss*)

liquidateur (*nm*): le **liquidateur judiciaire** vend les actifs de la société pour payer les créanciers (*official receiver*)

liquidation (*nf*): le tribunal de commerce de Pontoise prononce la **liquidation judiciaire** de la société (*winding-up [by decision of court]*)

liquider (*vt*): Immobilier: l'armée **liquide** son patrimoine (*sell off*); la France et l'Iran **liquident leur contentieux financier** (*settle their financial dispute*)

liquidités (*nfpl*): une crise mondiale des **liquidités** (*liquid assets; available funds; liquidity*)

lisibilité (*nf*): le manque de **lisibilité** de la politique du gouvernement (*clarity, coherence*)

liste (*nf*): la **liste** de la majorité présidentielle l'emporte dans l'Aveyron (*list of candidates*); SEE ALSO **conduire**, **scrutin**

litige (*nm*): la soumission du **litige** à l'arbitrage des Nations Unies (*dispute*); le **litige** qui oppose le chanteur à Universal Music (*lawsuit*)

litigieux, -euse (*adj*): un service des contentieux s'occupe des questions **litigieuses** (*disputed, contentious*)

livraison (*nf*): l'embargo sur la **livraison d'armes** à la Bosnie (*supplying of arms*); dans la dernière **livraison** de la revue, parue en mars (*issue [of periodical]*)

livre (*nm*): les objectifs du prochain **livre blanc** de la défense (*[Brit] White Paper*); un **livre vert** qui servira de document de réflexion (*[Brit] Green Paper, policy proposals document*); (*nf*): nouvelle baisse de la **livre sterling** (*[pound] sterling*)

livrer (*vt*): les malfaiteurs furent **livrés** à la police (*hand over, give up*); la Chine, accusée de **livrer** des matériaux nucléaires au Pakistan (*supply, deliver*); [**se**] (*vpr*): **se livrer** à des exactions contre la population civile (*carry out*)

livret (*nm*): titulaire d'un **livret de caisse d'épargne** (*[savings] bank-book*)

lobby (*nm*): se heurter à des **lobbies** puissants (*lobby*); le **lobby des armes** essuie une défaite (*arms lobby*)

lobbying (*nm*): **mener un lobbying intense** en faveur de l'avion français (*lobby intensively*)

local, -e *mpl* **-aux** (*adj/nm*): dans un **local associatif** dans la cité ouvrière (*community room*); (*pl*) les **locaux administratifs** du collège sont occupés depuis mardi (*administrative offices*); SEE ALSO **occupation**

locataire (*nmf*): le précédent **locataire** n'a pas encore vidé les lieux (*tenant, occupier*); l'obsession statistique du **locataire de la place Beauvau** (*[Fr] minister of the Interior*)

locatif, -ive (*adj*): le montant du loyer et des **charges locatives** (*rental charges*); le **revenu locatif** des immeubles (*rental, proceeds from rents*)

location (*nf*): préférer la **location** à l'accession à la propriété (*renting*)

lock-out (*nm*): le patron réplique par une menace de **lock-out** [fermeture d'usine] pour briser la grève (*lock-out*)

locomotive (*nf*): la France a perdu son rôle de **locomotive** de la zone euro (*engine/motor; pacesetter, pacemaker*)

logement (*nm*): un **logement social** réservé aux familles modestes (*local authority housing*); un salaire mensuel généreux et un **logement de fonction** (*company house/flat*); favoriser le **logement locatif** en milieu rural (*rented accommodation*); SEE ALSO **crise, épargne, indemnité, insalubre, parc, propriétaire, propriété**

loi (*nf*): faire campagne sur le thème de la **loi et l'ordre** (*law and order*); les grandes lignes de la **loi de finances** 2006 (*finance act/bill*); SEE ALSO **abrogation, enfreindre, prescription, projet, proposition, respecter, terme, texte, violer**

lotissement (*nm*): des banlieues couvertes de **lotissements pavillonnaires** (*housing estate*)

lourdeur (*nf*): la **lourdeur** bureaucratique et réglementaire (*red tape*); les chômeurs, confrontés aux **lourdeurs administratives** de l'ANPE (*administrative inefficiency*)

loyer (*nm*): la libération totale des **loyers** (*rent, rental*); n'ayant pas à **s'acquitter d'un loyer** (*pay rent*); SEE ALSO **arrérages, flambée, gratuité, habitation, hausse, impayé, libération, quittance**

lucratif, -ive (*adj*): un trafic **lucratif** de papiers falsifiés (*profitable*); un établissement privé **à but lucratif** (*profit-making*)

M

magasin (*nm*): de nouvelles mesures en faveur des **magasins de proximité** (*neighbourhood/local shops*); les **grands magasins**, victimes de la concurrence des hypermarchés (*department store*)

magazine (*nm*): la bonne santé de la **presse magazine** (*magazine press*); SEE ALSO **mensuel**

Maghreb (*nm*): les pays francophones du **Maghreb** (*the Maghreb, North Africa*)

maghrébin, -e (*adj/nm,f*): parmi les immigrés, les **Maghrébins** sont les plus nombreux (*Maghrebi*)

magistrat, -e (*nm,f*): un **magistrat** investi d'une autorité administrative ou politique (*officer, public servant*); les deux **magistrats instructeurs** chargés de l'enquête (*investigating judge*)

magistrature (*nf*): la **magistrature** est indépendante vis-à-vis de l'exécutif (*judiciary*); la première femme à accéder à la **magistrature suprême** du pays (*highest office [esp. presidency]*)

magouille (*nf*): l'Opposition parle de **magouille** à propos du redécoupage électoral (*election rigging*)

main (*nf*): **tendre la main** aux partis du centre (*make overtures*); la **reprise en main** des médias par le gouvernement (*re- taking control*)

main-d'œuvre (*nf*): avoir recours à la **main-d'œuvre** étrangère (*labour; work force*); dans les métiers souffrant de **pénurie de main-d'œuvre** (*labour shortage*)

mainmise (*nf*): freiner la **mainmise** du pouvoir sur la télévision (*control; hold*)

maintenir (*vt*): la direction **maintient** son projet de 12.500 suppressions d'emplois (*maintain, stand by*); [**se**] (*vpr*): la droite pourra-t-elle **se maintenir au pouvoir**? (*stay in power, retain power*); SEE ALSO **investissement**

maintien (*nm*): le préfet demeure chargé du **maintien de l'ordre** dans le département (*maintenance of law and order*)

maire (*nm*): dans le département de l'Allier, dix-sept femmes sont **maire** (*mayor*); SEE ALSO **député**, **sénateur**

mairie (*nf*): les Communistes ont le tiers des **mairies** (*town council*); c'est le FN qui **s'empare de la mairie de Dreux** (*win/take control of Dreux*)

maison (*nf*): filiale à 50% de la **maison mère** (*parent company*); être écroué à la **maison d'arrêt** de Toul (*holding/short-stay prison*); SEE ALSO **employé**, **rapport**

maître, -esse (*adj/nm,f*): la mairie de Vendôme est **maître-d'œuvre** du projet (*main contractor; project manager*); la commune, agissant en tant que **maître-d'ouvrage** (*contracting authority; developer*); SEE ALSO **pièce**

maîtrise (*nf*): la **maîtrise** de l'immigration (*control*); une **maîtrise** de philo, et un stage d'informatique (*Master's degree*); l'équipe lauréate **aura la maîtrise-d'œuvre complète du projet** (*will be the main contractor*); les travaux dont la **maîtrise-d'ouvrage** incombe au département (*[role of] contracting authority*); SEE ALSO **agent**

maîtriser (*vt*): on a à peu près **maîtrisé** l'inflation (*bring under control*); une immigration **mal maîtrisée** (*out-of-control*)

majeur, -e (*adj/nm,f*): le scrutin s'est déroulé sans incident **majeur** (*major, serious*); on est **majeur** à 18 ans (*person having attained his majority*)

major (*nm*): étudiant en médecine, et **major** de sa promotion (*top of the class*); les **majors** du bâtiment et des travaux publics (*leading name; [major] company*)

majoration (*nf*): une **majoration** pour retard de paiement (*surcharge*); il n'y aura pas de **majorations de prix** (*price increase*)

majorer (*vt*): les constructeurs **majorent leurs prix** en janvier (*raise prices*)

majoritaire (*adj*): le PCF, **majoritaire** dans le canton (*having a majority*); SEE ALSO **pondéré**, **uninominal**

majorité (*nf*): cinq députés sur six de l'ancienne **majorité** (*party in power, governing party*); avant, la **majorité** était de 21 ans (*coming of age, majority*); **prendre la majorité dans le capital** de la société (*take a controlling stake*); SEE ALSO **verdict**

mal *pl* **maux** (*nm*): les **maux** de l'université française sont désormais bien connus (*defects, shortcomings*); le **mal de vivre** dans les grands ensembles (*depression [esp. caused by life in high-density housing]*)

maladie (*nf*): l'abrogation d'un règlement sur les **congés-maladie** (*sick leave*)

malaise (*nm*): on parle du **malaise des cités**, de la violence, de l'insécurité (*[Fr] living conditions in deprived suburban housing estates*)

mal-être (*nm*): le **mal-être urbain** que nous connaissons (*urban malaise*)

malfaiteur (*nm*): un des **malfaiteurs** a tiré à cinq reprises sur lui (*law-breaker; criminal*); SEE ALSO **association**

mal-logé (*nm,f*): le nombre des sans-abris et des **mal-logés** dans la capitale (*person living in substandard housing*)

maltraitance (*nf*): la **maltraitance** des personnes âgées dans des lieux d'accueil (*ill-treatment*); la lutte contre la **maltraitance à enfants** (*child abuse*)

malvenu, -e (*adj*): l'armée française **malvenue** dans son ancienne colonie au Rwanda (*unwelcome*)

malversation (*nf*): inculpé après la découverte de **malversations financières** (*financial malpractice; embezzlement*)

mal-vivre (*nm*): ceux qui souffrent du **mal-vivre** des grands ensembles (*poor living conditions*)

manchette (*nf*): l'annonce **a fait la manchette** de la presse (*made the headlines*)

mandant, -e (*nm,f*): les syndicats ouvriers doivent rendre des comptes à leurs **mandants** (*members*)

mandat (*nm*): son **mandat** est de cinq ans (*term of office*); le procureur avait lancé un **mandat d'amener** contre les deux hommes (*summons, arrest warrant*); le **mandat de comparaître** lui a été communiqué à son domicile (*summons to appear; subpoena*); un seul **mandat de dépôt** a été prononcé (*committal order*); sous le coup d'un **mandat d'arrêt international** (*international arrest warrant*); SEE ALSO **cumul**, **électif**, **moitié**

mandater (*vt*): le député, **mandaté** pour représenter ses électeurs à Paris (*mandated*)

mandature (*nf*): un dossier essentiel de sa **mandature** (*period of office*)

manifestant, -e (*nm,f*): des combats opposant **manifestants** et forces de l'ordre (*demonstrator*)

manifestation (*nf*): la présence de l'armée a directement inspiré la **manifestation** (*demonstration; unrest*)

manifester (*vi*): une centaine de personnes **manifestent** devant l'ambassade (*demonstrate*); (*vt*): **manifester sa colère** dans les rues (*demonstrate one's anger*)

manne (*nf*): la Roumanie reçoit une **manne européenne** de 390 milliards d'euros (*windfall from the UE budget*); faire bénéficier les Iraniens de l'énorme **manne pétrolière** (*oil revenues*)

manœuvre (*nm*): la disparition progressive des postes de **manœuvres** et d'ouvriers spécialisés (*manual/unskilled worker*); (*nf*): toutes les **manœuvres électorales** sont bonnes (*vote-catching manœuvre*)

manque (*nm*): un **manque à gagner** estimé à 75 millions d'euros (*loss of [expected] income*); SEE ALSO **avancée**, **prévoyance**

manqué, -e (*adj*): après le **coup d'état manqué** de juin 1992 (*failed coup*)

manquement (*nm*): par négligence ou **manquement aux règles de sécurité** (*breach of safety regulations*)

manufacture (*nf*): une **manufacture** de tabac, entreprise employant 2.000 personnes (*factory*)

manufacturier, -ière (*adj*): l'**activité manufacturière** ralentit sérieusement (*manufacturing activity*)

maquette (*nf*): la **maquette** a été rénovée, la pagination passe de 44 à 60 pages (*paste-up, layout [of newspaper]*)

marasme (*nm*): le **marasme** actuel du marché (*slump, stagnation*)

marchand, -e (*adj/nm,f*): entre **marchands de canons** la bataille sera féroce (*arms supplier/dealer*); SEE ALSO **valeur**

marchandage (*nm*): après des mois de **marchandage diplomatique** à New York (*diplomatic bargaining*)

marche (*nf*): une **marche de protestation** aura lieu dimanche (*protest march*); un droit d'information sur la **marche de l'entreprise** (*running of the company*)

marché (*nm*): le **marché** qu'il a proposé à la Pologne (*deal*); l'entreprise espagnole, leader sur son **marché** (*market sector*); **passer d'importants marchés** auprès d'entreprises locales (*place large orders*); conquérir des **marchés à l'exportation** (*export markets*); l'arrivée des jeunes **sur le marché du travail** (*in the job market*); partout dans l'ex-URSS les **marchés noirs** fleurissent (*black market*); SEE ALSO **attribuer, attribution, créneau, enlever, entente, leader, obtention, part, passation, porteur**

marge (*nf*): les **marges bénéficiaires** des entreprises sont en hausse (*profit/trading margin*); SEE ALSO **laminer**

marginal, -e *pl* **-aux** (*adj/nm*): certains sont des **marginaux**, qui refusent toute aide (*fringe elements of society, dropout*)

marginalité (*nf*): en situation de pauvreté et de **marginalité sociale** (*life on the margins of society*)

mariage (*nm*): un réseau de **mariages blancs** a été démantelé (*contracting marriage [esp. to obtain residence permit]*); SEE ALSO **naître, reculer**

maroquin (*nm*): un autre **maroquin** éphémère, celui du secrétaire d'Etat chargé des travailleurs immigrés (*[ministerial] portfolio*)

masse (*nf*): la nouvelle charge augmentera d'autant la **masse salariale** (*wage bill*)

maternité (*nf*): le **congé maternité** passera à trente semaines pour toute naissance multiple (*maternity leave*)

matière (*nf*): profitant de l'envolée du prix des **matières premières** (*raw materials*)

maussade (*adj*): une année **maussade** pour l'industrie automobile (*sluggish, lacklustre*)

mécontentement (*nm*): le **mécontentement** du président russe (*displeasure*); canaliser le **mécontentement** populaire (*discontent*)

mécontenter (*vt*): les propositions de Moscou **mécontentent** les dirigeants baltes (*displease*)

média (*nm*): la plupart des **médias** [quotidiens, radios et chaînes de télévision] (*[mass] media*); l'ex-candidate s'exprime **par médias interposés** (*via the media*)

médiateur, -trice (*adj/nm,f*): la Syrie, **médiatrice** entre le Hamas et le Fatah (*mediator*); le **médiateur** défend les intérêts des citoyens face à l'administration (*mediator, Ombudsman*); **être le médiateur** entre le gouvernement, les élus et les acteurs socio-économiques (*mediate*)

médiation (*nf*): après six mois de conflit, la **médiation** mise en place par le gouvernement a réussi (*mediation; arbitration*)

médiatique (*adj*): provoquer un écho **médiatique** (*in the media*); SEE ALSO **battage, emballement, exploitation, tapage**

médiatisation (*nf*): la **médiatisation** des agressions contre les forces de l'ordre (*media coverage*); devant la **médiatisation à outrance** de cette affaire (*media hype*)

médiatiser (*vt*): l'insécurité, un des thèmes les plus **médiatisés** en 2006; ces sommets exagérément **médiatisés** (*give/receive media coverage*)

mêler (*vt*): **être mêlé** à un trafic de devises (*be involved*); **[se]** (*vpr*): et maintenant les grandes puissances **s'en mêlent** (*get involved; intervene*)

membre (*nm*): devenir **membre à part entière** de l'édifice européen (*full member*); les **pays membres** de la Communauté (*member state*); SEE ALSO **convoquer, fondateur**

ménage (*nm*): plus d'allégements fiscaux pour les **ménages** (*household*); Juifs et Arabes ont souvent **fait bon ménage** (*get on well together*); SEE ALSO **dette, faible**

ménager, -ère (*adj/nf*): SEE **eau, ordure, panier**

mendicité (*nf*): le nouveau code pénal ne considère plus la **mendicité** comme un délit (*begging*)

menées (*nfpl*): se livrer à des **menées subversives** contre son pays (*subversive activities*)

mener (*vt*): **mener** une stratégie de diversification osée (*carry out*); **mener à bien** un vaste programme de réhabilitation (*carry out [successfully]; implement*); **mener à terme** les négociations avec les Palestiniens (*see through, bring to a [successful] conclusion*); SEE ALSO **lobbying**

meneur, -euse (*nm,f*): des **meneurs** qui entretiennent la violence dans la rue (*leader; agitator*)

mensualisation (*nf*): la **mensualisation des salaires** s'est généralisée à partir de 1969 (*payment on a monthly basis*)

mensualité (*nf*): aider les ménages à payer leurs **mensualités de remboursement** (*monthly repayment/instalment*)

mensuel, -elle (*adj/nm*): salaire **mensuel**: 10.200 euros (*monthly*); un [magazine] **mensuel** consacré aux questions financières (*monthly [magazine]*)

menu, -e (*adj*): sans compter les **menus frais** (*incidental/minor expenses*); commettre des **menus larcins** (*petty theft*)

mère (*nf*): l'abolition de toute aide aux jeunes **mères célibataires** (*single/unmarried mother*); la question controversée des **mères porteuses** (*surrogate mother*); SEE ALSO **maison**

méridional, -e *mpl* **-aux** (*adj/nm,f*): dans les régions **méridionales** de la péninsule (*southern*)

mesure (*nf*): décider une série de **mesures concrètes** (*practical measures*); SEE ALSO **coercition, coup, draconien, incitatif, kyrielle, paquet, ponctuel, rétorsion**

mesurer (*vt*): on **mesure** ainsi l'ampleur du problème (*measure, gauge; assess*)

métier (*nm*): apprendre un **métier** (*trade, profession*); SEE ALSO **armée**

métis, - isse (*adj/nm,f*) 30% de la population sont constitués de **métis** (*person of mixed race*)

métropole (*nf*): dans les quatre lycées de la **métropole** lilloise (*metropolis; regional capital*); les rapports tendus que les Corses entretiennent **avec la métropole** (*[Fr] with the French mainland*)

métropolitain, -e (*adj/nm,f*): en Afrique du Nord et en **France métropolitaine** (*mainland France*)

meurtre (*nm*): lors d'un récent **procès pour meurtre** (*murder trial*); SEE ALSO **conclure, préméditation**

meurtrier, -ière (*adj/nm,f*): des attaques plus sanglantes et plus **meurtrières** (*causing great loss of life*); un suivi médical pour les **meurtriers d'enfants** (*child murderer*)

mévente (*nf*): avec la **mévente** actuelle de l'avion supersonique (*slump in sales; poor sales*)

mieux (*nm*): léger **mieux** pour le déficit américain (*improvement*)

mieux-être (*nm*): pour la résorption du chômage, pour le **mieux-être** de tous (*greater welfare; wellbeing*)

milieu *pl* **-x** (*nm*): les **milieux d'affaires** allemands sont favorables à la monnaie unique (*business community*); dans les **milieux autorisés** français (*official circles*); SEE ALSO **rural**

militant, -e (*adj/nm,f*): les **militants** d'autrefois, dévoués corps et âme au parti (*activist, active member*); SEE ALSO **pur**

militantisme (*nm*): avoir derrière soi 20 ans de **militantisme** syndical (*militant action; activism*)

militer (*vi*): **militer** pour l'arrêt du projet d'autoroute (*fight; campaign*); tout en continuant à **militer au parti** (*be an [active] party member*)

milliard (*nm*): le montant dépasse le **milliard** d'euros (*billion; one thousand million*)

mineur, -e (*adj/nm,f*): les parents de **mineurs** suspectés d'actes de délinquance (*minor, under-age person*); SEE ALSO **délit**, **détournement**, **traitement**

minimal, -e *mpl* **-aux** (*adj*): fixer des **prix minimaux** aux frontières européennes (*minimum prices*)

minimum *pl* **-a** (*adj/nm*): ne disposer même pas du **minimum vital** (*minimum living wage*); les bénéficiaires du RMI et des autres **minima sociaux** (*basic welfare benefits*); SEE ALSO **revenu**, **vieillesse**

ministère (*nm*): sous le **ministère** Villepin (*premiership*); la plupart des **ministères** devront faire des économies (*government department, ministry*); le **ministère public** a requis une peine de deux ans (*public prosecutor*)

ministériel, -ielle (*adj*): une réunion **au niveau ministériel** (*at ministerial level*); SEE ALSO **liquidation**, **remaniement**

ministrable (*adj/nmf*): après sa victoire, il prend rang parmi les **premiers ministrables** (*possible Prime minister*)

ministre (*nmf*): conflits et divergences au sein de l'équipe de la nouvelle **ministre** (*minister*); l'ancien **ministre délégué à la Santé** (*minister of state responsible for health*); SEE ALSO **conseil**

minorer (*vt*): le montant des frais se trouve **minoré** d'autant (*cut, reduce*)

minoritaire (*adj*): un éventuel gouvernement **minoritaire** (*minority*)

minorité (*nf*): une réelle volonté de **mettre en avant les minorités** (*promote the interests of [ethnic] minorities*); le gouvernement risque d'**être mis en minorité** au Sénat (*be defeated*); conserver une **minorité de blocage** de 25% dans la compagnie (*minority blocking vote*)

mise (*nf*): la **mise initiale** est assez modique (*first payment*); SEE ALSO **application, avant, chantier, demeure, disposition, échec, écoper, épreuve, examen, fonds, garde, jour, œuvre, pied, place, point, route, sac, séquestre, valeur, veilleuse**

miser (*vt*): les socialistes **misent** sur les divisions de la droite (*count on, bank on*)

misère (*nf*): la montée de la précarité et de la **misère** (*extreme poverty; squalor*)

mission (*nf*): partir **en mission** à l'étranger (*on assignment*); l'Inde a fermé sa **mission commerciale** à Durban (*trade mission*); les emplois précaires, les **missions d'intérim** (*temporary work*); SEE ALSO **chargé**

mi-temps (*nm*): on offre aux plus de 50 ans un **[emploi à] mi-temps** (*part-time job*); une activité **à mi-temps** et sans perspective (*part-time*); SEE ALSO **préretraite**

mitigé, -e (*adj*): le bilan de l'action menée reste **mitigé** (*modest*); **satisfaction mitigée** dans les territoires occupés (*qualified satisfaction*)

mixité (*nf*): faut-il repenser la **mixité à l'école**? (*coeducational schooling*); le quartier cesse d'être un lieu de **mixité sociale** (*social mixing*)

mobile (*adj*): SEE **gendarmerie**

mobilier, -ière (*adj/nm*): SEE **bien**

mobilisation (*nf*): faible **mobilisation** syndicale à Paris et en province (*participation, turnout [industrial action, demonstration]*); la forte **mobilisation policière** y jouait pour beaucoup (*police presence*)

mobiliser (*vt*): l'appel CGT-FO a **mobilisé** moins de 40% de grévistes (*mobilize [esp. for strike action]*); [**se**] (*vpr*): le Sénégal **se mobilise** contre le nouveau fléau de la toxicomanie (*take action*)

mobilité (*nf*): un chiffre qui met en valeur une assez faible **mobilité professionnelle** (*mobility of labour; job mobility*)

modalité (*nf*): les **modalités** de remboursement des frais sont les suivantes (*method, procedure*)

modération (*nf*): du fait d'une extrême **modération salariale** outre-Rhin (*moderate pay awards*)

modéré, -e (*adj/nm,f*): les cinq autres pays arabes **dits modérés** (*so-called moderate*); renforcer le camp des **modérés** chez les Palestiniens (*[political] moderate*); SEE ALSO **aile**

modicité (*nf*): la **modicité** des impôts indirects (*low level*); la **modicité des contraventions** prévues par la loi (*small [parking] fines*)

modique (*adj*): pour la **somme modique** de 50 euros (*modest sum*)

modulation (*nf*): une **modulation** des prestations en fonction des revenus (*adjustment*)

moduler (*vt*): une réforme de la fiscalité visant à **moduler à la hausse** la taxe professionnelle (*raise; increase*)

mœurs (*nmpl*): les **mœurs politiques** très particuliers de l'époque (*political customs/behaviour*); SEE ALSO **affaire**, **outrage**, **police**

moins-value (*nf*): provoquant une **moins-value** des appartements de 30% (*fall in value, depreciation*)

moitié (*nf*): un volume de transactions **moitié moindre** (*smaller by half, half as big/great*); l'Allemagne veut **réduire de moitié** le nombre de chômeurs (*halve, reduce by half*); la **réduction de moitié** de l'effectif actuel de 500 personnes (*halving*); SEE ALSO **amputer**

mondial, -e *mpl* **-aux** (*adj*): les stocks **mondiaux** ont diminué de moitié (*world; world-wide*)

mondialisation (*nf*): dans un environnement international marqué par la **mondialisation** (*globalization*); SEE ALSO **défi**, **heure**

monnaie (*nf*): baisse de la **monnaie américaine** (*US dollar*); depuis la mise en place de la **monnaie unique** (*single European currency/euro*)

monoparental, -e *mpl* **-aux** (*adj*): les **foyers monoparentaux** représentent 35% des allocataires du RMI (*one-parent household*); SEE ALSO **famille**

monopartisme (*nm*): le **monopartisme** est terminé au Zaïre (*one-party political system*)

monopole (*nm*): disposer d'un **monopole** en matière de radio et de télévision (*monopoly*); le **monopole d'embauche syndical** est illégal en France (*closed shop*)

montant, -e (*adj/nm*): il dénonça la **criminalité montante** (*rising crime rate*); pour un **montant total** de 20.000 euros (*total [sum]*); SEE ALSO **global**

montée (*nf*): un risque de **montée** de l'extrémisme (*rise, increase*); dans un contexte de **montée de chômage** (*rising unemployment*)

monter (*vt*): il avait **monté** sa propre société de carrosserie (*set up [business]*); [**se**] (*vpr*): la perte de salaire **se montait** à 500 euros par jour (*amount [to]*); SEE ALSO **créneau**, **épingle**, **flèche**

moralisation (*nf*): la **moralisation** du financement de la vie politique (*cleaning up*)

moraliser (*vt*): ces deux textes vont **moraliser** le financement de la vie politique (*clean up; reform*)

morceler (*vt*): une agglomération **morcelée** en une quarantaine de communes (*split, fragment*)

morcellement (*nm*): le remembrement a résolu les problèmes causés par le **morcellement des terres** (*division of land into small units*)

morose (*adj*): après cinq années **moroses**, le marché a bondi cette année (*lacklustre*)

morosité (*nf*): la **morosité** du secteur automobile persiste (*depressed mood; sluggishness [esp. of market]*); malgré la **morosité du climat politique** (*gloomy political mood of the country*); SEE ALSO **heure**

mot d'ordre (*nm*): manifester, mais sans **mot d'ordre** ni objectif déterminé (*slogan*); il a lancé un **mot d'ordre de grève** (*strike call*)

moteur, -trice (*adj/nm,f*): il jouait un **rôle moteur** dans la réforme des institutions (*leading role*); le principal **moteur** de la croissance en 2006 (*driving force*)

motif (*nm*): selon ses proches, elle aurait des **motifs de divorce** (*grounds for divorce*); SEE ALSO **exposé**

motion (*nf*): la **motion de censure** déposée par la gauche contre le gouvernement, en mai 2006 (*censure motion*); les communistes ont décidé de **voter la motion de censure** (*pass a vote of no confidence*)

motivé, -e (*adj*): un éventuel refus doit être **motivé** (*well-founded; justifiable*)

motiver (*vt*): on leur demanda de **motiver leur décision** (*explain their decision*)

mouiller (*vi*): la flotte **mouille** en rade de Brest (*be at anchor*); [**se**] (*vpr*): **se mouiller** dans une affaire de pots-de-vin (*be implicated/involved*)

mouture (*nf*): la **première mouture** de ces propositions (*first draft/version*)

mouvance (*nf*): le dialogue entre le pouvoir et la **mouvance islamique** (*Islamic circles*)

mouvement (*nm*): ce **mouvement ministériel** était attendu (*ministerial reshuffle*); des **mouvements de grève** ont paralysé hier les transports parisiens (*strike*); l'extension des **mouvements sociaux** (*industrial action in pursuit of workers' demands*); SEE ALSO **contestataire**, **guérilla**, **haussier**, **revendicatif**, **séparatiste**

mouvementé, -e (*adj*): dans un contexte social et politique **mouvementé** (*turbulent*)

moyen, -enne (*adj/nm,f*): l'Allemagne compte deux fois plus d'**entreprises moyennes** (*middle-sized companies*); les étudiants réclament **plus de moyens** pour les universités (*more resources/funding*); le chômage y est inférieur à la **moyenne nationale** (*national average*); SEE ALSO **ancienneté**, **faiblesse**

muet, -ette (*adj*): malaise au sein de **la grande muette** (*[Fr] the army*)

multipartisme (*nm*): la transition d'un régime de parti unique au **multipartisme** (*multi-party system/politics*)

multipartite (*adj*): des pourparlers **multipartites** sur le projet d'élections en Irlande du Nord (*cross-party*)

multiplication (*nf*): la **multiplication des contacts** entre les deux parties (*increasing contacts*); la **multiplication des candidatures** pourrait-elle nuire aux chances du parti? (*large number of candidates*)

multiplier (*vt*): Londres **multiplie les avertissements** à Téhéran (*give repeated warnings*); [**se**] (*vpr*): dans le Caucase russe, les disparitions d'opposants **se multiplient** (*are on the increase*)

multirécidiviste (*adj/nmf*): des centres destinés aux jeunes **multirécidivistes** (*habitual offender*)

municipal, -e *mpl* **-aux** (*adj/nfpl*): en vue des [élections] **municipales** (*municipal elections*); SEE ALSO **arrêté**, **conseil municipal**, **receveur**, **régie**

municipalité (*nf*): les deux **municipalités** vont se retrouver pour discuter de la question (*town/city council*)

munir (*vt*): des jeunes **munis d'un CAP** [certificat d'aptitude professionnelle] (*equipped with a vocational training qualification*); [**se**] (*vpr*): il est conseillé de **se munir d'une assurance médicale** privée (*obtain medical insurance*)

musclé,-e (*adj*): des interpellations **musclées** (*vigorous, forceful*); Washington **lance un avertissement musclé** aux ayatollahs (*send a strong warning*)

mutation (*nf*): face à un monde **en mutation** (*changing*); refuser une **mutation** pour raisons d'ordre familial (*job transfer*)

muter (*vt*): en poste à Lille, il a été **muté** en Alsace; **muté** disciplinairement de Nîmes à Lyon (*transfer*)

mutisme (*nm*): il est enfin sorti de son **mutisme** (*silence*); depuis son arrestation, la presse **observe un mutisme total** (*is maintaining complete silence/a blackout on the subject*)

mutualisme (*nm*): écrire l'histoire du **mutualisme** français (*mutual benefit insurance system*)

mutualiste (*nm*): un Français sur deux est **mutualiste** (*member of a mutual insurance company*)

mutualité (*nf*): la **mutualité**, l'assurance maladie complémentaire à celle de la Sécurité sociale (*[Fr] mutual benefit insurance scheme*)

mutuel, -elle (*adj/nf*): les **mutuelles** complètent les remboursements de la Sécurité sociale (*[Fr] complementary insurance scheme*); SEE ALSO **consentement, respect**

mutuellement (*adv*): les deux pays **s'accusent mutuellement** (*accuse one another*)

N

naissance (*nf*): SEE **bulletin, extrait, taux**

naître (*vi*): un enfant sur deux **naît hors mariage** pour les mères de moins de 25 ans (*be born out of wedlock*)

nanti, -e (*adj*): le fossé qui sépare les pays **nantis** et les pays pauvres (*rich, prosperous*); une commune particulièrement **bien nantie** (*well provided, well equipped*); (*nmpl*) par rapport aux autres salariés, ils sont des **nantis** (*affluent, well-to-do*)

natalité (*nf*): le **taux de natalité** est partout en baisse (*birth rate*)

national, -e *mpl* **-aux** (*adj/nm,f*): prendre la **nationale** 10 en direction de Chartres (*[Brit] trunk road*); réservé aux **nationaux** de ces deux pays (*national*); SEE ALSO **assemblée, assise, service**

nationaliser (*vt*): **nationaliser** les biens des anciens colons (*nationalize*)

nationalité (*nf*): acquérir la **nationalité française** (*French nationality*); SEE ALSO **accès**

naturalisation (*nf*): les tests imposés aux candidats à la **nationalisation** (*naturalization*)

naturaliser (*vt*): les étrangers voulant **se faire naturaliser français** (*acquire French nationality/citizenship*)

navette (*nf*): le projet de loi a **fait la navette** entre l'Assemblée et le Sénat (*shuttle backwards and forwards*); une première **navette diplomatique** Belgrade-Pristina (*diplomatic shuttle*)

nécessiteux, -euse (*adj/nm,f*): les familles **nécessiteuses**, vivant dans le dénuement le plus complet (*needy, poor*); venir en aide aux **nécessiteux** (*the needy/poor*)

néfaste (*adj*): une nouvelle évolution **néfaste** pour l'Europe (*harmful, dangerous*); pour atténuer les **effets néfastes** de la croissance (*harmful effects/consequences*)

négoce (*nm*): **faire du négoce** avec des pays asiatiques (*trade, do business*); le **négoce des céréales** continue entre eux (*trade in grain/cereals*)

négociant (*nm*): un célèbre **négociant** en vins du Bordelais (*merchant*); un **négociant en gros** du Havre (*wholesaler*)

négociation (*nf*): les **négociations commerciales** ont repris (*trade talks*); l'échec des **négociations salariales** (*pay talks*); SEE ALSO **séance**, **table**

négocier [**se**] (*vpr*): le titre **se négocie** peu au-dessus de son coût le plus bas de l'année (*change hands, sell*)

nervosité (*nf*): la **nervosité** du pouvoir, face à la contestation (*irritability; touchiness*); **nervosité** à la Bourse de Paris hier (*nervous trading*)

nettoyage (*nm*): le **nettoyage ethnique** mené en Yougoslavie (*ethnic cleansing*)

nier (*vt*): le président iranien **nie** toute livraison d'armes aux talibans (*deny*); l'accusé n'a pas cessé de **nier les faits** (*deny the charges*)

niveau *pl* **-x** (*nm*): élévation sensible du **niveau de vie** (*living standards*); discussions bilatérales **au plus haut niveau** (*top-level*); SEE ALSO **ministériel**, **remise**

niveler (*vt*): il faut **niveler par le haut** les normes environnement-ales existantes (*level up*)

nivellement (*nm*): ce projet risque d'imposer un **nivellement par le bas** au lieu d'une harmonisation par le haut (*levelling down*); les producteurs de l'émission se défendent de tout **nivellement par le bas** (*dumbing-down*)

nocturne (*adj/nf*): **nocturne** hebdomadaire, vendredi jusqu'à 22h (*late opening; late-night shopping*); SEE ALSO **tapage**

noir, -e (*adj*): SEE **caisse**, **marché**, **or**, **travail**

nommément (*adv*): le rapport les met **nommément** en cause (*by name*)

nommer (*vt*): sans le **nommer** ouvertement (*name, mention by name*); des enseignants titulaires nouvellement **nommés** (*appoint [to a post]*)

non-aligné, -e (*adj/nm*): lors de la conférence au sommet des [pays] **non-alignés** (*nonaligned countries*)

non-assistance (*nf*): inculpé de coups et blessures et de **non-assistance à personne en danger** (*failing to come to the aid of a person in danger*)

non autorisé, -e (*adj*): sa participation à une manifestation **non autorisée** (*unauthorized; illegal*)

non conforme (*adj*): déclarer un texte **non conforme à la constitution** (*unconstitutional*)

non-droit (*nm*): **un pays de non-droit** où règne l'anarchie la plus totale (*a country where human rights are not respected; a lawless country*); entre banlieues chaudes et **zones de non-droit** (*urban areas where law and order has broken down*)

non-ingérence (*nf*): au nom de la **non-ingérence** dans les affaires d'un autre pays (*non-interference*)

non-inscrit, -e (*adj*): le député **non-inscrit** du Vaucluse (*deputy without party affiliation*)

non-lieu *pl* -**x** (*nm*): le juge d'instruction a **rendu une ordonnance de non-lieu** (*dismiss a case [for lack of evidence]; decide there is no case to answer*)

non-observation (*nf*): la **non-observation du règlement** peut exposer à des poursuites (*failure to comply with regulations*)

non-paiement (*nm*): un mouvement de protestation contre le **non-paiement** de leurs salaires (*non-payment*)

non-port (*nm*): le **non-port de la ceinture de sécurité** ou du casque (*failure to wear a seat-belt*)

non-recevoir (*nm*): **opposer une fin de non-recevoir** à tout projet d'augmentation d'impôts (*flatly refuse*)

non rentable (*adj*): la fermeture systématique des **puits non rentables** (*unprofitable mines*)

non résolu, -e (*adj*): le nombre d'affaires criminelles **non résolues** (*unsolved*)

non-respect (*nm*): dans les cas de **non-respect de la loi** (*infringement of the law*); le principal reproche des usagers, c'est le **non-respect des horaires** (*poor punctuality; failure to run on time*)

non-satisfaction (*nf*): **en cas de non-satisfaction des revendications**, une nouvelle grève sera lancée (*if their demands are not met*)

normalien, -ienne (*adj/nm,f*): diplômé de l'ENA et **normalien** (*[Fr] graduate of the* Ecole normale supérieure)

normalisation (*nf*): l'accord de **normalisation des relations** entre la Grèce et la Macédoine (*normalizing of relations*); on va vers une **normalisation** des législations nationales (*standardization*)

normaliser (*vt*): il faudra **normaliser** l'écartement des voies de chemin de fer en Europe (*standardize*); le Maroc **normalise ses relations** avec Israël (*normalize relations*); [**se**] (*vpr*): depuis, l'approvisionnement **s'est normalisé** (*return to normal*)

norme (*nf*): compte tenu des **normes** nationales et internationales (*norms, standards*); **mettre aux normes** le patrimoine existant (*bring up to standard*)

notable (*adj/nm*): être désigné par un collège de **notables** (*notable; important personality*)

notation (*nf*): la **notation** des professeurs par leurs étudiants; la promotion dépend de ces **notations** (*grading; assessment*)

note (*nf*): rédiger une **note interne** (*memorandum, memo*); présenter sa **note de frais** (*claim for expenses*)

noter (*vt*): les militaires sont **notés** par leur supérieur hiérarchique (*assess; grade*)

notifier (*vt*): **se faire notifier** sa mise en examen par le juge (*be notified, receive notification*); si votre propriétaire vous a **notifié votre congé** (*give notice to leave/quit*)

notoriété (*nf*): outre-Manche, la **notoriété** de ces vins reste très faible (*fame; reputation*)

noyau *pl* **-x** (*nm*): le **noyau dur** des chômeurs de longue durée (*hard core*)

noyautage (*nm*): le **noyautage du pouvoir** par les communistes (*infiltration of government*)

noyauter (*vt*): le parti au pouvoir veut **noyauter** la radio et la télévision (*infiltrate*)

nuancé, -e (*adj*): adopter une position plus **nuancée** (*subtle; balanced; finely shaded*)

nue-propriété (*nf*): la **nue-propriété**: le droit de posséder un bien sans avoir le droit de l'utiliser (*ownership without usufruct; freehold*)

nuire (*vt*): un fanatisme qui **nuit fortement** à l'image de l'islam (*do great harm*); éliminer le dictateur en le **mettant hors d'état de nuire** (*neutralize*)

nuisance (*nf*): le problème des **nuisances sonores** que subissent les riverains d'aéroports (*noise pollution*); les produits **sans nuisance pour l'environnement** (*environmentally harmless*)

nuisible (*adj*): avoir des conséquences **nuisibles** sur l'économie (*harmful*)

nul, nulle (*adj*): ses chances de gagner sont **nulles** (*nil, non-existent*); s'abstenir ou **voter nul** (*spoil a voting paper*); déclarer **nulle et non avenue** la consultation populaire proposée (*null and void*); SEE ALSO **bulletin, croissance**

numéraire (*adj/nm*): exiger d'être payé **en numéraire** (*in cash*)

numérique (*adj*): le progrés de la cartographie **numérique** (*digital*)

numérisation (*nf*): la **numérisation** du cadastre départemental (*digitization*)

numériser (*vt*): **numériser** le cadastre; le projet consiste à **numériser** des millions d'ouvrages à travers le monde (*digitize*)

numéro (*nm*): le quotidien *Libération*, dans son **numéro** du 28 mars (*issue, edition*); des cas d'abus sexuels, signalés au **numéro Vert** (*freephone number*); SEE ALSO **un**

O

---

obédience (*nf*): parmi les musulmans **de stricte obédience** (*devout*)

objectif (*nm*): son **objectif**: 1,3 millions d'abonnés (*aim, target*); il annonce un **objectif de croissance** de 8% (*growth target*); l'aviation bombarda plusieurs **objectifs industriels** (*industrial target*)

obligation (*nf*): convertir la dette en **obligations** négociables sur le marché international (*bond; debenture; fixed-interest stock*); la loi **fait obligation** aux associations de tenir des comptes (*oblige*)

obtempérer (*vi*): devant leur **refus d'obtempérer**, le policier fit usage de son arme (*refusal to obey [instruction/order]*)

obtention (*nf*): l'**obtention** d'un visa de travail (*obtaining*); l'**obtention d'un important marché d'armement** en Chine (*winning of a large arms contract*)

occidental, -e *mpl* **-aux** (*adj/nm,f*): le premier chef d'Etat **occidental** à s'y rendre (*Western*); face aux Serbes, **les Occidentaux** opposent hésitations et incohérences (*the Western powers; the West*); SEE ALSO **ouvrir**

occulte (*adj*): des commissions **occultes** dégagées sur des marchés publics (*undisclosed; under-the-counter*)

occulter (*vt*): le régime tenta d'**occulter** ces années de quasi-guerre civile (*gloss over; conceal*)

occupation (*nf*): des grèves d'étudiants, avec **occupation de locaux** (*sit-in*); le **taux d'occupation** des hôtels de luxe (*occupancy rate*)

occuper (*vt*): une centaine de grévistes **occupent les lieux** (*occupy the premises*)

octroi (*nm*): décider l'**octroi** d'un jour de congé; l'**octroi** d'une aide iranienne au Hamas (*granting*)

octroyer (*vt*): une prime **octroyée** au personnel (*grant, award*); [**s'**] (*vpr*): **s'octroyer** une indemnité de départ de 5 millions d'euros (*award oneself; claim*)

œuvre (*nf*): la décentralisation fut l'**œuvre** de l'ancien ministre de l'Intérieur (*work, achievement*); cette réforme était difficile à **mettre en œuvre** (*implement*); SEE ALSO **maître, maîtrise**

œuvrer (*vi*): ils s'engagent à **œuvrer** ensemble à la recherche de solutions (*work [for]*)

office (*nm*): les employés de l'**Office** des HLM (*bureau, office*); le nouveau Premier ministre **fera office** aussi de ministre de la Justice (*hold office; serve as*); SEE ALSO **cartel**

officialiser (*vt*): un décret qui **officialise** le droit au multipartisme (*make official; formalize*)

officieux, -ieuse (*adj*): établir des contacts **officieux** entre les belligérants (*unofficial*); faire un voyage **à titre officieux** à Bonn (*in an unofficial capacity; unofficially*)

offrant (*nm*): l'**offrant** ne peut revenir sur son offre (*bidder, offeror*); vendre **au plus offrant** (*to the highest bidder*)

offre (*nf*): l'**offre** crée sa propre demande (*supply*); le nombre d'**offres d'emploi** est en forte progression (*job vacancy*); en lançant une OPA [**offre publique d'achat**] sur le grand quotidien (*take-over bid*); SEE ALSO **appel**

omnipraticien, -ienne (*nm,f*): 6.000 généralistes, soit 18% de l'ensemble des **omnipraticiens** (*general [medical] practitioner*)

onéreux, -euse (*adj*): les traites à payer sembleront à long terme très **onéreuses** (*expensive, costly*); sous peine d'**amendes onéreuses** (*heavy fines*)

onusien, -ienne (*adj*): Jérusalem rejette les conclusions des **experts onusiens** (*UN experts*)

opérer (*vt*): **opérer** une transition en douceur (*effect*); [**s'**] (*vpr*): un transfert des compétences **s'est opéré** du préfet vers le président du conseil général (*take place; come about*)

opinion (*nf*): une bonne partie de l'**opinion** prend position en faveur du ministre (*public opinion*); en prison pour **délit d'opinion** (*expressing subversive views*); SEE ALSO **décalé, enquête, liberté, presse, prisonnier, sensibiliser, sondage**

opportunité (*nf*): **saisir les opportunités** qu'offre le marché unique de 1993 (*seize the opportunity*); mettre en question l'**opportunité** de cette mesure (*timeliness; appropriateness*);

opposant, -e (*adj/nm,f*): dix **opposants** iraniens expulsés de France (*opponent; member of the opposition*)

opposer (*vt*): des heurts ont **opposé** étudiants et policiers (*bring into conflict*); [**s'**] (*vpr*): l'Arabie Saoudite et l'Iran **s'opposent** sur les quotas de production de pétrole (*clash, disagree*); faire grève pour **s'opposer** au projet de fusion (*oppose, resist*); SEE ALSO **non-recevoir**, **véto**

opposition (*nf*): les **chefs de l'opposition** demandent la démission du président (*opposition leaders*); SEE ALSO **formation**, **siéger**

opprimé, -e (*adj/nm,f*): un pays refuge pour les **opprimés** (*oppressed person*)

optimal, -e *mpl* **-aux** (*adj*): pour une gestion **optimale** des ressources (*optimum, optimal*)

optimiser (*vt*): essayer d'**optimiser les bénéfices** (*maximize profits*)

optique (*nf*): **dans l'optique américaine**, l'affaire est plus compliquée (*from the American perspective*)

or (*nm*): en raison de l'appétit d'**or noir** des pays émergents (*oil, black gold*)

ordonnance (*nf*): un projet de loi autorisant le gouvernement à recourir aux **ordonnances** (*[government] order/edict*); SEE ALSO **injonction**, **non-lieu**

ordonner (*vt*): un juge de la cour d'appel avait **ordonné** sa libération (*order*)

ordre (*nm*): l'**ordre** et la répression, une obsession de la droite (*[law and] order*); SEE ALSO **force**, **loi**, **maintien**, **trouble**, **troubler**

ordre du jour (*nm*): Londres souhaite **inscrire** la question palestinienne **à l'ordre du jour** du sommet (*put on the agenda*); la réduction du temps de travail **revient à l'ordre du jour** (*is back on the agenda*)

organe (*nm*): le Conseil des ministres, l'**organe décisionnel** de l'Union européenne (*decision-making body*)

organisme (*nm*): une initiative subventionnée par les **organismes** régionaux et départementaux (*body, organisation*)

oriental, -e *mpl* **-aux** *(adj/nm,f)*: les pays d'Europe centrale et **orientale** *(Eastern)*

orientation *(nf)*: définir les **grandes orientations** de sa politique étrangère *(main [policy] direction; main thrust)*

orienter *(vt)*: **orienter** un élève vers la vie active *(direct, steer [esp. in careers advice])*; **[s']** *(vpr)*: le marché **s'oriente à la hausse** *(is on a rising trend)*

otage *(nm)*: la **prise en otage** des deux soldats israéliens *(taking hostage)*

outrage *(nm)*: il comparut sous l'inculpation d'**outrages aux forces de l'ordre** *(insulting behaviour to police officers)*; coupable d'**outrage aux bonnes mœurs** *(affront to public decency; publication of obscene material)*; le juge d'instruction l'a inculpé d'**outrage public à la pudeur** *(gross indecency; indecent exposure)*

outrance *(nf)*: la majorité se mobilise contre les **outrances de son discours** *(his/her extreme views)*; SEE ALSO **médiatisation**

outrancier, -ière *(adj)*: sans pour autant donner dans un patriotisme **outrancier** *(excessive, extreme)*

outre *(prep)*: ceci a été abondamment commenté **outre-Manche** *(across the Channel, in Britain)*; **outre-Atlantique**, on est en période d'élections *(across the Atlantic, in the United States)*; aussi bien en France qu'**outre-Pyrénées** *(in Spain)*; avec nos voisins **d'outre-Rhin** *(German)*; SEE ALSO **passer**

outremer *(adv/nm)*: un nouveau ministre de l'**Outremer** *(overseas territories)*

outrepasser *(vt)*: le Premier ministre avait **outrepassé** son pouvoir *(exceed/go beyond, overstep)*

ouverture *(nf)*: demander l'**ouverture** d'une enquête *(opening)*; prévoyant l'**ouverture** totale du ciel européen à la concurrence *(opening up)*; le débat sur l'**ouverture dominicale** rebondit *(Sunday trading)*; Syrie multiplie les **ouvertures en direction d'Israël** *(overtures towards Israel)*

ouvrable *(adj)*: on appelle **jours ouvrables** tous les jours de la semaine sauf celui consacré au repos hebdomadaire *(working day)*

ouvré, -e *(adj)*: on appelle **jours ouvrés** les jours du lundi au vendredi inclus *(working day)*

ouvrier, -ière (*adj/nm,f*): 20.000 emplois d'**ouvrier qualifié** (OQ) ne trouvent pas preneurs (*skilled worker*); un maçon qui est devenu OS (**ouvrier spécialisé**) dans l'automobile (*unskilled/semi-skilled worker*); SEE ALSO **banlieue, polyvalent, syndicat**

ouvrir [**s'**] (*vpr*): le congrès qui doit **s'ouvrir** dimanche (*open, begin*); l'Irak semble prêt à **s'ouvrir aux occidentaux** (*open up to Western firms/to the West*)

P

---

pacsé, -e (*adj*): les **couples pacsés**, ainsi que les concubins, sont concernés par cet impôt (*[Fr] couples who have signed a civil partnership contract [PACS]*)

pactole (*nm*): 30 millions de dollars: le **pactole** qu'Israël va recevoir sous forme de dons (*windfall*)

paie (*nf*): on ne verse plus de **paie** au personnel réduit à l'inactivité (*wage, pay*); SEE ALSO **feuille, fiche**

paiement (*nm*): le **paiement** des indemnités auxquelles il a droit (*payment*); SEE ALSO **balance, cessation, défaut, échelonner**

paix (*nf*): comment **ramener la paix** en Irak? (*restore peace*); SEE ALSO **aboutir, accord, gardien, juge, maintien, plan, pourparlers, processus**

palliatif (*nm*): les nouvelles mesures ne sont que des **palliatifs** (*stop-gap measure*)

pallier (*vt*): pour **pallier** cette honteuse carence (*compensate [for]*)

palmarès (*nm*): la société bretonne s'est hissée à la première place du **palmarès** de l'agro-alimentaire (*order of merit; honours list*)

panier (*nm*): le **panier de la ménagère**, mesure de l'évolution des prix à la consommation (*housewife's shopping basket*)

paquet (*nm*): un **paquet de mesures** de relance (*package of measures*); le **paquet fiscal** représente un allégement de 11 milliards d'euros (*package of tax cuts*)

parachutage (*nm*): la pratique du **parachutage**, mal acceptée par les instances locales du parti (*imposing an outside electoral candidate*)

parachuter (*vt*): **parachuté** dans l'Oise, il fut battu sans appel dans les élections (*brought in from outside [esp. election candidate]*)

paradis (*nm*): le système des **paradis fiscaux** (*tax haven*)

parapher (*vt*): la CGT refuse de **parapher l'accord** (*sign the agreement*)

parc (*nm*): le **parc français du logement** a doublé en dix ans (*French housing market*); le maintien et le renouvellement du **parc nucléaire français** (*all of France's nuclear power stations*); un **parc d'activités** de 66 hectares (*business park; enterprise zone*)

parcelle (*nf*): s'acheter une **parcelle de terre** (*plot of land*); un lotissement de douze **parcelles privatives** (*individual plot*)

parent, -e (*nm,f*): les contentieux entre parents par le sang et **parents adoptifs** (*adoptive/foster parents*); **parent isolé** avec un enfant à charge (*lone parent*)

parental, -e *mpl* **-aux** (*adj*): avoir droit à un **congé parental d'éducation** (*parental right to time off work without pay after birth of child*); SEE ALSO **autorité**

pari (*nm*): un **pari** économique, mais aussi un défi politique (*gamble; challenge*)

paritaire (*adj*): une **gestion paritaire** patronat-syndicats (*joint management*)

parité (*nf*): la loi sur la **parité** entre les hommes et les femmes (*equality*); leur exigence principale, la **parité des salaires** (*equal pay*)

parlement (*nm*): renforcer le rôle des **parlements** nationaux (*parliament*); SEE ALSO **dissoudre, unicaméral**

parquet (*nm*): le **parquet** a ordonné l'ouverture d'une enquête (*office of the public prosecutor*); **sur le parquet**, les titres s'échangeaient à un rythme soutenu (*on the trading floor [Stock Exchange]*); SEE ALSO **déférer**

parrain (*nm*): les Etats-Unis, **parrain** du processus de paix (*sponsor*)

parrainage (*nm*): le **parrainage** d'une équipe cycliste professionnelle (*sponsorship*); faire campagne pour obtenir les **parrainages** des maires (*[electoral] sponsorship*)

parrainer (*vt*): les 500 élus qui **parrainent** la candidature de l'écologiste (*back, sponsor*)

part (*nf*): la **part** des hydrocarbures dans les exportations est tombée à 50% (*share*); de nouveaux pays producteurs pourront **prendre de grosses parts de marché** (*take a large market share*); SEE ALSO **audience, membre, tailler**

partage (*nm*): le vote sur le **partage** de la Palestine (*division, partition*); un **partage du pouvoir** avec les communistes (*power sharing*); l'accord sur le **partage du travail** évitera des licenciements (*work sharing*)

partagé, -e (*adj*): les spécialistes restent très **partagés** (*divided*)

partenaire (*nm*): plusieurs **partenaires** qui détiennent globalement 27% du capital (*partner; associate*); le ministre discuta de l'affaire avec tous les **partenaires sociaux** (*management and labour/unions*)

partenariat (*nm*): un **partenariat** industriel franco-espagnol (*partnership; association*); un **partenariat civil** ouvrant les mêmes droits que le mariage (*civil partnership*)

parti (*nm*): le **régime du parti unique** est un facteur de cohésion (*one-party regime*); hésiter à **prendre parti** dans la dispute (*take sides*); SEE ALSO **cacique, militer, permanent**

participation (*nf*): il nie toute **participation** à fusillade (*involvement*); certains actionnaires ont déjà accru leurs **participations** (*share holding, stake*); la faible **participation électorale** impose un second tour (*voter turnout*)

particularisme (*nm*): une preuve du **particularisme** régional bavarois (*distinctive identity*)

particulier, -ière (*adj/nm*): la production de voitures **particulières** (*private, privately owned*); le nombre de **particuliers** à détenir directement des actions (*person, private individual*); SEE ALSO **hôtel**

partie (*nf*): les avocats de la **partie adverse** (*opposing party*); faire venir les **parties belligérantes** autour d'une table (*warring faction*); la Chine **est partie prenante** à tout règlement cambodgien (*be directly concerned*); notre armement nucléaire est une **partie intégrante** de la sécurité européenne (*integral part*)

partiel, -ielle (*adj*): des [élections] **partielles** auront lieu dans le Doubs (*by-election*); SEE ALSO **chômage, temps**

partisan, -e (*adj/nm,f*): quelle que soit leur préférence **partisane** (*party-political*); beaucoup de ses **partisans** sont passés à l'opposition (*supporter*); SEE ALSO **affiliation, farouche**

partition (*nf*): depuis les accords de Genève et la **partition** du Vietnam (*partition*)

passage (*nm*): le **passage** à la monnaie unique (*change, transition*); lors de leur **passage à la douane** (*passing through customs*); SEE ALSO **privé, tabac**

passation (*nf*): la **passation des pouvoirs** s'est déroulée hier à Matignon (*transfer of power*); soupçonné d'avoir perçu 30.000 euros lors de la **passation d'un marché** (*negotiation of a contract*)

passer (*vi*): l'allocation **passe** à 400 euros (*rise/be increased [to]*); il faut utiliser différents moyens pour **faire passer son message** (*put across one's message*); le gouvernement est parvenu à **faire passer** plusieurs réformes importantes (*push through [legislation]*); Taiwan, **passant outre** au véto de Pékin (*defy; disregard*); SEE ALSO **acte, aveu, baccalauréat, marché, rouge, tabac**

passerelle (*nf*): de nouvelles façons de créer des **passerelles** entre la société et les marginaux (*bridge, link*)

passible (*adj*): tout contrevenant sera **passible d'une amende** (*liable to a fine*); les contrevenants **sont passibles des tribunaux** (*are liable to prosecution*)

passif, -ive (*adj/nm*): le **passif** atteint 3 milliards d'euros (*deficit; debt*); SEE ALSO **apurer**

pâtir (*vi*): le tourisme **pâtit** de la désaffection des étrangers (*suffer [from]*)

patrimoine (*nm*): objectif: exonérer 95% des **patrimoines** des droits de succession (*personal fortune*); la mise en valeur du **patrimoine bâti** (*architectural heritage*); SEE ALSO **transparence**

patron, -onne (*nm,f*): le **patron** d'une petite société de micro-informatique de Tours (*boss, owner*)

patronal, -e *mpl* **-aux** (*adj*): SEE **contribution, grève**

patronner (*vt*): les firmes qui **patronnent** des spectacles et des manifestations sportives (*sponsor*)

paupérisation (*nf*): résultat: **la paupérisation de l'éducation nationale** (*the education system is starved of resources*)

paupériser (*vt*): la lente progression des salaires **paupérise** les classes moyennes (*impoverish*); [**se**] (*vpr*): une population qui **se paupérise** (*become impoverished*)

pauvreté (*nf*): la lutte contre la **grande pauvreté** (*extreme poverty*); le nombre de Français **qui vivent en dessous du seuil de pauvreté** (*living below the poverty line*); une nouvelle **pauvreté urbaine** a fait son apparition (*urban poverty*); SEE ALSO **seuil**

pavillon (*nm*): habiter un **pavillon** de banlieue (*[detached] house*); les armateurs placent souvent leurs navires sous **pavillon de complaisance** (*flag of convenience*); SEE ALSO **onusien**

pavillonnaire (*adj*): le centre ancien, et les **zones pavillonnaires** (*area of low-rise housing; housing estate*); SEE ALSO **lotissement**

payant, -e (*adj*): SEE **tiers**

payer (*vt*): Taïwan **paye comptant** ses achats d'armements (*pay cash down*); des versements officieux **payés en liquide** (*paid in cash*)

payeur, -euse (*adj/nm,f*): des sanctions automatiques contre les **mauvais payeurs** (*bad debtor*)

pays (*nm*): SEE **accueil**, **arrière-pays**, **conduire**, **contrôle**, **endettement**, **fuir**, **non-droit**, **producteur**, **répartir**, **riverain**, **ruine**, **voie**

paysage (*nm*): **le paysage politique d'Afrique** s'en est trouvé profondément remanié (*the political map of Africa*); France 2 doit s'adapter au nouveau **paysage audiovisuel** (*broadcasting environment*)

paysan, -anne (*adj/nm,f*): propositions agricoles: les **paysans** sont-ils sacrifiés? (*small farmers; peasantry*)

paysannerie (*nf*): le niveau de vie de la **paysannerie** suisse (*small farmers*)

peine (*nf*): pédophilie: vers des **peines aggravées** (*stiffer penalties*); l'instauration de **peines plancher** pour les récidivistes (*minimum sentence*); SEE ALSO **confusion**, **cumul**, **encourir**, **incompressible**, **prononcé**, **purger**, **remise**, **renforcer**, **valoir**

peiner (*vi*): les syndicats **peinent à s'entendre** pour la grève du 8 novembre (*struggle to reach agreement*)

pénal, -e *mpl* **-aux** (*adj*): la législation civile et **pénale** (*criminal*); les honoraires des avocats **en matière pénale** (*in criminal cases*); la **population pénale** est en hausse de 10% (*prison population*); SEE ALSO **chambre**, **code**, **droit**, **responsabilité**, **traitement**

pénaliser (*vt*): une mesure qui **pénalise** les plus démunis (*disadvantage*); **pénaliser** l'usage de drogues (*punish by law*)

pénalité (*nf*): le **renforcement des pénalités** pour crimes de violence (*stiffer penalties*)

pénibilité (*nf*): la définition et la prise en compte de la **pénibilité au travail** (*unpleasant/hard working conditions*)

pénible (*adj*): les salariés exerçant un métier **pénible** (*hard, [physically] demanding*)

pénitentiaire (*adj*): l'**administration pénitentiaire** voit ses crédits augmentés d'un tiers (*prison authorities*)

pensée (*nf*): la France est soumise à la dictature de la **pensée unique** (*doctrinaire approach [in politics]*)

pension (*nf*): recevoir une **pension de retraite à taux plein** (*full [retirement] pension*); avoir droit à une **pension d'invalidité** (*disability pension*); la **pension alimentaire** qu'il doit à son ancienne épouse (*alimony, maintenance*); SEE ALSO **bloquer**, **veuf**

pénurie (*nf*): certains biens, sujets à de fréquentes **pénuries** (*shortage, scarcity*); SEE ALSO **main-d'œuvre**

percée (*nf*): **percée** de l'extrême droite en Allemagne (*breakthrough*); **réaliser une percée** sur le marché américain (*make a breakthrough*)

percepteur (*nm*): la suppression du poste de **percepteur** (*tax collector*)

perception (*nf*): le ministre veut moderniser la **perception** de la redevance (*collection; levying [of tax/charge]*); aller à la **perception** payer ses contributions (*tax collector's office, tax office*)

percer (*vi*): Média: la presse libre a du mal à **percer** (*make a breakthrough*); (*vt*): pour **percer** le marché intérieur américain (*penetrate, break into*)

percevoir (*vt*): soupçonné d'avoir **perçu** des dessous-de-table (*receive [esp. payment]*); la façon dont ceci **est perçu** par les partenaires sociaux (*is perceived*)

perchoir (*nm*): l'ancien Premier ministre a été investi pour le **perchoir** (*[Fr] seat/office of President of the National Assembly*)

perdurer (*vi*): le chômage a baissé en Allemagne, mais la précarité **perdure** (*continue*)

pérenniser (*vt*): avoir pour objectif de **pérenniser** le régime actuel (*ensure the continuance [of], retain*)

pérennité (*nf*): des incidents qui prouvent la **pérennité** du sentiment raciste (*permanence; durability*)

performant, -e (*adj*): les entreprises les plus **performantes** (*high-performance; outstanding*)

péricliter (*vi*): faute de dynamisme, l'entreprise **périclite** (*be in a bad way; go downhill*)

période (*nf*): pendant la **période électorale** (*election time*); embauché après une **période d'essai** (*trial period*)

périodicité (*nf*): la **périodicité** peut être semestrielle ou trimestrielle (*periodicity; interval, frequency*)

permanence (*nf*): devant la **permanence** et l'ampleur des troubles en Cisjordanie (*persistence*); le député **tient une permanence** le samedi matin dans sa circonscription (*hold a surgery*)

permanent, -e (*adj/nm*): élu **permanent** fédéral CFDT pour la branche Tourisme (*[union] official*); devenu **permanent du parti** (*party worker*)

permis (*nm*): un **permis** de construire a été accordé (*permit, licence*); se procurer un **permis de travail** (*work permit*)

perpétrer (*vt*): deux attentats à la bombe **perpétrés** simultanément (*carry out, commit*)

perpétuité (*nf*): condamné à la **prison à perpétuité**; une **perpétuité** réelle pour assassinat de mineur précédé de viol (*life sentence; prison for life*)

perquisition (*nf*): la police a opéré une **perquisition** chez l'accusé (*search of premises [by police]*)

perquisitionner (*vi*): la police **perquisitionna** à son domicile (*carry out a search*)

personne (*nf*): les dons de **personnes morales**, entreprise ou fédération, sont interdits (*legal entity; corporate body*); cette allocation est soumise à un plafond de 10.000 euros pour une **personne physique** (*person; individual*); SEE ALSO **atteinte, circulation, dépendant, droit, troisième âge, valide**

personnel, -elle (*adj/nm*): l'ensemble du **personnel** est prêt à faire grève (*staff, personnel*); SEE ALSO **actionnariat, apport, compression, équipe, prévoyance, réduction, rotation, vacataire**

perspective (*nf*): une **perspective** peu séduisante pour Paris (*prospect*); l'absence complète de **perspectives d'emploi** (*employment prospects*)

perte (*nf*): on annonce de **fortes pertes** pour la filiale allemande (*heavy losses*); SEE ALSO **alourdissement**

perturbation (*nf*): de nouvelles **perturbations** dans le trafic aérien (*disruption*)

perturber (*vt*): les services des Finances **perturbés** par des arrêts de travail (*disrupt; disorganize*)

pervers, -e (*adj*): dénoncer les **effets pervers** des 35 heures (*pernicious effects*)

peser (*vi*): l'UE sera capable de **peser** sur la scène internationale (*exert influence*); les charges sociales excessives qui **pèsent** sur les salaires (*be a heavy burden*);

pétition (*nf*): apposer sa signature sur une **pétition** (*petition*)

pétitionner (*vi*): **pétitionner** contre l'implantation d'une aire de nomades (*petition; organise a petition*)

pic (*nm*): le **pic** ayant été atteint en 2004, avec 36% (*peak; high point*)

pièce (*nf*): se munir d'une **pièce d'identité** (*identity papers; means of identification*); Washington a fait de Riyad la **pièce maîtresse** de son dispositif au Proche-Orient (*cornerstone, key element*); SEE ALSO **annexe**

pied (*nm*): la société de Rennes a **mis à pied** plus de 400 employés (*lay off*); la direction décida la **mise à pied** immédiate des grévistes (*suspension*); la **mise sur pied** d'une commission parlementaire (*setting up, forming*)

pied noir (*nm*): cette décision tranche en faveur des **pieds noirs** et d'autres rapatriés d'Afrique (*Algerian of European stock; French settler in North Africa, especially Algeria*)

piégé, -e (*adj*): Paris: **attentat à la voiture piégée** (*car-bombing*)

piège (*nm*): les civils, **pris au piège des combats** (*caught up in the fighting*); la diplomatie américaine **prise au piège du Darfour** (*embroiled in the Darfour problem*)

pierre (*nf*): la Constitution reste la **pierre angulaire** de l'édifice politique américain (*cornerstone*); la **pierre d'achoppement** qui empêche de faire avancer les négociations (*stumbling block, obstacle*); SEE ALSO **jet**

piétinement (*nm*): pour masquer le **piétinement de l'enquête** (*slow progress of the investigation*)

piétiner (*vi*): les négociations sur le Kosovo **piétinent** (*make little progress*); (*vt*): les droits de l'homme sont quotidiennement **piétinés** (*trample under foot*)

pilotage (*nm*): le **comité de pilotage** définit le programme de travail (*steering group*)

pilote (*adj*): le tourisme, **secteur pilote** de l'économie (*leading sector*); SEE ALSO **expérience**

piquet (*nm*): installer un **piquet de grève** devant les portes de l'usine (*strike picket, picket line*)

piratage (*nm*): le **piratage informatique** entraîne une peine de trois ans de prison (*computer crime*)

pirate (*nm*): les **pirates de l'air** impliqués dans le détournement de l'avion (*hijacker*)

pirater (*vt*): le système informatique du FN a bien été **piraté** (*hack into [computer]*)

piraterie (*nf*): la **piraterie** en matière de droits d'auteur (*pirating; illegal copying*)

placard (*nm*): insérer un **placard pleine page** dans cinq quotidiens (*full-page advertisement*)

placarder (*vt*): des affichettes, avec le portrait de l'enfant, **placardées** sur les murs de la ville (*stick up, post*)

place (*nf*): chercher une **place** d'employé de maison (*position, situation*); **mettre en place** un plan de réformes économiques (*establish; put in place*); la **mise en place** de ces mesures sera très coûteuse (*implementation*); comme toutes les **places** asiatiques, Bombay a accusé une forte baisse (*[stock] market*); SEE ALSO **postuler**

placement (*nm*): le juge d'enfants décide un **placement** dans une famille d'accueil (*placement*); ces actions constituent un **placement** très sûr (*investment*)

placer (*vt*): **placer** un enfant en danger (*find a placement for, place [esp. with foster family]*); SEE ALSO **assistance**

plafond (*nm*): le **plafond** pour le calcul des cotisations (*ceiling, upper limit*); des prestations familiales versées sans **plafond de ressources** (*upper limit on income*); SEE ALSO **cours**

plafonnement (*nm*): en refusant le **plafonnement** des dépenses de santé (*setting of upper limit/ceiling*); on assiste à un **plafonnement** des recettes publicitaires (*levelling-off*)

plafonner (*vi*): la croissance française **plafonne** à 2% en 2006 (*reach a ceiling*); (*vt*): une retraite qui serait **plafonnée** à trois fois le Smic (*be subject to a ceiling/upper limit*)

plage (*nf*): la nouvelle **plage horaire** (*broadcasting slot*); les émissions sont interrompues par des **plages publicitaires** (*commercial break*)

plaider (*vt*): la défense **plaide l'acquittement** (*plead not guilty*); pris en flagrant délit, il **plaide coupable** (*plead guilty*); SEE ALSO **circonstance, foi, relaxe**

plaideur, -euse (*nm,f*): le **plaideur** refuse l'assistance d'un avocat (*litigant*)

plaidoirie (*nf*): après les **plaidoiries** de l'avocat de la défense (*plea*)

plaidoyer (*nm*): [*fig*] se livrer à un vibrant **plaidoyer** en faveur du désarmement (*plea*)

plaignant, -e (*adj/nm,f*): la **partie plaignante** a eu gain de cause (*litigant*); le **plaignant** fut débouté de sa plainte (*plaintiff, complainant*); SEE ALSO **débouter, raison**

plainte (*nf*): **porter plainte** pour incitation à la haine raciale; le principal du collège a **déposé plainte** (*lodge an official complaint*)

plan (*nm*): le **plan de paix** qui entérine la partition de la Bosnie (*peace plan*); le **plan social** offre à tout licencié 10.000 euros de dédommagement (*planned redundancy scheme*); SEE ALSO **cadastral, épargne, prévoyance, rigueur, sauvetage**

plancher (*nm*): SEE **cours, peine**

plancher (*vi*): [*fam*] 517.000 jeunes ont **planché** hier sur l'épreuve de philosophie (*sit [esp. examination]*)

planification (*nf*): la **planification à la française** est de conception assez souple (*French economic planning*); l'encouragement à la **planification familiale** (*family planning*)

planifier (*vt*): les attentats auraient été **planifiés** depuis l'étranger (*plan*)

planning (*nm*): établir un **planning** (*programme, schedule*); le libre accès des femmes au **planning familial** (*family planning*)

plaque (*nf*): [*fig*] véritable **plaque tournante** du commerce international (*hub, centre*)

plaquette (*nf*): éditer une nouvelle **plaquette** d'information (*booklet*)

plastiquage (*nm*): après le **plastiquage** d'un poste de police près de Bastia (*bomb attack [on], bombing*)

plastiquer (*vt*): des immeubles d'habitation **plastiqués** (*bombed, blown up*)

plat, -e (*adj*): il propose de **remettre à plat** le système fiscal (*re-examine thoroughly*); attribution des logements sociaux: **une mise à plat s'impose** (*the whole question needs a thorough examination*)

plate-forme (*nf*): appliquer la **plate-forme [électorale]** de la gauche (*electoral programme*)

plébisciter (*vt*): les militants socialistes l'avaient **plébiscité** (*elect by an overwhelming majority*)

plein, -e (*adj*): l'objectif: le retour au **plein-emploi**, d'ici à cinq ans (*full employment*); SEE ALSO **temps**

plénier, -ière (*adj*): SEE **séance**

pléthorique (*adj*): gonflant ainsi une fonction publique déjà **pléthorique** (*bloated, excessive*)

plier [se] (*vpr*): si le Hamas ne **se plie** pas à ces trois conditions (*abide [by]*); Chirac: Pékin doit **se plier aux droits de l'homme** (*respect human rights*)

pluralisme (*nm*): s'engager sur la voie du **pluralisme politique** (*multi-party political system*)

pluraliste (*adj*): les premières **élections pluralistes** que le pays a connues (*multi-party elections*)

pluralité (*nf*): **en cas de pluralité d'infractions**, les peines s'additionnent (*if more than one offence has been committed*)

pluripartisme (*nm*): les pays de l'Est s'ouvrent au **pluripartisme** (*multi-party political system*)

plus-value (*nf*): l'Etat réalisera ainsi une **plus-value** substantielle (*profit*); la **plus-value** sera alors totalement exonérée (*capital gain*); SEE ALSO **juteux**

poids (*nm*): réduire le **poids** des cotisations sociales (*burden*); le **poids** croissant de l'Iran dans la région (*importance; influence*)

point (*nm*): le porte-parole de l'Elysée tiendra chaque semaine un **point de presse** (*press briefing*); le quai d'Orsay **diffusa une mise au point** hier (*issue a statement [to clarify a point]*); et maintenant, **le point sur les grèves** (*an update on the strike situation*); la Poste, forte de ses 17.000 **points de vente** (*sales outlet*)

pointage (*nm*): au dernier **pointage**, un train sur cinq circulait en région parisienne (*at the last/most recent check*)

pointe (*nf*): après une **pointe**, le titre a fait marche arrière (*high spot; peak*); l'Europe **en pointe** contre les pollutions chimiques (*playing a leading role*); le Japon, **à la pointe** de l'innovation (*at the forefront*); leader dans les **technologies de pointe** (*leading-edge technology*)

pointer (*vi*): son mandat de député non-renouvelé, il a dû **pointer au chômage** (*register at the unemployment office*); (*vt*): un rapport **pointe** les défaillances de la CIA avant le 11 septembre 2001 (*point to/out*)

pointu, -e (*adj*): des formations spécifiques, très **pointues**; acquérir une spécialisation plus **pointue** (*specialized*)

pôle (*nm*): la création de **pôles de croissance** soigneusement situés (*growth centre*); la ville de Nîmes constitue un véritable **pôle régional** (*regional centre*)

polémique (*adj/nf*): essais nucléaires: la **polémique** continue (*debate, controversy*); une affaire qui **suscite une grosse polémique** au Royaume-Uni (*provoke fierce controversy*)

polémiquer (*vi*): éviter de **polémiquer** avec la direction du parti (*enter into a debate*)

police (*nf*): en l'absence d'une **police** internationale (*policing authority*); la **police judiciaire** [PJ] parisienne (*criminal investigation department*); la **police des mœurs** enquête sur les affaires crapuleuses (*vice squad*); plastiquage d'un **poste de police** en Corse (*police station*); SEE ALSO **préfet, proximité, quadriller, recenser, tribunal**

policier, -ière (*adj/nm*): quatre **policiers** dont un commissaire (*police officer*); SEE ALSO **bavure, dispositif, enquête, mobilisation, quadrillage, ripou**

politicien, -ienne (*adj/nm,f*): il récuse la **politique politicienne** (*politicking; politics for its own sake*)

politique (*adj/nf*): la **politique** qu'il a l'intention de mettre en œuvre (*policy*); la **politique intérieure** préoccupe le gouvernement (*domestic policy/politics*); SEE ALSO **classe, clivage, engager, étiquette, imprévoyance, inflexion, institution, mœurs, paysage, pluralisme, politicien, positionnement, récupération, réfugié, salarial, sanction**

politiquement (*adv*): oser aller à l'encontre du **politiquement correct** (*[what is] politically correct*)

polyvalence (*nf*): un poste exigeant **polyvalence** et motivation (*adaptability, versatility*)

polyvalent, -e (*adj*): une brigade d'intervention **polyvalente** (*all-purpose*); on hébergea les sinistrés dans une **salle polyvalente** mise à disposition par la mairie (*multi-purpose hall*); la création d'un poste d'**ouvrier polyvalent** à temps complet (*worker with flexible duties*)

ponction (*nf*): une inflation maîtrisée, et des **ponctions fiscales en baisse** (*lower taxes*)

ponctionner (*vt*): l'impôt sur le revenu en France **ponctionne** moins de 6% de la richesse nationale (*take out, tap*)

ponctuel, -elle (*adj*): des **mesures ponctuelles** pour lutter contre le chômage (*selective measures*)

ponctuellement (*adv*): convaincre ses adversaires de se rallier **ponctuellement** à tel ou tel projet (*selectively; in specific cases*)

pont (*nm*): avant le **pont** du 11 novembre; s'évader lors des **ponts** du mois prochain (*long weekend made by bridging a public holiday and a weekend*); SEE ALSO **bâtir**

population (*nf*): le chômage a atteint 10% de la **population active** (*population of working age*); SEE ALSO **pénal, vieillissement**

port (*nm*): interdire le **port** des signes religieux à l'école (*wearing*); SEE ALSO **défaut, non-port, voile**

porte-à-faux (*adv*): le syndicat se trouve **en porte-à-faux** avec sa base (*out of step; at odds*)

portée (*nf*): la **portée** de ses remarques n'a pas échappé à ses interlocuteurs (*import, significance*)

portefeuille (*nm*): le difficile **portefeuille** de l'Intérieur (*ministerial portfolio*); la gestion d'un **portefeuille** d'un montant de 2 milliards d'euros (*share portfolio*); SEE ALSO **gérer**

porte-parole (*nm*): selon le **porte-parole** de la commission d'enquête (*spokesperson*)

porter (*vt*): l'interdiction de **porter** le niqab, le voile intégral (*wear [item of clothing]*); le coup d'état qui **porta au pouvoir** le régime militariste (*bring to/put in power*); [**se**] (*vpr*): il décida de ne pas **se porter candidat** à l'investiture socialiste (*stand, be a candidate*); SEE ALSO **acquéreur, garant, plainte, préjudice**

porteur, -euse (*adj/nm,f*): investir dans les marchés les plus **porteurs** (*buoyant; booming*); 400.000 **petits porteurs** sont devenus actionnaires de la chaîne privatisée (*small shareholder*); SEE ALSO **créneau, mère**

position (*nf*): **prendre position** contre la dénucléarisation de l'Europe (*take a stance; declare oneself*); sa **prise de position** en faveur des minorités opprimées (*stand; position*); SEE ALSO **assouplir, dirigeant, raidir**

positionnement (*nm*): quel est le vrai **positionnement politique** des Verts? (*political stance/position*)

positionner [**se**] (*vpr*): la société essaie de **se positionner** sur ce nouveau créneau (*occupy a [market] slot*)

possédant, -e (*adj/nm,f*): l'explosion de la Bourse a fait la joie des **possédants** (*property-owning class*)

posséder (*vt*): **posséder** sa résidence principale demeure un bon investissement (*own, possess*)

poste (*nm*): les dépenses, réparties en différents **postes** (*[budget] heading; item*); permettant de créer 6.000 **postes de travail** (*job*); un seul ministre de Tony Blair **reste à son poste** (*keeps his job*); SEE ALSO **cadre, clé, création, débloquer, exclure, honorifique, police, pourvoir, responsabilité, suppression**

poste (*nf*): une employée des **Postes** (*[Fr] post office service*); on va vers la **privatisation des postes** (*privatizing postal services*)

posté, -e (*adj*): des salariés **postés** (*on shift work*); ceux qui **travaillent en posté** (*do shift work, work shifts*)

postulant, -e (*nm,f*): pour 4.000 **postulants**, on propose 400 places (*applicant*)

postuler (*vt*): **postuler** à un poste vacant, et soumettre un dossier de candidature; **postuler** une place de représentant (*apply [for job/position]*)

pot-de-vin (*nm*): les poursuites pour versement de **pots-de-vin** (*bribe, sweetener; backhander*); **toucher des pots-de-vin** pour l'obtention de marchés (*accept bribes*)

poumon (*nm*): le puits fut longtemps le **poumon économique de la région** (*economic lifeblood of the region*)

pourcentage (*nm*): rémunération: fixe plus **pourcentage** sur le chiffre d'affaires réalisé (*percentage, commission*)

pourparlers (*nmpl*): les **pourparlers de paix** sur le Darfour (*peace talks*)

pourrir (*vi*): au risque de **laisser pourrir la situation** (*allow the situation to deteriorate*)

pourrissement (*nm*): le gouvernement a choisi la stratégie du **pourrissement** (*allowing a situation to deteriorate*)

pourriture (*nf*): un des symptômes de la **pourriture** de notre système universitaire (*rottenness*)

poursuite (*nf*): les autorités redoutent une **poursuite des affrontements** (*further clashes*); la société a fait l'objet de **poursuites en justice** (*legal proceedings*)

poursuivre (*vt*): les dirigeants de la secte sont **poursuivis** pour escroquerie (*prosecute*); [**se**] (*vpr*): cette tendance devrait **se poursuivre** cette année encore (*continue*)

pourvoi (*nm*): le **pourvoi** a été rejeté (*appeal*); le défenseur a **déposé un pourvoi en cassation** contre le verdict de la cour (*take a case to the supreme court of appeal*)

pourvoir (*vt*): 600 emplois sont créés pour **pourvoir** aux besoins immédiats (*cater for; satisfy*); douze sièges sont encore à **pourvoir** (*fill, allot*); [**se**] (*vpr*): condamné en appel, il **se pourvoit en cassation** (*take a case to the court of appeal*)

pourvoyeur, -euse (*nm,f*): principal **pourvoyeur en armes** des rebelles (*arms supplier*)

poussée (*nf*): s'opposer aux **poussées** autonomistes flamandes (*pressure*); la **poussée** des inégalités sociales (*increase*)

pousser (*vt*): les Serbes **poussent** à un arrêt des combats (*push/press [for]*)

pouvoir (*nm*): les **pouvoirs publics** ont décrété le couvre-feu (*authorities*); facilitant ainsi la **prise de pouvoir** des communistes (*seizure of power*); des gains de **pouvoir d'achat** consécutifs à une progression des salaires (*purchasing power*); SEE ALSO **accaparer, accrocher, blocage, coulisse, décision, écarter, élargi, étendu, éviction, fondé, inféoder, maintenir, noyautage, partage, passation, porter, usure, venue**

pratique (*nf*): la **pratique [religieuse]** dominicale est en baisse en France (*church attendance*); SEE ALSO **discriminatoire**

pratiquer (*vt*): inférieurs aux **taux pratiqués la semaine dernière** (*last week's rates*); [**se**] (*vpr*): les **prix qui se pratiquent à Paris** sont très chers (*Paris prices*)

préalable (*adj/nm*): exiger le retrait **préalable** des troupes (*prior*); de vraies négociations, **sans préalable** (*without preconditions*); (*adv*): faire arrêter **au préalable** un certain nombre de gens (*as a preliminary*)

préalablement (*adv*): donner **préalablement** son accord (*first, beforehand*)

préavis (*nm*): le licenciement sans **préavis** de 19 ouvriers (*warning, notice*); partir sans **effectuer son préavis** (*work one's notice*); le syndicat des cheminots **dépose un préavis de grève** pour le 15 mars (*give notice of strike action*)

précaire (*adj*): entassés dans des logements **précaires** et insalubres (*unsafe*); une société où **l'emploi est si précaire** (*the job situation is so uncertain*); les intérimaires et autres **travailleurs précaires** (*person without job security*)

précarité (*nf*): la **précarité de l'emploi** s'est accentuée (*lack of job security*)

préciser (*vt*): à une date qui reste à **préciser** (*fix; decide*); le ministre **précise** son calendrier de réforme de l'université (*clarify, spell out*); [**se**] (*vpr*): si l'offre **se précise** d'ici à la fin du mois (*is confirmed*)

précision (*nf*): le communiqué **n'a fourni aucune précision** (*gave no [further] details*)

préconiser (*vt*): l'Algérie **préconise** une augmentation des quotas de production (*advocate, be in favour of*)

prédateur, -trice (*nm,f*): toutes les valeurs susceptibles d'intéresser les grands **prédateurs** (*predator, corporate raider*)

préemption (*nf*): la municipalité fait usage de son **droit de préemption** pour acquérir ce terrain (*pre-emptive right to acquire*)

préfectoral,-e *mpl* **-aux** (*adj*): des **arrêtés préfectoraux** appellent aux économies d'eau (*edict from the* préfet)

préfecture (*nf*): interdit par un arrêté pris par la **préfecture** (*office of* préfet); Créteil, ville-**préfecture** du Val-de-Marne [*prefecture; main administrative town in* département); à Marseille, devant la **préfecture** (*residence of the* préfet)

préférence (*nf*): le candidat du FN veut généraliser la **préférence française**, un de ses thèmes de prédilection (*discrimination in favour of France [trade, commerce, society]*)

préfet (*nm*): les maires ne craignent plus la tutelle du **préfet** (*préfet; administrative head of* département); le **préfet de police** dépend hiérarchiquement du ministre de l'Intérieur (*prefect of police*); SEE ALSO **truchement, valse**

préjudice (*nm*): obtenir réparation d'un **préjudice** subi (*loss, damage*); l'attraction de Paris **porte préjudice** au développement des autres grands centres (*be detrimental*)

préjudiciable (*adj*): une décision très **préjudiciable** pour le tourisme régional (*harmful, prejudicial*)

prélèvement (*nm*): un **prélèvement** de 1,5% sur tous les revenus (*deduction, levy*); les **prélèvements obligatoires** [impôts et cotisations sociales] vont augmenter (*tax and social security deductions*); régler une facture par **prélèvement automatique** sur compte bancaire (*direct debit*)

prélever (*vt*): les versements peuvent être **prélevés** automatiquement sur un compte bancaire (*deduct*)

préméditation (*nf*): le tribunal n'a pas retenu la **préméditation** (*premeditation; intent [to commit a crime]*); inculpé de **meurtre avec préméditation** (*premeditated/first-degree murder*)

prendre (*vt*): ces dispositions **prennent acte** de la nouvelle configuration des frontières (*take account [of]*); [**s'en**] (*vpr*): Darfour: le Soudan **s'en prend** à l'ONU (*attack, criticize, denounce*); SEE ALSO **fait, parti**

prépondérance (*nf*): ceci leur y a garanti une **prépondérance économique** (*dominant [economic] position*)

prépondérant, -e (*adj*): **jouer un rôle prépondérant** dans la recherche d'une solution pacifique (*play a major role*); SEE ALSO **voix**

préposé, -e (*nm,f*): le **préposé des postes** doit absolument vérifier votre identité (*post office clerk/employee*)

préretraite (*nf*): des **préretraites** massives et de plus en plus précoces (*early retirement*)

préretraité, -e (*nm,f*): la Communauté compte 20 millions de **préretraités** (*person having taken early retirement*)

prérogative (*nf*): il abuse des **prérogatives** présidentielles (*privilege, prerogative*)

prescription (*nf*): selon les **prescriptions de la loi** (*terms of the law*); la promotion du produit incite à des **prescriptions (médicales)** abusives (*medical prescription*)

prescrire (*vt*): la liberté de **prescrire** des médecins sera encadrée (*prescribe [medicine/treatment]*)

présenter [se] (*vpr*): le maire décida de ne pas **se présenter** (*stand [for election]*)

présidence (*nf*): une femme a été nommée à la **présidence** (*presidency, chairmanship*); lors des élections à la **présidence de la République** (*presidency of the Republic*); SEE ALSO **prétendant, tournant**

président, -e (*nm,f*): **président** du conseil de direction (*chairman*); c'est le P-DG (**président-directeur général**) lui-même qui annonça la nomination (*chairman and managing director*); SEE ALSO **relever**

présidentiable (*adj/nmf*): il est, de l'avis de tous, le meilleur **présidentiable** (*potential presidential candidate*)

présidentialisme (*nm*): le **présidentialisme** à la française (*presidential regime*)

présidentiel, -ielle (*adj*): l'ex-candidate à la **présidentielle**, Ségolène Royal (*presidential election*); SEE ALSO **mouvance**

présomption (*nf*): bénéficier de la **présomption d'innocence** (*presumption of innocence*); les accusations s'appuyaient sur un faible **faisceau de présomptions** (*body of evidence*)

presse (*nf*): une année décisive pour la **presse écrite** (*press, newspaper industry*); les ventes de la **presse hebdomadaire d'information** en baisse (*news weeklies*); SEE ALSO **baron, délit, liberté, magazine, point**

pressentir (*vt*): **pressenti** à la succession par le maire lui-même (*approached [to stand for office]*); la liste des **pressentis** s'allonge (*[person] sounded out*)

presser (*vt*): les Etats-Unis **pressent** leurs alliés de s'impliquer davantage en Afghanistan (*urge*)

pression (*nf*): les **pressions** politiques dont ils sont l'objet (*pressure*); **exercer des pressions** sur le gouvernement pour obtenir leur libération (*bring pressure to bear*); une aggravation de la **pression fiscale** (*tax burden*); SEE ALSO **groupe**

prestataire (*nm*): le nombre de **prestataires** a augmenté de 25%, en deux ans (*recipient of a state benefit*); les **prestataires de services** indépendants s'estiment lésés par cette loi (*supplier of a service*)

prestation (*nf*): la directive européenne sur la libre **prestation de services** (*supplying of a service*); vivre uniquement des **prestations sociales** (*social security benefits*); Suisse: **prestation de serment** du gouvernement (*taking of oath*)

présumé, -e (*adj*): les responsables **présumés** de ces attentats (*alleged, presumed*); l'**assassin présumé** a été écroué (*murder suspect*)

prêt (*nm*): obtenir un nouveau **prêt** (*loan*); l'attribution de logements HLM et de **prêts immobiliers** (*housing loan*); une fois remboursés ses **prêts hypothécaires** (*mortgage loan*); SEE ALSO **annuité**

prétendant, -e (*nm,f*): l'assassinat du **prétendant à la présidence** (*presidential candidate*)

prétendre (*vt*): il **prétend** incarner l'ancrage à gauche du parti socialiste (*claim*)

prétendu, -e (*adj*): les **prétendus** excès de la politique commerciale de la CE (*alleged*)

prétendument (*adv*): lors d'une opération **prétendument** antiterroriste (*allegedly*)

prétention (*nf*): l'Italie n'a aucune **prétention territoriale** sur la Dalmatie (*territorial claim*)

prêter (*vt*): le gouvernement a **prêté serment** devant le Président (*swear an oath*); les propos **prêtés au ministre** (*attributed to the minister*); 200 bénévoles **prêteront leur concours** (*give their help, lend support*); SEE ALSO **confusion**

prétoire (*nm*): la bataille va donc se poursuivre **dans les prétoires** (*in the courts*)

preuve (*nf*): après audition des témoins et examen des **preuves** (*evidence*)

prévaloir (*vi*): le souci de ne pas isoler la Russie **prévaut** à Washington (*prevail; be the prime consideration*); [**se**] (*vpr*): Tokyo a pu **se prévaloir** d'une très forte croissance (*boast a high growth rate*)

prévenir (*vt*): afin de **prévenir** toute augmentation du prix du brut (*anticipate*); dans la perspective de **prévenir** d'éventuels conflits (*avert, prevent*)

préventif, -ive (*adj/nf*): un raid **préventif** serait-il justifié? (*preemptive*); être maintenu **en détention préventive** (*in detention pending trial*); **faire de la préventive**, en attendant son jugement (*be remanded in custody*)

prévention (*nf*): le projet de loi relatif à la **prévention** du licenciement économique (*prevention*); adjoint au maire chargé de la sécurité et de la **prévention** (*crime prevention*); comment lever les **préventions bruxelloises**? (*opposition from Brussels*)

prévenu, -e (*adj/nm,f*): un **prévenu** en attente de son jugement (*accused [person]; defendant*); SEE ALSO **banc**

prévisible (*adj*): il s'agit d'anticiper l'augmentation **prévisible** de la population (*likely, predictable*)

prévision (*nf*): la **prévision** d'une croissance de 6% en 2010 paraît optimiste (*forecast, prediction*)

prévisionnel, -elle (*adj*): un chiffre d'affaires **prévisionnel** pour 2009 de 200 millions de dollars (*projected/estimated*)

prévisionniste (*nm*): les **prévisionnistes** parient sur une nouvelle explosion du chômage (*[economic] forecaster*)

prévoir (*vt*): les accords **prévoient** deux réunions par an (*provide for, envisage*); le groupe **prévoit** un chiffre d'affaires de 4,5 milliards pour 2007 (*anticipate; expect*)

prévoyance (*nf*): son **manque de prévoyance**, sa mauvaise stratégie politique (*lack of foresight*); Jonquille: votre **plan de prévoyance** personnalisé (*savings and insurance scheme*)

primaire (*adj/nf*): désigner, dans des [élections) **primaires**, le candidat unique (*primary; eliminating contest*)

primauté (*nf*): la **primauté** du droit français sur le droit européen (*primacy; pre-eminence*)

prime (*nf*): le syndicat réclame le versement d'une **prime d'ancienneté** (*seniority bonus*); toucher une **prime d'intéressement** égale à 20% de son salaire annuel (*profit-sharing bonus*); toucher des **primes de rendement** (*efficiency bonus*); recevoir une **prime de départ** de 150.000 euros (*golden handshake*); recevoir une **prime de licenciement** (*severance pay*)

principal, -e *mpl* **-aux** (*adj/nm*): les **principaux de collège** et les proviseurs de lycée (*college principal*)

principauté (*nf*): la **principauté** d'Andorre quitte la tutelle de la France et de l'Espagne (*principality*)

prise (*nf*): la **prise** de la ville par les rebelles (*seizure, capture*); SEE ALSO **bénéfice, charge, commande, position, pouvoir**

prison (*nf*): SEE **encombrement, ferme, peine, perpétuité, surpopulation**

prisonnier, -ière (*adj/nm,f*): une centaine de ces détenus sont des **prisonniers d'opinion**; la libération de nombreux **prisonniers de conscience** (*political prisoner*); SEE ALSO **constituer**

privation (*nf*): avec **privation du droit de vote** et inéligibilité pour cinq ans (*loss/forfeiture of voting rights*); condamné à cinq années de **privation de ses droits civiques** (*forfeiture of civil rights*)

privatisation (*nf*): relancer la **privatisation des terres** (*private ownership of land*); SEE ALSO **poste**

privatiser (*vt*): l'idée de **privatiser** les établissements pénitentiaires (*privatize*)

privé, -e (*adj/nm*): le retour au [secteur] **privé** de Rhône-Poulenc (*private sector*); les syndicats de l'entreprise ont accepté le **passage au privé** (*privatization*); SEE ALSO **intimité, vente**

priver (*vt*): la récente loi les **prive** de certains droits essentiels (*deprive*)

privilégié, -e (*adj/nm,f*): un allié **privilégié** dans la région du Golfe (*special; privileged*)

privilégier (*vt*): Iran: les Européens **privilégient** une approche diplomatique (*favour*); **privilégier** la lutte contre la drogue (*give priority to*)

prix (*nm*): les **prix de détail** n'ont progressé que de 0,1% (*retail prices*); se procurer des marchandises **au prix de gros** (*at wholesale prices*); après la fixation du **prix de vente** (*selling price*); le **prix de revient** est donc de cinq euros la pièce (*cost price; production cost*); des articles vendus **à prix coûtant** (*at cost price*); SEE ALSO **avantageux, blocage, bond, casser, casseur, concurrence, dissuasif, écraser, envolée, guerre, indexer, majoration, majorer, minimal, pratiquer, réglementation, soutenir, vérité**

probant, -e (*adj*): la démonstration paraît **peu probante** (*unconvincing*)

probatoire (*adj*): pendant une période **probatoire** (*trial; probationary*); il s'était soustrait aux obligations du **contrôle probatoire** (*probation*)

procédé (*nm*): se refuser à de tels **procédés** (*methods, practices*); le **procédé** [de fabrication] est protégé par un brevet exclusif (*manufacturing process*)

procéder (*vt*): vont-ils **procéder à un essai nucléaire** (*carry out a nuclear test*); SEE ALSO **constatation, recensement**

procédure (*nf*): réformer le Code pénal et aussi amender la **procédure** (*legal procedure*); éviter la **procédure judiciaire** (*legal proceedings*); engager une **procédure au civil** en dommages et intérêts (*civil action*); SEE ALSO **frais, vice**

procès (*nm*): détenir **sans procès** des étrangers soupçonnés de terrorisme (*without trial*); lors du **procès d'appel** (*appeal hearing*); le maire envisage de **faire un procès** à la Caisse des dépôts et consignations (*bring a court action [against], sue*); SEE ALSO **diffamation, intenter, intention, meurtre**

processus (*nm*): faire avancer le **processus de paix** au Proche-Orient (*peace process*)

procès-verbal (*nm*): extrait du **procès-verbal** des délibérations du conseil municipal (*minutes*); la contractuelle de service lui a **dressé un procès-verbal** pour stationnement interdit (*issue a parking ticket*)

prochain, -e (*adj/nm*): la **prochaine** suppression de 22.000 lits d'hôpitaux (*impending; imminent*)

proche (*adj/nm*): un **proche** du ministre le nie formellement (*person/source close to*)

procuration (*nf*): avoir une **procuration** sur le compte en banque de sa femme (*have authorization [esp. to operate a bank account]*); un Français d'outre-mer peut **voter par procuration** (*vote by proxy*)

procureur (*nm*): le **procureur** (**de la République**) a requis trois ans de prison ferme (*public prosecutor*)

producteur, -trice (*adj/nm*): la concurrence de nouveaux **pays producteurs de café** (*coffee-producing countries*)

productivité (*nf*): son ambition: **renouer avec la productivité** (*a return to greater productivity*); SEE ALSO **gain**

produit (*nm*): le **produit** des taxes sur les cartes grises (*proceeds, yield; [tax] revenue*); la Belgique exporte 70% de son **produit intérieur brut**, ou PIB (*gross domestic product*); la progression du **produit national brut**, ou PNB, a été de 1,7% en 2007 (*gross national product*)

profit (*nm*): améliorer le **profit** des entreprises (*profit, profitability*); le **retour au profit** est pour cette année (*return to profitability*)

profondeur (*nf*): procéder à une réforme **en profondeur** du financement de la protection sociale (*in-depth*)

progresser (*vi*): les prix à la consommation ont **progressé** de 0.9% (*increase, rise*)

progression (*nf*): la forte **progression** dans les ventes de magnétoscopes (*increase, rise*); les dépenses d'éducation, **en progression** de 14,5% (*up, higher*)

progressiste (*adj*): lors de la constitution de la nouvelle **alliance progressiste** (*alliance for progress*)

projet (*nm*): un **projet libéral** susceptible d'attirer des électeurs (*liberal programme*); un **projet de société**, basé sur la justice et l'égalité (*project for society*); le **projet d'extension** de l'aéroport de Roissy (*planned extension*); SEE ALSO **cohérence**

projet de loi (*nm*): un **projet de loi** sur la réforme des universités sera déposé en automne (*[government] bill*)

projeter (*vt*): la firme **projette** de fermer son usine de Gien (*plan*)

prolongation (*nf*): obtenir une **prolongation** de la trêve (*extension*)

prolongement (*nm*): l'UEO constitue le **prolongement** militaire de l'Union européenne (*extension*)

prolonger (*vt*): l'état d'urgence a été **prolongé** de six mois (*extend, prolong*)

promotion (*nf*): sortir major de sa **promotion** à HEC (*year, intake*); la **promotion sociale** des enfants issus de l'immigration (*upward mobility*)

promouvoir (*vt*): abaisser les barrières commerciales et ainsi **promouvoir** le commerce mondial (*promote, foster*); il a été **promu** au grade d'adjudant-chef (*promote, raise*)

promulguer (*vt*): de nouvelles législations ont été **promulguées** (*enact [legislation]*)

prôner (*vt*): contre ceux qui **prônent** le fanatisme religieux (*preach*); la Russie **prône** une solution négociée (*advocate, recommend*)

prononcé (*nm*): au moment du **prononcé du verdict** (*announcement of the verdict*)

prononcer (*vt*): les peines **prononcées** à l'encontre des putschistes (*pass, pronounce [sentence]*); [**se**] (*vpr*): la Cour suprême **se prononcera** sur leur sort (*decide, reach a verdict*); en **se prononçant** contre la construction d'un second porte-avions (*come out [for/against]*)

pronostic (*nm*): son **pronostic de croissance** a été révisé à la baisse (*growth forecast*)

pronostiquer (*vt*): tous deux **pronostiquent** une aggravation de la tension dans le pays (*forecast; foresee*)

proportionnel, -elle (*adj*): le scrutin majoritaire avec une dose de [représentation] **proportionnelle** (*proportional representation*); SEE ALSO **rétablir**

propos (*nmpl*): les réactions suscitées par ses **propos** (*remarks, words*); après les **propos tenus sur l'islam** (*remarks made about Islam*)

proposition (*nf*): Sénat: **propositions** sur la nationalité (*proposal*); la **proposition de loi** émane d'un groupe de socialistes (*[Brit] private member's bill*)

propriétaire (*nmf*): nouvelle loi sur le logement: les **propriétaires** mécontents (*landlord; owner*); 70% d'entre eux sont **propriétaires de leur logement** (*homeowner, householder*)

propriété (*nf*): le gouvernement a démocratisé la **propriété du logement** (*home ownership*); SEE ALSO **accédant, accéder, accession, titre**

prorogation (*nf*): le locataire peut demander une **prorogation du bail** (*extension of the lease*)

proroger (*vt*): le gouvernement a annoncé qu'il **proroge** de 30 jours supplémentaires la trêve (*extend, continue*)

protection (*nf*): une réforme du financement de la **protection sociale** (*state-provided social welfare*)

protestataire (*adj/nmf*): l'électorat rural, **volontiers protestataire** (*inclined to protest*); SEE ALSO **vote**

protestation (*nf*): arrêter le travail **en signe de protestation** (*as a protest*); SEE ALSO **marche**

protocole (*nm*): un **protocole d'accord** a été signé (*outline/draft agreement*); SEE ALSO **enterrer**

provenance (*nf*): nous avons pu nous assurer de sa **provenance** (*place of origin*)

provenir (*vi*): le tiers du PNB allemand **provient** de l'exportation; 45% de ses recettes **proviennent** de l'assurance-maladie (*come [from]*)

province (*nf*): une série d'attentats dans la capitale et **en province** (*in the provinces*); SEE ALSO **délocaliser**

proviseur (*nm*): principaux et **proviseurs** veulent une répression accrue de la violence à l'école (*headmaster, principal*)

provision (*nf*): le non-paiement d'un chèque en raison d'une **insuffisance de provision** (*insufficient funds*); SEE ALSO **chèque**

provisoire (*adj*): SEE **détention**, **liberté**

provocateur, -trice (*adj/nm,f*): rejeter la responsabilité sur d'éventuels **provocateurs** (*agitator, troublemaker*)

provocation (*nf*): la nouvelle infraction de **provocation à la haine ou à la violence raciale** (*inciting racial hatred or violence*)

provoquer (*vt*): l'attentat a **provoqué** d'importants dégâts matériels (*cause*); SEE ALSO **tollé**

proxénète (*nmf*): **proxénète**, il obligeait sa propre femme à se livrer à la prostitution (*procurer*)

proxénétisme (*nm*): inculpé de **proxénétisme** (*living off immoral earnings*)

proximité (*nf*): la **proximité** des élections (*imminence*); la **police de proximité** ne se résume pas à l'îlotage (*local/community policing*); SEE ALSO **magasin**

prudence (*nf*): appel à la **prudence salariale** (*moderation in pay claims/awards*)

prudent, -e (*adj*): Gatt: la France reste **prudente** (*cautious*)

prud'homal, -e *mpl* **-aux** (*adj*): le **juge prud'homal**, le juge des litiges liés au contrat de travail (*judge on industrial tribunal*)

prud'homme (*nm*): la CGT respecte la décision des **prud' hommes**; condamné par le **tribunal des prud'hommes** pour le licenciement d'un employé (*industrial disputes tribunal*)

public, -que (*adj/nm*): **dans le [secteur] public** les augmentations ont été rares (*in the public/state sector*); le géant européen de l'**électronique grand public** (*consumer electronics*); SEE ALSO **argent, dépense, école, finance, fonction, fonds, huée, ministère, rumeur, subside, utilité**

publicitaire (*adj*): SEE **encart, plage**

publicité (*nf*): poursuivi pour **publicité mensongère**; il s'estime victime d'une **publicité trompeuse** (*misleading advertising*)

pudeur (*nf*): SEE **attentat, outrage**

puissance (*nf*): une reconnaissance de leur statut de **grande puissance** (*major power*); SEE ALSO **équilibre**

puissant, -e (*adj*): face à un exécutif fort, il faut un Parlement **puissant** (*powerful*)

pur, -e (*adj/nm,f*): la grève **pure et dure** (*hardline, uncompromising*); quelques **purs et durs** du parti (*hardliner*)

purge (*nf*): procéder à une **purge** d'éléments politiquement indésirables (*purge*)

purger (*vt*): l'établissement où il va **purger sa peine** (*serve his sentence*)

putsch (*nm*): au moment du **putsch raté** d'août 1991 (*failed coup*); SEE ALSO **tentative**

pyramide (*nf*): la **pyramide des âges** est éloquente (*age pyramid*)

pyromane (*adj/nmf*): un **pyromane** serait à l'origine des incendies dans le Midi (*arsonist, pyromaniac*)

Q

quadrillage (*nm*): le **quadrillage policier** de la ville s'est encore accentué (*tight police control*)

quadriller (*vt*): les miliciens du Hamas **quadrillent** tout le quartier (*place under tight control*)

qualification (*nf*): l'insertion professionnelle de jeunes sans diplôme ou **sans qualification** (*unqualified*)

qualifié, -e (*adj*): une pénurie d'ouvriers **très qualifiés** (*highly skilled*); un monde de travail qui rejette **les moins qualifiés** (*those with least skills*)

qualifier (*vt*): Londres **qualifie** de prématurée la décision palestinienne (*label, term, call*)

qualité (*nf*): on lui avait refusé la **qualité** de réfugié (*status*); **avoir qualité** pour signer les traités (*be competent*); l'amélioration de la **qualité de la vie** (*quality of life*)

quart monde (*nm*): toutes les catégories sociales, des oubliés du **quart monde** aux nantis (*the most deprived sector of a wealthy country's population*)

quartier (*nm*): des demandes de subventions venues des associations **de quartier** (*local; neighbourhood*); dans le **quartier des affaires** (*business district*); un collège situé dans un **quartier difficile** (*deprived area*)

quémander (*vt*): les associations **quémandent** des subventions (*beg for*)

querelle (*nf*): le réveil de la **querelle** algéro-marocaine (*dispute*); l'opposition, divisée par ses **querelles intestines** (*internal wrangling*)

question (*nf*): la séance de **questions orales** (*oral questions [in Parliament]*); au Vietnam, on ne semble pas vouloir **remettre en question** le parti unique (*challenge, call into question*); une **remise en question** de la sécurité nucléaire (*reappraisal; reassessment*); SEE ALSO **non-accord**, **sécuritaire**

quête (*nf*): Kouchner en Irak **en quête d'une solution pacifique** (*in search of a peaceful solution*)

quêter (*vi*): **quêter** dans la rue pour soutenir les grévistes (*collect money*)

quinquennal, -e *mpl* **-aux** (*adj*): on fit voter la loi **quinquennale** pour l'emploi en 1993 (*quinquennial, five-year*)

quinquennat (*nm*): il préconise le **quinquennat** pour tous les mandats électifs (*five-year term of office*)

quittance (*nf*): une **quittance** d'électricité à laquelle on ne peut faire face (*bill*); pour pouvoir être inscrit, on demande une **quittance de loyer** (*rent receipt*)

quitter (*vt*): il est prêt à **quitter ses fonctions** (*resign, leave office, stand down*)

quolibet (*nm*): il partit sous les **quolibets** de ses adversaires (*gibe, jeer*)

quorum (*nm*): l'absence de **quorum** dans un comité plénier (*quorum*)

quota (*nm*): protéger un marché par des **quotas d'importation** (*import quotas*); la **mise en place de quotas** d'émissions de gaz à effet de serre (*setting/fixing quotas*); SEE ALSO **instauration**

quote-part (*nf*): la **quote-part** des Etats-Unis était de 40% en 1945 (*share*)

quotidien, -ienne (*adj/nm*): responsable de la **gestion quotidienne** (*day-to-day management*); le vandalisme, devenu le **quotidien** des quartiers en difficulté (*everyday experience*); la France a besoin d'un grand **quotidien** économique (*daily [newspaper]*)

quotient (*nm*): la suppression du **quotient familial** dans le calcul de l'impôt sur le revenu (*dependents' allowance set against tax*)

R

rabais (*nm*): accorder un **rabais** pour paiement au comptant (*discount*); SEE ALSO **consentir**

raccordement (*nm*): la taxe de **raccordement** au tout-à-l'égout (*connection, linking [up]*); SEE ALSO **bretelle**

raccorder (*vt*): demander un devis pour faire **raccorder** deux canalisations (*connect together*); [**se**] (*vpr*): la nouvelle ligne pourra par la suite **se raccorder au réseau** du TGV (*be connected*)

rachat (*nm*): le **rachat** en bourse de 5% des actions (*purchase, acquisition*); un autre candidat potentiel au **rachat** (*buy-out*)

racheter (*vt*): une société **rachetée** par une firme allemande (*take over [a company]*)

racisme (*nm*): le **racisme**, un délit puni par la loi (*racism, racial prejudice*)

raciste (*adj*): des écrits à caractère **raciste** et antisémite (*racist*); SEE ALSO **injure**

racket (*nm*): dans des collèges où sévissent la drogue, l'intimidation et le **racket** (*racketeering; extortion through blackmail*)

racolage (*nm*): arrêtée pour **racolage sur la voie publique** (*soliciting for purposes of prostitution*)

racoler (*vt*): le quartier dans lequel **racolaient** les prostituées (*solicit [esp. for prostitution]*)

radiation (*nf*): pratiquer des **radiations** des listes de l'ANPE (*striking off [register, list]*)

radical, -e *mpl* **-aux** (*adj/nm,f*): les plus **radicaux** des intégristes (*extreme, radical*); quelques **radicaux** seront un appoint précieux pour les Socialistes (*Radical*); SEE ALSO **aile**

radicalisation (*nf*): une **radicalisation** du conflit (*hardening of attitude*)

radicaliser [**se**] (*vpr*): les positions **se radicalisent** dans ce conflit (*become more extreme; harden*)

radicalisme (*nm*): face à la montée du **radicalisme** intégriste (*extremism*)

radier (*vt*): **radier** les jeunes chômeurs qui refusent un emploi (*cross off, strike off [list, register]*)

raffermir [**se**] (*vpr*): la monnaie américaine **s'est raffermie** hier (*strengthen*)

raffermissement (*nm*): cette bonne nouvelle a contribué au **raffermissement** de Wall Street (*strengthening; steadying*)

rafle (*nf*): le juge ordonna une **rafle** de tous les établissements du quartier (*[police] raid*)

rafler (*vt*): la liste arrivant en tête **rafle tous les sièges** (*win all the seats*)

raid (*nm*): une fièvre d'acquisitions et de **raids** dans le monde des assurances (*corporate raid*); après l'échec du **raid boursier** contre les Galeries Lafayette (*surprise bid on the Stock Exchange*)

raider (*nm*): le groupe agro-alimentaire semble intéresser les **raiders** (*corporate raider*)

raidir (*vt*): Washington **raidit sa position** (*hardens her position*); [**se**] (*vpr*): si Tokyo **se raidit** sur la question de l'aide (*takes a tougher line*)

raidissement (*nm*): comment s'expliquer le brusque **raidissement** de l'Iran? (*taking a tougher line*)

raison (*nf*): le tribunal a **donné raison au plaignant** (*find for the plaintiff*); les **raisons sociales** successives du groupe (*corporate name*)

ralenti (*nm*): les chantiers navals **tournent au ralenti** (*idle; run at less than full capacity*)

ralentir (*vi*): la croissance française a nettement **ralenti** au deuxième trimestre (*slow down*)

ralentissement (*nm*): le **ralentissement** de l'inflation dans la zone euro (*slowing down*)

ralliement (*nm*): Congo: **ralliement** du principal parti d'opposition (*conversion [to cause/party]*)

rallier (*vt*): sans surprise, il **rallie** le parti de l'ordre (*join, go over [to]*); la France veut **rallier** ses partenaires à l'idée d'un pacte européen de l'immigration (*win over [to]*); [**se**] (*vpr*): la Grèce **s'est ralliée** au compromis adopté hier à Paris (*rally [to]; come round [to]*)

rallonge (*nf*): obtenir une **rallonge** de cent mille euros (*additional sum/grant*)

rallonger (*vt*): inciter les entreprises à **rallonger** leurs horaires de travail (*lengthen, extend*)

ramener (*vt*): l'objectif d'un taux de chômage **ramené à 5%** en 2012 (*brought down to 5%*); SEE ALSO **paix**

rang (*nm*): la France doit pouvoir **tenir son rang** dans le monde (*maintain one's rank*); un diplomate **de haut rang** (*senior, high-ranking*); SEE ALSO **serrer**

ranger [**se**] (*vpr*): d'autres **se rangent au point de vue français** (*adopt/agree with the French position*)

rapatrié, -e (*adj/nm,f*): les mesures prises en faveur des **rapatriés** (*repatriated person*)

rapatriement (*nm*): le **rapatriement** des clandestins étrangers (*repatriation*)

rapatrier (*vt*): on propose de **rapatrier** ce trop-plein d'immigrés (*repatriate*)

rappel (*nm*): Paris annonce le **rappel** de son ambassadeur (*recall*); à la suite d'une augmentation, il touche un **rappel de salaire** de 2.000 euros (*back pay; retroactive pay rise*)

rappeler (*vt*): la Chine **rappelle** son ambassadeur (*recall, call back*)

rapport (*nm*): le **rapport** établira la vérité sur l'affaire (*report*); des placements **d'un faible rapport** (*giving a poor return*); SEE ALSO **décloisonner, envenimer, expertise**

rapporter (*vt*): une nouvelle **rapportée** par l'agence Reuter (*report*); l'impôt sur le capital **rapporte** 100 milliards par an (*yield, earn*); la proportion des chômeurs **rapportée à la population totale** (*in relation to the total population*)

rapporteur (*nm*): nommé **rapporteur** de la Commission des finances (*chairman [of a committee]*)

rapprochement (*nm*): un **rapprochement** inattendu entre les écologistes et la droite (*alliance*); l'accord vise à favoriser des **rapprochements d'entreprises** (*collaboration between companies*)

rapprocher (*vt*): le travail pour **rapprocher les communautés** a été négligé (*bring communities closer together*); [**se**] (*vpr*): les positions des négociateurs **se sont rapprochées** (*converge*)

rapt (*nm*): une condamnation pour **rapt** et détournement de mineur (*abduction; kidnapping*)

ras-le-bol (*nm*): comment canaliser le **ras-le-bol** des étudiants? (*dissatisfaction; frustration*)

rassemblement (*nm*): envisager la création d'un gouvernement de **rassemblement** (*union; unity*); la CGT organise des **rassemblements** pour rappeler ses revendications (*rally, meeting*); SEE ALSO **unitaire**

rassembler (*vt*): le seul à pouvoir **rassembler** toute la gauche (*unite, unify*)

ratissage (*nm*): lors d'une opération de **ratissage** de l'armée israélienne (*thorough search/combing of an area*)

ratisser (*vt*): les gendarmes avaient **ratissé le secteur** (*comb/search the area thoroughly*)

ratonnade (*nf*): des **ratonnades** dirigées contre les Pakistanais (*racially motivated beating*)

rattrapage (*nm*): le personnel navigant réclame un **rattrapage salarial** (*pay rise [to catch up with cost of living]*)

rattraper (*vt*): les prix dans les magasins **rattrapent** le pouvoir d'achat (*catch up [with]*); SEE ALSO **retard**

ravir (*vt*): pour **ravir** la municipalité de Nanterre aux communistes (*seize [from]*); SEE ALSO **vedette**

ravisseur, -euse (*nm,f*): onze otages sont encore aux mains de leurs **ravisseurs** (*kidnapper; abductor*)

ravitaillement (*nm*): pour assurer le **ravitaillement en essence** (*provision of fuel supplies*)

ravitailler (*vt*): comment **ravitailler** en eau ces populations? (*supply*); [**se**] (*vpr*): la France **se ravitaille** difficilement en sources énergétiques (*obtain supplies; be supplied*)

raz-de-marée (*nm*): le **raz-de-marée** socialiste n'épargne pas le Midi (*[electoral] landslide*)

réactualisation (*nf*): une **réactualisation** des données de l'INSEE (*updating*)

réactualiser (*vt*): on **réactualise** tous les chiffres au 31 décembre (*update*)

réalisation (*nf*): la **réalisation** de travaux de voirie (*carrying out; completion*); le ministre souligna les **réalisations** de son gouvernement (*achievement*)

réaliser (*vt*): le premier essai nucléaire **réalisé** par la Chine (*carry out*); il tente en vain de **réaliser** l'unité arabe (*achieve, bring about*); [**se**] (*vpr*): comment va **se réaliser** l'union monétaire? (*come about*); SEE ALSO **bénéfice**, **percée**

réaménagement (*nm*): des mesures de **réaménagement** des quartiers les plus défavorisés (*renovation; redevelopment*)

réaménager (*vt*): une priorité: **réaménager** le quartier du Marais (*re-develop, renovate*)

rebelle (*adj/nmf*): proche de la frontière ivoirienne, **sous contrôle rebelle** (*under rebel control*)

rébellion (*nf*): un attentat imputé à la **rébellion** séparatiste (*rebel movement, rebels*); placé en garde à vue pour **rébellion** et outrage à agent (*resisting arrest*)

rebond (*nm*): la croissance **a connu un rebond plus fort que prévu** en 2006 (*has made a stronger than expected recovery*)

rebondir (*vi*): la polémique vient de **rebondir** (*start up again*); Affiches racistes: **l'affaire rebondit** (*new developments [in the racist poster case]*)

rebondissement (*nm*): l'enquête vient de connaître un **nouveau rebondissement** (*new development*)

recaser (*vt*): le tiers des ouvriers licenciés **ont pu être recasés** (*have been found new jobs*)

recel (*nm*): impliqué dans de nombreuses affaires de **recel** (*receiving/being in possession of stolen goods*)

receleur (*nm*): soupçonnés d'être d'importants **receleurs d'objets volés** (*receiver of stolen goods*)

recensement (*nm*): **procéder à un recensement** des habitants (*carry out a census; do a count*)

recenser (*vt*): on a **recensé** plus de 200 offres d'emploi (*compile [an inventory of]*); les trois millions de faits de délinquance **recensés par la police** (*on police files*)

recentrage (*nm*): le **recentrage** de la gauche opéré par le Président (*occupation of/move to the centre ground*); le **recentrage** du groupe sur l'agro-alimentaire (*focusing [on core activities]*)

recentrer (*vt*): **recentrer** la politique sociale sur les plus défavorisés (*concentrate, focus*); [**se**] (*vpr*): Accor veut **se recentrer** sur l'hôtellerie et les services (*refocus*)

récession (*nf*): sur fond de **récession** mondiale (*recession*); l'Europe **connaît la pire récession** depuis un demi-siècle (*experience its worst recession*); SEE ALSO **sortie**

recette (*nf*): les **recettes pétrolières** du Mexique (*oil revenue*); les **recettes fiscales** rentrent toujours aussi mal (*tax revenue*); travailler à la **recette des impôts** (*tax office, revenue office*)

recevable (*adj*): le vote de la motion de censure, pour être **recevable**, doit être signé par 58 députés (*admissible, allowable*)

receveur, -euse (*nm,f*): au bureau du **receveur** municipal (*tax collector*); payable au **receveur des Postes** (*postmaster*)

réchauffement (*nm*): le **réchauffement des relations** entre Washington et Pékin (*improvement in relations*); les dangers que représente le **réchauffement de la planète** (*global warming*)

réchauffer (*vt*): le Qatar cherche à **réchauffer ses relations** avec l'Arabie Saoudite (*improve relations*); [**se**] (*vpr*): **les relations se réchauffent** entre Moscou et Paris (*relations improve*)

rechute (*nf*): la **rechute** des prix de l'immobilier (*fall back, fall*)

récidive (*nf*): le fort **taux de récidive** parmi les jeunes délinquants (*re-offending rate*)

récidiver (*vi*): 97% des jeunes qui vont en prison **récidivent** (*commit a further offence*)

récidiviste (*adj/nmf*): Yvelines: le violeur **récidiviste** inculpé (*repeat offender*)

réclamation (*nf*): inutile de **faire une réclamation** (*lodge a complaint*)

réclamer (*vt*): les nationalistes **réclament** le statut de république (*call for, demand*); [**se**] (*vpr*): sur l'essentiel, le Front national **se réclame des mêmes valeurs** que la majorité (*claim to hold the same values*)

reclassement (*nm*): la CGT exige un **reclassement** des partants dans les entreprises locales (*transfer, redeployment*)

reclasser (*vt*): on compte **reclasser** les deux tiers des sureffectifs dans d'autres emplois (*redeploy [esp. worker]*); les salariés de 45 à 55 ans **se reclassent difficilement** (*are difficult to place in a job*)

réclusion (*nf*): une peine de 15 ans de **réclusion criminelle** (*imprisonment*)

recommander [**se**] (*vpr*): dans les pays qui **se recommandent de l'Islam** (*claim allegiance to Islam*)

reconductible (*adj*): une grève de 24 heures, **reconductible** tous les jours (*renewable*)

reconduction (*nf*): le P-DG obtient la **reconduction** de son mandat d'administrateur (*renewal, extension*)

reconduire (*vt*):); le cessez-le-feu a été **reconduit** indéfiniment (*extend; renew*); le ministre **a été reconduit dans ses fonctions** (*has been re-appointed*); **être reconduit à la frontière** ou incarcéré (*be escorted back to the frontier [by the police]*)

reconduite (*nf*): ressortissants étrangers: 44 affaires de **reconduite à la frontière** (*expulsion [of illegal immigrant]*)

reconnaître (*vt*): l'Irak a **reconnu** l'indépendance du Koweït (*recognize*); il a **reconnu les faits** au cours de sa garde à vue (*admit to the deed; confess*)

reconversion (*nf*): un programme d'aide à la **reconversion** des bassins miniers (*redevelopment*); les suppressions d'emplois se feront par départs en préretraite et **reconversions** (*redeployment [of staff]*)

reconvertir (*vt*): les Charbonnages ont **reconverti** près de 10.000 salariés (*redeploy [staff]*); [**se**] (*vpr*): se recycler, ou **se reconvertir** dans les nouvelles technologies informatiques (*switch [to a trade/profession/sector]*)

recourir (*vt*): ils **recourent à la violence** en désespoir de cause (*resort to violence*)

recours (*nm*): l'ultime **recours en appel** s'est soldé par une fin de non-recevoir (*appeal against a verdict*); **déposer un recours** devant le Conseil constitutionnel (*register an appeal*); **avoir recours** à des moyens illégaux (*resort [to]*); SEE ALSO **voie**

recouvrement (*nm*): la lutte pour le **recouvrement** des droits palestiniens inaliénables (*recovery*); le **recouvrement** ou la perception de sommes dues (*levying, collecting [money, taxes]*)

recouvrer (*vt*): une amnistie leur a permis de **recouvrer** leurs droits civiques (*recover, regain*); **recouvrer** les arriérés d'impôts (*collect [unpaid tax]*)

recrudescence (*nf*): on assiste à une **recrudescence de la guérilla** (*renewed outbreak of guerrilla activity*)

recrue (*nf*): une armée mixte mêlant à parité cadres de métier et **recrues du contingent** (*national service recruit*)

recrutement (*nm*): le **recrutement** se fait sur concours (*recruitment*); le **recrutement des apprentis** par les entreprises (*taking on apprentices*); SEE ALSO **apprenti**

recruter (*vt*): des formations d'ingénieurs qui **recrutent** des diplômés Bac +2 (*take on, recruit*)

recteur (*nm*): rencontre du grand rabbin et du **recteur** de la mosquée de Lyon (*rector*); la compétence d'un **recteur d'académie** (*[Fr] chief regional education officer*)

rectificatif, -ive (*adj/nm,f*): *Le Monde* publia un **rectificatif** dans son numéro de mardi (*correction, amendment*)

rectoral, -e *mpl* **-aux** (*adj*): l'épiscopat attaque deux **décisions rectorales** supprimant le congé du mercredi (*[Fr] decisions taken by the regional education authority*)

rectorat (*nm*): une concertation entre l'Assemblée régionale, les **rectorats** et les enseignants (*[Fr] regional education authority*)

recueillement (*nm*): une journée de deuil et de **recueillement** (*meditation; reverence*)

recul (*nm*): le **recul** du pouvoir d'achat est supérieur à 10% (*decline*); le **recul** de l'âge de la retraite est jugé inévitable (*putting back*); les Libéraux sont **en recul** (*on the decline/in retreat*)

reculade (*nf*): Bruxelles: nouvelle **reculade** de la Grande-Bretagne (*climb-down*)

reculer (*vi*): le commerce mondial du pétrole a fortement **reculé** depuis 1973 (*decline, regress*); (*vt*): on parle de **reculer** le scrutin au 13 janvier (*put off, postpone*)

récupération (*nf*): déplorer la **récupération** d'un meurtre à des fins racistes (*exploitation*); CPE: **récupération politique** d'une jeunesse démobilisée? (*exploiting for political ends*); la **récupération** des déchets d'emballage (*recycling for re-use*)

récupérer (*vt*): **récupérer** de la ferraille (*salvage; reprocess*); leur intention est de **récupérer** le mouvement (*hijack, take over [esp. for political ends]*)

récuser (*vt*): l'aile gauche du parti **récuse** tout libéralisme excessif (*reject*); l'accusé **récuse** les compétences de la cour (*challenge*)

recyclage (*nm*): le **recyclage** des matériaux d'emballage (*recycling*); le développement technique impose un **recyclage** périodique (*retraining*)

recycler (*vt*): **recycler de l'argent** provenant d'un trafic de cocaïne (*launder money*); [**se**] (*vpr*): tenter de **se recycler** dans l'immobilier (*move into [another sector/profession]*)

rédacteur, -trice (*nm,f*): l'un des **rédacteurs** du code de procédure civile (*drafter*)

rédaction (*nf*): la **rédaction** du futur traité européen (*drawing up, drafting*); la **rédaction** est composée d'une centaine de journalistes (*editorial staff*)

reddition (*nf*): tenter d'obtenir la **reddition** des rebelles (*surrender*)

redécoupage (*nm*): le **redécoupage du calendrier scolaire** a été bien accueilli (*reorganization of the school year*); le projet de **redécoupage électoral** (*redrawing of electoral boundaries*)

redémarrage (*nm*): un **redémarrage** de l'activité industrielle (*take-off, resurgence*)

redémarrer (*vi*): la production **redémarre**, les commandes affluent (*take off*)

redéploiement (*nm*): devant la chute des commandes, la société envisageait un **redéploiement** industriel (*diversification; conversion*)

redéployer [**se**] (*vpr*): contraint de **se redéployer** pour sortir de la crise (*diversify*)

redevable (*adj*): les **redevables** de l'impôt de solidarité sur la fortune (*person liable [for tax]*)

redevance (*nf*): la société payera une **redevance** pour l'utilisation des brevets (*licence fee; royalties*); la **redevance audiovisuelle** augmentera de 4,5% en 2009 (*radio/TV licence fee*)

rédiger (*vt*): un rapport **rédigé** par son supérieur hiérarchique (*draft; write*)

redressement (*nm*): démographie: le **redressement** se confirme (*recovery*); la société **a été placée en redressement judiciaire** (*be put into receivership/administration*); le fisc lui a imposé un **redressement fiscal** pour les deux exercices écoulés (*tax adjustment; notification of arrears of tax*)

redresser (*vt*): réussir à **redresser** l'économie nationale (*redress, put right*)

réduction (*nf*): des **réductions de personnel** sont annoncées (*staff cutbacks*); une **réduction d'impôt** pour garde d'enfant (*tax allowance*); SEE ALSO **moitié**

réduire (*vt*): la France compte **réduire** son aide (*reduce, cut*); SEE ALSO **moitié**

réévaluation (*nf*): une **réévaluation à la hausse** des salaires des infirmières (*upgrade, upgrading, increase*)

réévaluer (*vt*): si l'euro est **réévalué**, le dollar le sera dans les mêmes proportions (*revalue*)

réfection (*nf*): procéder à la **réfection** des toitures (*repairing, rebuilding*)

référé (*nm*): une procédure simplifiée, le **référé**, permet d'obtenir d'une juridiction une décision provisoire (*summary court hearing*)

référendaire (*adj*): au fur et à mesure de la **campagne référendaire** (*referendum campaign*)

référendum (*nm*): soumettre une question à **référendum** (*referendum*)

réfléchir (*vt*): la commission chargée de **réfléchir** à une réforme de la procédure pénale (*consider; study*)

réflexion (*nf*): une **réflexion** en profondeur sur l'efficacité de l'ensemble de l'éducation (*debate*); les travaux de la **commission de réflexion** sur le système éducatif (*working group*); SEE ALSO **cellule**

reflux (*nm*): nouveau **reflux** du dollar (*fall [in value]*)

refondre (*vt*): il faudrait **refondre** l'ensemble du système (*overhaul*)

refonte (*nf*): Université: un rapport plaide pour une **refonte** du système de bourses (*overhaul, reform*)

réformateur, -trice (*adj/nm,f*): fier de l'œuvre **réformatrice** de la gauche (*reforming*)

réforme (*nf*): un rapport propose une **réforme de l'impôt** (*tax reform*); certains projets, comme la **réforme des retraites** (*pension reform*); SEE ALSO **abandon, enterrement, enterrer, geler, train**

réformiste (*adj*): un parti profondément divisé entre ses ailes **réformiste** et orthodoxe (*reforming*)

refoulement (*nm*): le **refoulement** d'étrangers se rendant en France (*turning-back, expulsion [esp. illegal immigrants]*)

refouler (*vt*): il risque d'**être refoulé** à la frontière (*be sent/turned back*)

réfractaire (*adj/nmf*): les **réfractaires au protocole de Kyoto** sont prêts à signer un accord climatique (*[countries] who refuse to sign the Kyoto agreements*)

réfugié, -e (*nm,f*): le statut de **réfugié politique** (*political refugee*)

refuser (*vt*): thèse que le gouvernement **refuse en bloc** (*reject absolutely*); [**se**] (*vpr*): son porte-parole **se refuse à tout commentaire** (*decline to comment*)

réfuter (*vt*): avant de **réfuter** les accusations portées contre lui (*refute*)

regain (*nm*): le **regain** du catholicisme aux Etats-Unis serait dû aux Hispaniques (*revival*); l'Ulster connaît un brusque **regain de tension** (*renewed tension*)

régie (*nf*): la transformation des services postaux en une **régie (d'Etat)** (*partly state-owned company*)

régime (*nm*): le **régime** en place est soutenu par l'étranger (*regime; government*); peut-on modifier un **régime matrimonial** après le mariage? (*marriage contract*); SEE ALSO **dérogatoire**

région (*nf*): la **région**, une collectivité territoriale à part entière (*region*); SEE ALSO **ancrage**, **limitrophe**

régional, -e (*adj*): SEE **schéma**

régir (*vt*): les nouvelles règles qui **régissent** son fonctionnement (*govern, control*)

règle (*nf*): la **règle de droit** s'applique à tous (*rule of law*); posséder un titre de séjour **en règle** (*valid*); SEE ALSO **assouplir**, **avertissement**, **déroger**, **dumping**

règlement (*nm*): les **règlements** internationaux s'en trouvent facilités (*settlement, payment*); parvenir à un **règlement négocié** du problème (*negotiated settlement*); six morts dans un **règlement de compte** mafieux (*settling of scores*); la société est **en règlement judiciaire** (*in compulsory liquidation*); SEE ALSO **amiable**, **comptant**, **entorse**, **non-observation**

réglementation (*nf*): plus de flexibilité sur le marché du travail, moins de **réglementation** (*regulation; laws*); aucun de ces pays n'a recouru à la **réglementation des prix** (*price controls*); SEE ALSO **déroger**, **répressif**

réglementer (*vt*): l'impossibilité de **réglementer** la publicité subliminale (*regulate, control*); alors que le travail dominical reste **réglementé** (*regulated, controlled*)

régler (*vt*): pour **régler** le problème des sureffectifs (*solve, settle*); en lui **réglant** les indemnités prévues à son contrat (*pay [out]*)

régresser (*vi*): les infractions à la législation sur les stupéfiants ont nettement **régressé** (*fall/decline in numbers*)

régression (*nf*): nette **régression** des valeurs minières (*decline, fall in value*); le pouvoir d'achat du consommateur **en régression** (*declining*)

regroupement (*nm*): autorisés à séjourner en France **au titre du regroupement familial** (*under a scheme for family entry and settlement*)

regrouper (*vt*): la francophonie **regroupe** un ensemble de communautés et de peuples (*bring together*); l'agglomération **regroupe** entre 40.000 et 50.000 habitants (*comprise, contain*)

régularisation (*nf*): afin d'**obtenir une régularisation de sa situation** (*regularize one's situation; put one's papers in order*)

régulariser (*vt*): l'Allemagne **régularise** certaines catégories d'immigés; permettre à 130.000 étrangers de **régulariser leur situation** (*make their [immigration] situation legal*)

régularité (*nf*): contrôler la **régularité** du séjour des étrangers en France (*legality*); veiller à la **régularité du scrutin** (*fairness of the election*)

régulation (*nf*): la nouvelle **instance de régulation** de l'audiovisuel (*regulatory body*)

réguler (*vt*): une autorité indépendante chargée de **réguler** le marché de l'électricité (*regulate*)

régulier, -ière (*adj*): ces premières élections ont-elles été **régulières**? (*properly conducted*); apporter la preuve de cinq années de **résidence régulière** en France (*lawful residence*)

régulièrement (*adv*): arrivé **régulièrement** en France en 2005 (*legally, lawfully*)

réhabilitation (*nf*): une opération de **réhabilitation** de l'habitat ancien (*regeneration; restoration*)

réhabiliter (*vt*): on va **réhabiliter** les habitations dégradées (*rehabilitate, restore*)

réinsérer (*vt*): les chômeurs les plus difficiles à **réinsérer** (*find new employment for*); [**se**] (*vpr*): aider les drogués à **se réinsérer dans la société** (*become rehabilitated into society*)

réinsertion (*nf*): la **réinsertion** des anciens détenus dans la société (*re-integration; rehabilitation*); les difficultés de la **réinsertion des chômeurs de longue durée** (*putting back to work the long-term unemployed*)

réintégration (*nf*): la **réintégration** du Caire au sein de la Ligue arabe (*readmission; re-entry*); la **réintégration** automatique du salarié licencié (*reinstatement*)

réintégrer (*vt*): **réintégrer** les employés renvoyés par l'ancienne direction (*reinstate, re-engage*); la femme refusa de **réintégrer le domicile conjugal** (*return to the marital home*)

rejoindre (*vt*): la Croatie pourrait **rejoindre** l'UE en 2010 (*join*)

réjouir [**se**] (*vpr*): officiellement, Tokyo **s'est réjoui** des engagements pris par Pyongyang (*express pleasure [at]*)

relâche (*nm*): lutter **sans relâche** contre de tels abus (*without let-up; relentlessly*)

relâchement (*nm*): il critique un **relâchement** dans la lutte contre l'inflation (*slackening; laxity*)

relâcher (*vt*): Israël s'engage à **relâcher** 250 prisonniers palestiniens (*release*)

relais (*nm*): les Chinois vont **prendre le relais** des Japonais; les services y ont **pris le relais** de l'agriculture (*take over from; replace*)

relance (*nf*): la **relance de l'économie** se fait toujours attendre (*boost to/revival of the economy*); une possible **relance** du processus de paix (*reopening; revival*)

relancer (*vt*): pour **relancer** à l'Est le rôle politique de la France (*revive, boost*); l'Allemagne refuse de **relancer**, mais accepte une réévaluation de sa monnaie (*stimulate the economy*)

relation (*nf*): les **relations** de la Colombie avec les Etats-Unis (*relations*); SEE ALSO **assainir**, **inamical**, **ménager**, **normalisation**, **normaliser**, **réchauffement**, **réchauffer**

relativiser (*vt*): le score du Front national doit être **relativisé** par l'abstention massive des électeurs (*put into perspective*)

relaxe (*nf*): les avocats de la défense **plaident la relaxe** (*ask for the acquittal of a defendant*)

relaxer (*vt*): deux des prévenus ont été **relaxés** (*acquit, discharge*)

relève (*nf*): une élite indigène qui pourra **prendre la relève** au moment de l'indépendance (*take over*)

relèvement (*nm*): un **relèvement** de la cotisation vieillesse (*raising, increase*); on assiste à un **relèvement spectaculaire** de l'économie (*spectacular recovery*)

relever (*vi*): les zones non urbaines **relèvent de la gendarmerie** (*come within the competence of the* gendarmerie); (*vt*): **relever le défi** des nouvelles technologies (*take up the challenge*); une force de paix de 50.000 hommes va **relever** les Casques bleus (*relieve, take over from*); le Président l'a **relevé de ses fonctions** (*dismiss, sack*)

remaniement (*nm*): toute la défense de l'OTAN **est en cours de remaniement** (*is being reorganized*); un **remaniement ministériel** est intervenu à Bonn (*cabinet reshuffle*)

remanier (*vt*): la législation a été **remaniée** à plusieurs reprises (*revise, amend*); un gouvernement largement **remanié** et rajeuni (*reshuffle*)

remboursement (*nm*): le **remboursement** d'une dette (*reimbursement, repayment*); SEE ALSO **mensualité**

rembourser (*vt*): les frais d'hospitalisation sont **remboursés** à 80% (*reimburse*)

remédier (*vt*): pour **remédier** au surpeuplement dans les prisons (*find a remedy for; cure*)

remembrement (*nm*): grâce au **remembrement**, les exploitations seront d'une taille rentable (*restructuring [of land]*)

remercier (*vt*): le gouvernement **remercie** le P-DG d'Elf-Aquitaine (*sack, dismiss*)

remettre (*vt*): le rapport qu'il vient de **remettre** au ministre (*submit, hand in*); son adjoint aux finances **remet sa démission** (*tender one's resignation*); la société **remet à plus tard** son introduction en Bourse (*postpone*); SEE ALSO **cause, huitaine, indéterminé, plat**

remise (*nf*): consentir des **remises** importantes (*discount, reduction*); la **remise en état** des infastructures (*repair*); des formations de **remise à niveau des connaissances** (*refresher course*); solliciter une **remise de peine** (*reduction of sentence; remission*); SEE ALSO **cause, question**

remontée (*nf*): la **remontée** du chômage; rechute du dollar, **remontée** du yen (*rise*)

remonter (*vi*): le chômage **remonte**, on assiste à une baisse des reprises d'emploi (*rise again, go up again*); (*vt*): la Banque centrale envisage toujours de **remonter ses taux** (*raise interest rates*)

remporter (*vt*): Sierra Leone: l'opposition **remporte** les élections législatives (*win*); la France pourrait **remporter de gros contrats** en Chine (*win major contracts/orders*)

rémunération (*nf*): avoir droit à une **rémunération** décente de son travail (*pay, earnings*); SEE ALSO **évolutif, fourchette, moindre**

rémunérer (*vt*): la banque **rémunère** les compte-chèques de 6 à 7% (*pay interest on*); un travail **mal rémunéré** (*poorly paid*); SEE ALSO **compte**

renchérir (*vi*): on a vu le brut **renchérir** constamment (*increase in price*); **renchérir** sur toute OPA lancée sur le fabricant de whisky (*bid higher, outbid*)

renchérissement (*nm*): le **renchérissement** très sensible du coût de l'habitat (*rise in price/cost*); le Japon, ébranlé par le **renchérissement de l'énergie** (*rise in energy costs*)

rendement (*nm*): son **rendement** est passé de 20 milliards en 2000 à 50 en 2006 (*yield, output*); l'usine travaillait **à plein rendement** (*at full capacity*); SEE ALSO **course, prime**

rendre [**se**] (*vpr*): les deux pirates de l'air **se sont rendus** aux autorités (*surrender*)

renforcement (*nm*): le **renforcement** des troupes cubaines en Afrique australe (*strengthening, reinforcement*); SEE ALSO **pénalité**

renforcer (*vt*): les Etats-Unis **renforcent** l'embargo sur Haïti (*reinforce*); **renforcer les peines** prévues pour la fabrication de faux documents (*set stiffer penalties*); [**se**] (*vpr*): Lafarge **se renforce** en Espagne (*strengthen its trading position; expand*); SEE ALSO **lien**

renfort (*nm*): des **renforts** occidentaux, dont un millier de soldats français (*reinforcements*)

reniement (*nm*): les **reniements** du maire, et sa gestion incohérente (*broken promises*)

renier (*vt*): **renier** les idées de son prédécesseur (*disown, repudiate*); [**se**] (*vpr*): écouter la base, **sans se renier** (*without going back on what one has said/done*)

renouer (*vt*): **renouer le dialogue** sans perdre la face (*reopen talks*); la France voudrait **renouer** avec Canberra (*get back on good terms*); Ford **renoue avec les bénéfices** (*return to profitability*); SEE ALSO **productivité**

renouveau *pl* **-x** (*nm*): accusé d'être le saboteur du **renouveau économique** (*economic regeneration*); **renouveau de tension** indo-pakistanais (*renewed tension*)

renouveler (*vt*): les élections permettront de **renouveler** le personnel (*renew, replace, change*); onze sièges **sont à renouveler** (*are up for re-election*)

renouvellement (*nm*): le **renouvellement** partiel du comité central (*renewal, replacement*); lors d'un **renouvellement de bail** (*renewing of a lease*)

rénovateur, -trice (*adj/nm,f*): les **rénovateurs** refusent de voter pour la liste communiste (*reformer, modernizer*)

rénovation (*nf*): la **rénovation** de l'habitat ancien (*renovation, restoration*); participer à la **rénovation** de la gauche française (*reform*)

rénover (*vt*): le conseil général décide de **rénover** le collège d'Etampes (*renovate, refurbish*)

renseignement (*nm*): la France accroît fortement ses moyens de **renseignement** (*intelligence*); la police judiciaire, en liaison avec les **Renseignements généraux** (*[Fr] general intelligence service*)

rentabiliser (*vt*): pouvoir **rentabiliser** au mieux son investissement (*make profitable*)

rentabilité (*nf*): par souci de **rentabilité** et d'économie (*profitability*); SEE ALSO **seuil**

rentable (*adj*): un investissement qui sera **rentable** à long terme (*profitable*)

rente (*nf*): vivre largement de ses **rentes** (*unearned income*); percevoir une **rente viagère** (*life annuity*); pour une gestion transparente de la **rente pétrolière** (*oil revenue*)

rentier, -ière (*nm,f*): c'est la France des **rentiers** contre la France qui travaille (*person of independent/private means*)

rentrée (*nf*): les dépenses étaient supérieures aux **rentrées** (*income; revenue*); se procurer de précieuses **rentrées de devises** (*foreign currency revenue*); la **rentrée sociale sera agitée** encore cette année (*the return to work [after the summer holiday] will be troubled*); SEE ALSO **irrégularité**

renversement (*nm*): l'opposition appelle au **renversement** militaire du régime (*overthrow*)

renverser (*vt*): les auteurs du putsch qui a **renversé** le régime nigérien (*overthrow, topple*)

renvoi (*nm*): il souhaite le **renvoi** des travailleurs étrangers (*sending back; expulsion*); son **renvoi** devant une cour d'assises (*committal [for trial]*); le **renvoi** de la discussion au lendemain (*postponement*)

renvoyer (*vt*): pas question de **renvoyer** jusqu'après 2012 cette question cruciale (*put off, postpone*); GB: l'institutrice voilée a été **renvoyée** (*dismiss, sack*); les inculpés sont **renvoyés** devant la cour d'assises (*send, refer*); SEE ALSO **barreau**

répartir (*vt*): mettre en place un réseau de distribution **réparti sur tout le pays** (*across the whole country*)

répartition (*nf*): une **répartition** plus équilibrée du logement social (*division; sharing-out*); la mise en place d'un **plan de répartition des profits** (*profit-sharing scheme*)

répercussion (*nf*): les **répercussions** des mouvements du dollar sur les prix (*repercussion, knock-on effect*)

répercuter (*vt*): les entrepreneurs **répercutent** souvent ces augmentations dans leurs prix (*pass on*); **[se]** (*vpr*): ces incidents **se répercutent** sur la vie de chaque Français (*have repercussions*)

repli (*nm*): le **repli** des observateurs de l'ONU (*withdrawal*); la consommation des biens manufacturés a connu un **repli** sensible (*reduction, fall*); suscitant un certain **repli** nationaliste (*retreat into nationalism*); SEE ALSO **solution**

replier [se] (*vpr*): les forces gouvernementales **se sont repliées** provisoirement (*withdraw, fall back*); la bourse d'Amsterdam **s'est repliée**, dans un marché terne (*fall back*)

report (*nm*): demander le **report** de la conférence (*postponement*); un **report d'incorporation** pour cause d'études supérieures (*deferment of national service*); il compte sur un bon **report de voix** du PCF (*transfer of votes*)

reporter (*vt*): **reporter** la scolarité obligatoire jusqu'à l'âge de 18 ans (*put back*); l'élection présidentielle au Liban a été **reportée** (*postpone, put off*)

repousser (*vt*): les femmes ont le droit de **repousser** l'âge de la maternité (*put back, postpone*); la motion de censure **fut repoussée** par 130 voix à 105 (*was defeated*); SEE ALSO **requête**

reprendre (*vi*): le travail **reprend** dans l'usine de Belfort (*restart, resume*); (*vt*): les autorités de Zagreb **reprennent** la Krajina aux Serbes (*retake, recapture*); **reprendre** l'entreprise en perdition (*take over; acquire*); les fonctionnaires **reprennent le travail** (*go back to work*); SEE ALSO **dessus**

repreneur (*nm*): le **repreneur** désigné devra injecter 15 millions d'euros (*new owner*)

représailles (*nfpl*): la menace de **représailles** aériennes (*reprisals*); SEE ALSO **éventuel**

représentation (*nf*): le Parlement, en France, assure la **représentation** du peuple (*representation*); SEE ALSO **proportionnel**

représenter [**se**] (*vpr*): le président **se représentera** aux prochaines élections (*stand again*)

répressif, -ive (*adj*): c'est un texte **répressif**, certes, mais aussi dissuasif (*repressive*)

répression (*nf*): à la **répression** préférer la négociation (*repressive measures*); les dépenses pour la **répression de la criminalité** (*dealing with crime*)

réprimer (*vt*): une loi destinée à **réprimer** la violence dans les stades (*curb, crack down on*); un rassemblement d'opposants au Hamas a été durement **réprimé** (*suppress*)

repris (*nm*): un **repris de justice** notoire, activement recherché par la police (*known criminal; person with previous convictions*)

reprise (*nf*): réunification chypriote: **reprise du dialogue** (*resumption of talks*); les salariés votent la **reprise du travail** (*return to work*); la **reprise** amorcée s'est poursuivie en 2006 (*recovery*); après l'échec du projet de **reprise** de la firme allemande (*take over; acquisition*); SEE ALSO **appel, main**

reprocher (*vt*): SEE **fait**

requérant, -e (*adj/nm,f*): le tribunal débouta les **requérants** (*plaintiff; claimant*)

requérir (*vt*): l'avocat général a **requis** une peine de prison de dix ans (*call for [sentence]*); SEE ALSO **anonymat**

requête (*nf*): la Haute cour de justice **repoussa la requête** des plaignants (*reject the appeal*)

réquisition (*nf*): la **réquisition** du parquet est accablante pour lui (*closing speech [for prosecution]*)

réquisitoire (*nm*): dans son **réquisitoire**, l'avocat général a insisté sur l'horreur du crime (*charge*); [*fig*] un véritable **réquisitoire** contre la politique de son prédécesseur (*indictment [of]*)

réseau *pl* **-x** (*nm*): grève SNCF: **réseau** perturbé hier (*[transport] network*); un **réseau d'espionnage** opérant au profit de la Chine (*spy ring*)

réserve (*nf*): les autres Etats, quant à eux, **ont émis des réserves** (*expressed reservations*); la Banque de France doit reconstituer ses **réserves de change** (*foreign currency reserves*)

résidence (*nf*): le **placement en résidence surveillée** du chef du parti de l'opposition (*placing under house arrest*); SEE ALSO **assignation, assigner, délai, régulier**

résiliation (*nf*): la **résiliation** d'un contrat de location (*termination, cancellation*)

résilier (*vt*): il est possible de **résilier un contrat** souscrit avec un fournisseur d'accès (*terminate/cancel a contract*)

résolution (*nf*): chercher une **résolution pacifique** du conflit (*peaceful resolution*); selon la **résolution 232 de l'ONU** (*UN resolution 232*)

résorber (*vt*): **résorber** la violence urbaine (*reduce, bring down*); [**se**] (*vpr*): la crise de recrutement d'enseignants a tendance à **se résorber** (*resolve itself*)

résorption (*nf*): la **résorption du chômage** tarde à se réaliser (*bringing down of unemployment*)

résoudre (*vt*): criminalité en hausse: une affaire sur quatre seulement **résolue** (*solve [a case]*); **résoudre un conflit** à l'amiable (*settle/ resolve a dispute*)

respect (*nm*): des relations de **respect mutuel** et de bon voisinage (*mutual respect*); une force de paix chargée de surveiller le **respect du cessez-le-feu** (*observance of the cease-fire*)

respecter (*vt*): être là pour **faire respecter la loi** (*enforce the law*)

responsabilité (*nf*): établir la **responsabilité pénale** de la mère (*criminal responsibility*); voir davantage de femmes **à des postes à responsabilité** (*in senior positions*)

responsable (*adj/nmf*): un **responsable** américain a démenti cette affirmation (*official representative*); être à la fois délégué du personnel et **responsable syndical** (*trade-union official*)

ressentiment (*nm*): il n'y a pas de **ressentiment** ici contre les Américains (*resentment, ill-feeling*)

ressentir [**se**] (*vpr*): le couple franco-allemand **s'en ressentira** durablement (*will feel the effects*)

resserrement (*nm*): le **resserrement** de la politique monétaire vise à mettre fin à la faiblesse du mark (*tightening; squeeze*)

resserrer (*vt*): aux Etats-Unis, la Réserve fédérale a préféré **resserrer** sa politique du crédit (*tighten*); SEE ALSO **employer**

ressort (*nm*): utiliser tous les **ressorts** de la procédure parlementaire pour retarder l'adoption du. texte (*resource*); la défense **est du ressort du chef de l'Etat** (*falls within the competence of the head of state*)

ressortir (*vi*): c'est ce qui **ressort** du rapport des enquêteurs (*emerge*); les traitements nets **font ressortir** une baisse du pouvoir d'achat (*indicate, reveal*)

ressortissant, -e (*nm,f*): la protection des 10.000 **ressortissants français** en Côte d'Ivoire (*French national*)

ressource (*nf*): la principale **ressource** du pays est le pétrole (*resource*); père de trois enfants, **sans ressources** (*with no means of support*); une bonne gestion des **ressources humaines** (*human resources, staffing*); SEE ALSO **condition, plafond**

restituer (*vt*): **restituer** la péninsule du Sinaï à l'Egypte (*return, give back*)

restitution (*nf*): la **restitution** du chef du gouvernement déchu (*reinstatement*); la **restitution** de Hongkong à la Chine (*return, giving back*)

restreindre (*vt*): c'est le budget global qui **restreint** les dépenses hospitalières (*curb, limit*)

restreint, -e (*adj*): SEE **comité**

restriction (*nf*): la politique de **restrictions salariales** dans le secteur public (*wage restraint*)

restructuration (*nf*): 8% de la population active ont été touchés par les **restructurations** (*restructuring*)

restructurer [**se**] (*vpr*): le groupe **se restructure**: bilan, 400 personnes sans emploi (*restructure; reorganize*)

résultat (*nm*): baisse des **résultats** des constructeurs automobiles (*profit*); la firme enregistra un **résultat d'exploitation** de 5,2 millions d'euros (*operating profit*); SEE ALSO **intéressement**

rétablir (*vt*): **rétablir** des conditions de vie normales (*re-establish*); SEE ALSO **Etat**

rétablissement (*nm*): partisan du **rétablissement de la peine de mort** (*restoration of the death penalty*)

retard (*nm*): comment pourrons-nous **combler notre retard industriel**? (*close the gap in our industrial performance*); la priorité pour ces pays: **rattraper leur retard économique** (*catch up economically*)

retarder (*vt*): une tentative d'attentat à Belfast **retarde** le plan de paix (*hinder, set back*)

retenir (*vt*): la zone où sont **retenus** les otages (*detain, hold*); l'impôt sur le revenu sera **retenu à la source** (*deduct at source*); SEE ALSO **légitime**

rétention (*nf*): les conditions de **rétention des clandestins** en voie de reconduite à la frontière (*holding of illegal immigrants*)

retentissant, -e (*adj*): essuyer un échec **retentissant** (*resounding*); la Maison Blanche prend position dans une **retentissante** affaire de mœurs (*sensational*)

retenue (*nf*): la **retenue** dont avaient fait preuve les autorités (*restraint*); les **retenues** pour la Sécurité sociale étaient de 6,5% (*deduction, stoppage*)

réticence (*nf*): les **réticences** des Français vis-à-vis des 35 heures (*reservations*); malgré les **réticences syndicales** (*trade-union opposition*)

réticent, -e (*adj*): les partenaires de la France restent **réticents** (*hesitant, doubtful*); ce peuple, conservateur et **réticent au changement** (*opposed to change*)

retirer (*vt*): **retirer** une plainte (*withdraw, take back*); [**se**] (*vpr*): Inde: les communistes menacent de **se retirer** de la coalition au pouvoir (*withdraw*)

retombée (*nf*): des **retombées** du boom pétrolier (*beneficial effects*); cette mesure pourrait avoir des **retombées** politiques négatives (*consequences*)

rétorsion (*nf*): mettre en place des **mesures de rétorsion** économique (*retaliatory measures*)

retour (*nm*): la gauche, pour assurer à tout prix son **retour aux affaires** (*return to power*); SEE ALSO **profit**

retournement (*nm*): des entreprises en voie de **retournement** (*turn-round; recovery*); les constructeurs craignent un **retournement de conjoncture** (*change of economic conditions*)

retourner [se] (*vpr*): permettre au citoyen de **se retourner** contre l'Etat (*take legal action [against]*)

rétracter [se] (*vpr*): le principal témoin à charge **s'est rétracté** (*withdraw a statement*)

retrait (*nm*): le **retrait** du corps expéditionnaire libyen (*withdrawal*); effectuer un **retrait de fonds** de votre compte (*withdrawal of funds*); SEE ALSO **espèce**

retraite (*nf*): pour obtenir une **retraite à taux plein** (*full pension*); des militaires **à la retraite** (*retired, in retirement*); prendre une **retraite anticipée** (*early retirement*); SEE ALSO **départ, pension, réforme, régime**

retraité, -e (*nm,f*): la France comptera davantage de **retraités** que d'actifs (*retired person; pensioner*)

rétribuer (*vt*): il faut **rétribuer** le travail, et décourager le non-travail (*pay, reward*)

rétrocéder (*vt*): Hongkong fut **rétrocédé** à la Chine en 1997 (*retrocede, give back*)

rétrocession (*nf*): Israël accepte le principe de la **rétrocession** du Golan (*giving back*)

rétrograder (*vt*): douze fonctionnaires sont **rétrogradés** (*downgrade; demote*)

retrouver [se] (*vpr*): Occidentaux et Russes **se retrouvent** à Genève (*meet [again]*)

réunion (*nf*): une **réunion de crise** des ministres des Affaires étrangères (*emergency meeting*); SEE ALSO **compte, liberté, viol**

réunir (*vt*): des réunions **réunissant** plus de 40.000 personnes (*bring together*); [**se**] (*vpr*): une table ronde nationale devrait **se réunir** à la mi-juin (*meet, get together*)

revalorisation (*nf*): le comité sur la **revalorisation** du métier d'enseignant (*reasserting the value [of]*); ils demandent une **revalorisation de leur statut** (*regrading*); une **revalorisation de 10%** de l'indemnisation horaire (*10% increase*)

revaloriser (*vt*): il faut **revaloriser** le rôle du Parlement (*enhance, give greater importance to*); l'ensemble des rémunérations sera **revalorisé** de 1.500 euros au moins (*raise, increase*)

revendicateur, -trice (*adj/nm,f*): envoyer une **lettre revendicatrice** à la direction (*letter stating demands*)

revendicatif, -ive (*adj*): s'associer à d'éventuels **mouvements revendicatifs** (*protest movement; action in support of claims*)

revendication (*nf*): se limiter à des **revendications catégorielles** (*sectional demands*); face aux **revendications identitaires corses** (*demand for recognition of their Corsican identity*); SEE ALSO **salarial, solidaire**

revendiquer (*vt*): les Kurdes ne **revendiquent** pas l'attentat d'Ankara (*claim responsibility for*); territoire **revendiqué** par le Tchad (*claim*); les ouvriers **revendiquent** de nouvelles hausses de salaire (*demand, put in a claim for*)

revenir (*vi*): le gouvernement n'entend pas **revenir** sur la liberté totale des prix (*reconsider [decision, policy]*); le meurtrier présumé **revient sur ses aveux** (*retract his confession*); SEE ALSO **ordre du jour**

revenu (*nm*): seul le **revenu du travail** est imposable (*earned income*); pour ceux qui touchent le **revenu minimum d'insertion** [RMI] (*[Fr] minimum welfare payment made to person with no other income*); SEE ALSO **déclarer, disponible, faible, imposable, impôt**

revers (*nm*): un nouveau **revers** pour l'intégration européenne (*setback*); SEE ALSO **enregistrer, essuyer**

revirement (*nm*): un **revirement** de la politique étrangère que rien ne présageait (*change of mind; turnaround; U-turn*)

réviser (*vt*): l'INSEE **révise à la baisse** ses estimations (*revise downward*)

révocation (*nf*): sous peine de sanctions allant jusqu'à la **révocation** (*dismissal [of civil servant]; removal from office*)

revoir (*vt*): **revoir** un projet qui s'annonce trop coûteux (*re-examine, review*); l'OCDE **revoit à la hausse** ses prévisions (*revise upwards*)

révoquer (*vt*): le premier président d'industrie nationalisée à être **révoqué** (*sack, dismiss*)

rigide (*adj*): la Commission se défend d'être trop **rigide** (*strict, inflexible*)

rigidité (*nf*): la Finlande déçue par la **rigidité** de Paris (*inflexibility*)

rigueur (*nf*): une **rigueur** accrue contre les sectes (*strong measures, hard line*); les effets du **plan de rigueur** se font déjà sentir (*austerity measures*)

ripou *pl* **-x** (*nm*): [*fam*] au lendemain du guet-apens tendu aux **policiers ripoux** (*corrupt police officers*)

ristourne (*nf*): un dossier-clef: la **ristourne** accordée à la Grande-Bretagne (*rebate*); proposer une **ristourne** de 20% sur le prix affiché (*discount*)

riverain, -e (*adj/nm,f*): les dirigeants des **pays riverains de la Méditerranée** (*countries on the Mediterranean*); accès interdit, sauf aux **riverains** (*local resident*)

rocade (*nf*): l'ouverture de la **rocade** réduira le flux des camions (*bypass*); une seconde **rocade de contournement** de l'agglomération (*ring road*)

rompre (*vt*): Tel Aviv se défend de **rompre l'accord de cessez-le-feu** (*break the cease-fire agreement*); les relations diplomatiques avec l'Iran, **rompues** en 1980 (*broken off*); il faut **rompre** avec le courant libéral dominant au PS (*break [with]*)

rotation (*nf*): la **rotation du personnel** donne à penser que les cadences y sont trop élevées (*turnover/rotation of staff*)

rouge (*adj/nm*): beaucoup d'entreprises **passeront dans le rouge** (*will go into the red*): SEE ALSO **ceinture**

roulement (*nm*): travailler avec un **roulement** de trois équipes (*rota system; system of shift-working*)

route (*nf*): la **mise en route** de nouveaux chantiers (*starting-up*); SEE ALSO **compagnon**

rubrique (*nf*): il tenait longtemps la **rubrique financière** du *Monde* (*financial column*); SEE ALSO **fait divers**

rude (*adj*): la concurrence est **rude** dans ce secteur (*tough, fierce*); les prochains mois **s'annoncent rudes** (*promise to be difficult*)

rue (*nf*): une décision qui mécontente **la rue** (*the people*); Hongrie: **la rue ne désarme pas** (*the people keep up the pressure*); SEE ALSO **pignon**

ruine (*nf*): sa gestion désastreuse va **conduire son pays à la ruine** (*bankrupt his country*)

ruiner [se] (*vpr*): s'installer sans **se ruiner** (*go bankrupt*)

rumeur (*nf*): la **rumeur publique** l'accuse, malgré le démenti de ses amis (*hearsay; rumour*)

rupture (*nf*): une **rupture** de la coalition gouvernementale (*collapse*); une **rupture diplomatique** entre Londres et Damas (*breaking-off of diplomatic relations*); une **rupture** totale avec la politique suivie jusqu'alors (*break [with]; change*); des jeunes **en rupture familiale** (*affected by family breakdown; who have left the parental home*); SEE ALSO **ban**

rural, -e *mpl* **-aux** (*adj/nm,f*): s'installer **en milieu rural** (*in a rural area*); la fermeture de services publics **en zone rurale** (*in rural areas*); SEE ALSO **bourg**, **désertification**

rythme (*nm*): l'ampleur et le **rythme** des réformes sont déconcertants (*tempo, rate*); la réforme des **rythmes scolaires** (*pattern of school day/week*); les charges augmentent **sur le même rythme** en 2007 (*at the same rate*)

rythmer (*vt*): une année **rythmée par grèves** et arrêts de travail (*punctuated by strikes*)

S

sabbatique (*adj*): prendre un **congé sabbatique** d'une durée de six mois (*sabbatical leave*); le 'gap year', **année sabbatique** qui se prend avant ou après les études (*year off/out, gap year*)

sabotage (*nm*): le police exclut l'hypothèse d'une malveillance ou d'un **sabotage** (*sabotage*)

saboter (*vt*): [*fig*] veulent-ils **saboter** le processus de paix? (*sabotage*)

saccage (*nm*): l'armée tente de mettre fin au **saccage** de la capitale (*[wanton] destruction; vandalizing; sacking*)

saccager (*vt*): mairie **saccagée**, bâtiments publics pillés (*vandalize, wreck*)

sage (*adj/nm*): les **neuf sages** vont plancher sur le projet de loi gouvernemental (*[Fr] the nine members of the Constitutional Council*); SEE ALSO **palais**

sagesse (*nf*): une compression de la demande, et la **sagesse de la consommation** (*moderate level of consumer spending*)

saisie (*nf*): ordonner la **saisie** de l'hebdomadaire; les **saisies** de cocaïne effectuées au Sénégal (*seizure*); assurer la **saisie informatique** des résultats d'examen (*data capture, information input*)

saisine (*nf*): la **saisine** du Conseil constitutionnel par le simple citoyen (*seisin; submission of a case before a court*)

saisir (*vt*): ses créanciers ont **saisi** tous ses biens (*seize*); **saisir la justice** et demander des dommages et intérêts (*go to law*); [**se**] (*vpr*): le Sénat à son tour va **se saisir du dossier** (*examine the case*); SEE ALSO **opportunité**

saisonnier, -ière (*adj/nm,f*): des travailleurs agricoles **saisonniers** (*seasonal*); vérifier les contrats de travail des **saisonniers** (*seasonal worker*); SEE ALSO **donnée**

salaire (*nm*): un **salaire d'embauche** de 8.000 euros mensuels (*starting salary*); SEE ALSO **baisse, bas, égalité, éventail, gel, grille, hiérarchie, parité, rappel**

salarial, -e *mpl* **-aux** (*adj*): la **politique salariale** a été extrêmement sévère (*wage policy*); il s'agit, comme toujours, de **revendications salariales** (*wage demands*); SEE ALSO **augmentation, barème, coût, masse, modération, négociation, prudence, rattrapage, restriction**

salarié, -e (*adj/nm,f*): dix mois d'**activité salariée** (*paid employment*); un **salarié** sur cinq n'a pas un emploi stable (*salaried employee*)

sanction (*nf*): la **sanction** des infractions aux règles de la navigation (*penalty*); s'exposer à des **sanctions disciplinaires** (*disciplinary action*); ils craignent la **sanction** de l'opinion publique (*verdict, judgment*); l'efficacité de la **politique des sanctions** prônée par Washington (*sanctions policy*); SEE ALSO **durcissement, levée**

sanctionner (*vt*): des fautes qui devraient être **sanctionnées** (*punish; penalize*); le vote de confiance a **sanctionné** sa déclaration de politique générale (*ratify; endorse*)

sang (*nm*): en Allemagne, la nationalité s'obtient par le **droit du sang** (jus sanguinis, *right to citizenship by virtue of kinship*); SEE ALSO **effusion**

sanglant, -e (*adj*): les **sanglantes** émeutes d'octobre (*bloody*); une colonie éprouvée par une **sanglante guerre civile** (*bloody civil war*)

sanitaire (*adj*): une détérioration des **services sanitaires** dans ce pays (*health service*); SEE ALSO **schéma**

sans-abri (*nmf*): Soudan: plus d'un million de **sans-abri** à Khartoum (*homeless person*)

sans-emploi (*nmf*): au total, 16 millions de **sans-emploi** dans les pays de l'UE (*unemployed person*)

sans-papiers (*nmf*): 25.000 **sans-papiers** demandent leur régularisation (*illegal immigrant*)

satisfecit (*nm*): OCDE: **satisfecit** à l'économie française (*commendation*)

sauvage (*adj*): l'immigration **sauvage** ou clandestine (*unrestricted*); SEE ALSO **grève**

sauver (*vt*): peut-on encore **sauver** le Kosovo? (*save*)

sauvetage (*nm*): une tentative de **sauvetage** des otages (*rescue*); mettre au point un **plan de sauvetage** (*[company] rescue plan*)

savoir (*nm*): recentrer les programmes scolaires sur les **savoirs** essentiels (*skills, competences*)

savoir-faire (*nm*): un musée du **savoir-faire** artisanal (*skill, skills, know-how*)

scander (*vt*): les manifestants **scandaient des slogans** anti-américains (*chant slogans*)

schéma (*nm*): Bretagne: le **schéma sanitaire régional** inquiète élus et professionnels (*regional health plan*)

scinder [se] (*vpr*): le parti communiste lituanien **se scinde** en deux factions (*split*)

scission (*nm*): cette décision entraîna une **scission** au sein du parti (*split*); les socialistes refusent l'union de la gauche et **font scission** (*split, secede*)

scolaire (*adj/nmf*): SEE **cursus, échec, rythme**

scolariser (*vt*): le lycée **scolarise** la population la plus aisée (*provide schooling [for]*); une famille avec cinq **enfants scolarisés** (*children at school/receiving an education*)

scolarité (*nf*): terminer sa **scolarité** sans diplôme (*schooling, education*)

scrutin (*nm*): le nouveau **scrutin** impose un regroupement des partis (*vote, ballot*); le **scrutin de liste** dans le cadre de la représentation proportionnelle (*list system [for elections]*); SEE ALSO **dépouiller, régularité, tour, uninominal**

séance (*nf*): ces travaux seront présentés lors d'une **séance plénière** (*plenary session*); au terme de cinq **séances de négociations** (*negotiating session*)

sécession (*nf*): un canular annonçant la **sécession** de la partie flamande du pays (*secession*); Yougoslavie: le PC slovène **fait sécession** (*secede*)

secouer (*vt*): la crise des crédits immobiliers **qui secoue actuellement les Etats-Unis** (*which is currently hitting the USA*)

secourir (*vt*): on chiffre à 2.500 les personnes **secourues** (*aid, help*)

secours (*nm*): les pays occidentaux **viennent au secours** des Kurdes (*come to the aid of*)

sectaire (*adj*): un Islam de plus en plus **sectaire** (*doctrinaire*)

sectarisme (*nm*): un puissant lobby, connu pour son **sectarisme** (*sectarianism; intolerance*)

secteur (*nm*): les **secteurs** les plus touchés: la poste, l'enseignement (*area, sector*); SEE ALSO **pilote, privé, public, ratisser, valoriser**

section (*nf*): dans les **sections** et les fédérations du parti (*local grouping*); patronat et **section syndicale** [d'entreprise] sont accusés de complicité dans la mauvaise gestion de l'entreprise (*trade-union representation [in the workplace]*)

sectoriel, -ielle (*adj*): l'industrie souffrait de **difficultés sectorielles** (*problems in particular branches/sectors*)

séculaire (*adj*): les **haines séculaires** entre Allemands et Polonais renaissent (*centuries-old hatred*)

sécuriser (*vt*): pour **sécuriser** les frontières méxico-américaines (*make secure*)

sécuritaire (*adj*): la **question sécuritaire** figure en bonne place dans les manifestes des partis (*security issues*)

sécurité (*nf*): la **sécurité de l'emploi** sera un des principaux enjeux de l'élection (*job security*); SEE ALSO **dispositif**

séduire (*vt*): l'occasion de **séduire** trois millions d'électeurs potentiels (*win over*)

séduisant, -e (*adj*): une perspective **séduisante** pour les petits investisseurs (*attractive*)

séjour (*nm*): les conditions d'entrée et de **séjour** des étrangers en France (*residence*); SEE ALSO **autorisation, interdire, taxe, titre**

séjourner (*vi*): perdre le droit de **séjourner** en France (*stay, reside*)

sélection (*nf*): la **sélection à l'entrée** pratiquée par certaines écoles de commerce (*selective entry*)

sellette (*nf*): déjà **sur la sellette** à propos d'histoires de pots-de-vin (*under attack; in the hot seat*)

semaine (*nf*): EDF propose la **semaine** de 32 heures à ses agents (*working week*); pratiquer la **semaine anglaise** (*five-day working week*)

semestre (*nm*): la société a enregistré de très bons résultats pour le premier **semestre** (*half-year, six-month period*)

semestriel, -ielle (*adj*): SEE **bénéfice**

semonce (*nf*): [*fig*] ces abstentions constituent un **coup de semonce** pour le gouvernement (*warning shot across the bows*)

sénat (*nm*): le **Sénat**, la Chambre haute du parlement, siège au palais du Luxembourg (*[Fr] Senate*)

sénateur, -trice (*nm,f*): ancien **sénateur maire** de Tours (*senator and mayor*)

sénatorial, -e *mpl* **-aux** (*adj*): membre de plusieurs **commissions sénatoriales** (*senate committee*); les **sénatoriales** ont lieu tous les trois ans (*elections to the Senate*)

sens (*nm*): SEE **abonder, apaisement**

sensibilisation (*nf*): un problème de **sensibilisation des jeunes** (*increasing awareness among the young*)

sensibiliser (*vt*): **sensibiliser l'opinion** au sort des immigrés (*heighten public awareness*)

sensibilité (*nf*): le cabinet de Gordon Brown mêle les diverses **sensibilités** du travaillisme (*currents, shades of opinion*)

sensible (*adj*): une réduction **sensible** des effectifs (*noticeable, appreciable*); le ministère de l'intérieur, le poste le plus **politiquement sensible** (*politically sensitive*); SEE ALSO **banlieue, dossier, zone**

sensiblement (*adv*): la retraite à 60 ans n'a pas **sensiblement** abaissé l'âge réel de cessation d'activité (*noticeably; significantly*)

sentence (*nf*): la **sentence** a été rendue: deux ans de prison ferme (*sentence*)

séparation (*nf*): les époux mariés sous le régime de la **séparation de biens** (*matrimonial division of property*); la **séparation de corps** dispense les époux du devoir de cohabitation (*legal separation*)

séparatiste (*adj/nmf*): le principal **mouvement séparatiste** corse (*independence movement*)

séparer [**se**] (*vpr*): lorsque les parents divorcent ou **se séparent** (*split up, separate*); le conseil **s'est séparé** sans être arrivé à voter aucun des projets (*split up; break up*); Thomson **se sépare de ses activités financières** (*sell off its financial interests*)

septennat (*nm*): la fin du **septennat** s'approchait (*seven-year term of office*)

septentrional, -e *mpl* **-aux** (*adj*): SEE **frontière**

séquestre (*nm*): la **mise sous séquestre** de ses biens (*confiscation, impounding*)

séquestrer (*vt*): en son absence, tous ses biens furent **séquestrés** (*sequester; impound*)

serein, -e (*adj*): le candidat se dit **serein** et optimiste (*calm; confident*); pour un débat économique **serein** (*calm, dispassionate*)

sérénité (*nf*): appeler à la **sérénité** dans le débat sur le foulard (*calm, moderation*)

serment (*nm*): prononcer un **serment d'allégeance** à la couronne (*oath of allegiance*); SEE ALSO **prestation, prêter**

serré, -e (*adj*): au terme d'un scrutin **serré** (*tight, close-fought*)

serrer (*vt*): une stratégie pour **serrer les coûts de production** (*squeeze production costs*); on peut penser que le PS **serrera les rangs** (*close ranks*)

service (*nm*): tout dépend du **service** dans lequel on travaille (*department; section*); effectuer son **service national** (*national/military service*); (*pl*) les **services** sont les principaux bénéficiaires (*service industries*); SEE ALSO **bien, exempt, hygiène, prestataire, prestation, sanitaire**

session (*nf*): le projet de loi sera présenté au Parlement **à la session de printemps** (*in the spring session*)

seuil (*nm*): le **seuil de tolérance** a été largement dépassé (*threshold of tolerance*); décider le **seuil de rentabilité** (*break-even point*); SEE ALSO **pauvreté**

sévices (*nmpl*): les **sévices** subis par les femmes (*violence, ill-treatment*); soupçonné d'avoir **exercé des sévices** sur ses enfants (*ill-treat*)

sévir (*vi*): l'ampleur de la crise qui **sévit** dans l'ex-Union soviétique (*be rife*); le gouvernement va devoir **sévir durement** (*crack down*)

sexe (*nm*): SEE **discrimination**

sexuel, -elle (*adj*): SEE **abus, agression, harcèlement, sévices, vagabondage, violence**

siège (*nm*): perdre son **siège** de conseiller général (*seat*); les Ets Duforge ont leur **siège social** à Paris (*head office*); SEE ALSO **rafler**

siéger (*vi*): le Parlement européen **siège** à Strasbourg (*sit, meet*); il **siège dans l'opposition** (*sit on the Opposition benches*)

sinistre (*nm*): le **sinistre** a été rapidement maîtrisé (*fire, blaze*); SEE ALSO **déclaration**

sinistré, -e (*adj*): la reconversion des sites sidérurgiques **sinistrés** (*stricken; devastated [industry]*); l'aide aux **sinistrés** (*disaster victim [war, flood, earthquake]*); SEE ALSO **zone**

sinistrose (*nf*): après l'unification allemande, **sinistrose** à l'Est (*doom and gloom; pessimism*)

site (*nm*): l'entreprise, qui comprend deux **sites**, à Lille et à Douai (*factory, operation*); SEE ALSO **fermeture**

social, -e *mpl* **-aux** (*adj*): à l'issue d'une **semaine sociale agitée** (*a week in which social issues loomed large*); cette **Europe sociale** qu'il appelle de ses vœux (*Europe of social justice*); SEE ALSO **accompagnement, acquis, agitation, aide, animation, capital, cas, charge, cohésion, conflit, couverture, fléau, fracture, inégalité, insertion, logement, marginalité, mouvement, plan, prestation, promotion, protection, travailleur, volet**

sociétaire (*nmf*): la mutuelle regroupe 1.260 **sociétaires** (*member [of club/association]*)

société (*nf*): les rapports complexes entre les enseignants et la **société civile** (*society [as a whole]*); elle dirige une **société de conseil** en ressources humaines à Paris (*consultancy*); une entreprise d'Etat transformée en **société anonyme** (*public company*); SEE ALSO **ban, consommation, impôt, problème, réinsérer**

soin (*nm*): les besoins fondamentaux, comme les **soins médicaux** (*health care*); SEE ALSO **système**

sol (*nm*): un étranger expulsé du **sol français** peut faire appel (*French soil/territory*); le **droit du sol**: tout enfant né sur le territoire français est citoyen français (jus soli; *right of nationality by birth within that country*)

solde (*nm*): le **solde** doit être réglé un an plus tard (*balance, remainder, sum outstanding*); (*nf*): une **solde** correcte et des conditions de vie décentes (*pay [military]*); le Hezbollah libanais, des extrémistes chiites **à la solde de Téhéran** (*in the pay of Iran*)

solder (*vt*): des sommes utilisées pour **solder** les dettes de la campagne électorale (*discharge, settle, pay off*); [**se**] (*vpr*): [*fig*] l'affrontement **s'était soldé** par la mort de trois soldats (*result in*)

solidaire (*adj*): les médecins d'hôpital **sont solidaires des revendications des infirmières** (*support the nurses' demands*)

solidariser [**se**] (*vpr*): ils **se solidarisent** avec leurs collègues moins fortunés (*make common cause, sympathize [with]*)

solidarité (*nf*): ministre des Affaires sociales et de la **solidarité** (*national solidarity*); renoncer à certains avantages, **au nom de la solidarité** (*to show solidarity [with others]*)

solution (*nf*): il n'y a pas de **solution de rechange** à la coopération franco-allemande (*alternative, alternative solution*); avoir une **solution de repli** en cas d'échec (*fall-back solution*); SEE ALSO **adapté, amorce, quête**

solutionner (*vt*): une question qui n'est pas près d'être **solutionnée** (*solve, settle*)

solvabilité (*nf*): les problèmes de **solvabilité** des familles les plus démunies (*solvency, creditworthiness*)

solvable (*adj*): les banques prêtent de préférence à des débiteurs **solvables** (*solvent, credit worthy*)

sommation (*nf*): recevoir une **sommation** de quitter les lieux (*injunction*); le policier a tiré **sans sommation** (*without giving a warning*)

sommer (*vt*): un ultimatum **sommant** les étrangers de quitter le pays (*order, instruct*)

sommet (*nm*): après le **sommet** franco-allemand de Dijon (*summit [meeting]*)

sondage (*nm*): les **sondages d'opinion** lui donnent un avantage de neuf points (*opinion poll, survey*)

sondé, -e (*adj/nm,f*): 30% des **sondés** seraient prêts à abandonner leur droit de grève (*person taking part in an opinion poll*)

sonder (*vt*): on a **sondé** toutes les catégories de personnel (*canvass, poll the opinion of*)

sortant, -e (*adj/nm*): l'équipe municipale **sortante** (*retiring, outgoing*); Elections: le PS reconduit ses **sortants** (*sitting member, incumbent*)

sortie (*nf*): pas de **sortie de récession** sans une croissance rapide de la consommation (*way out of recession*); avant même sa **sortie en librairie** (*publication [of book]*); SEE ALSO **visa**

souche (*nf*): nos compatriotes **de souche nord-africaine** (*of North African stock*)

souci (*nm*): le **souci** du parti de se présenter comme le défenseur du peuple (*concern, desire*)

soucier [se] (*vpr*): sans avertir ses alliés ni **se soucier** des réactions du Congrès (*care/be concerned*)

soucieux, -ieuse (*adj*): l'Europe, **soucieuse** de se démarquer des Etats-Unis (*anxious [to]*)

soulèvement (*nm*): la tentative de **soulèvement** avortée de mars 2007 (*uprising*)

soulever (*vt*): en dépit de l'émotion que **soulève** cette affaire (*arouse; excite*); **soulever** le problème du monopole (*raise, bring up*); [**se**] (*vpr*): le peuple est prêt à **se soulever** contre le dictateur (*rise up, revolt*)

soumettre (*vt*): on **soumet** le peuple à des pressions intolérables (*subject*); le plan sera **soumis au Parlement** au printemps (*be put before Parliament*); [**se**] (*vpr*): le préfet est tenu de **se soumettre à l'avis de la commission** (*obey the committee's ruling*)

soumis, -e (*adj*): le régime, **soumis** à des pressions venues de l'extérieur (*subject [to]*); tous les contribuables **soumis à l'impôt sur la fortune** (*liable for wealth tax*); SEE ALSO **quota**

souple (*adj*): il a invité les deux pays à **se montrer plus souples** dans la négociation (*be more flexible*)

souplesse (*nf*): injecter plus de **souplesse** dans la gestion des universités (*flexibility*)

source (*nf*): **selon de bonnes sources**, Paris y serait favorable (*according to reliable sources*); SEE ALSO **retenir**

souscripteur, -trice (*nm,f*): la liste des **souscripteurs** s'allonge (*contributor, subscriber*); 70 millions de titres achetés par des **petits souscripteurs** (*small investor*)

souscrire (*vt*): être disposé à **souscrire** un contrat de vente (*sign [esp. contract]*)

sous-préfecture (*nf*): chef-lieu d'arrondissement et **sous-préfecture** (*[Fr] sub-prefecture, administrative subdivision of* département)

sous-préfet (*nm*): le **sous-préfet**, représentant de l'Etat (*sub-prefect*)

sous-traitance (*nf*): développer des activités de **sous-traitance** (*subcontracting*)

sous-traitant (*adj/nm*): des milliers de PME **sous-traitantes** (*subcontracting*); travailler pour un **sous-traitant** d'un chantier naval (*subcontractor*)

sous-traiter (*vt*): la firme **sous-traite** plus de 70% des travaux (*subcontract, contract out*)

soutenir (*vt*): Tripoli promet de ne pas **soutenir** les islamistes algériens (*give support to*)

soutenu, -e (*adj*): la demande reste **soutenue** (*buoyant, strong*); **croissance soutenue**, faible inflation (*sustained growth*)

soutien (*nm*): l'Occident, qui est le **soutien** d'Israël (*support, mainstay*); SEE ALSO **acquérir**

souverain, -e (*adj/nm,f*): la principauté de Monaco est un Etat **souverain** (*sovereign*)

souveraineté (*nf*): permettre au peuple le plein exercice de sa **souveraineté** (*sovereignty*); SEE ALSO **abandon, délégation**

sponsor (*nm*): la liste des **sponsors** du Parti républicain (*sponsor*)

sponsorat (*nm*): les entreprises se convertissent au **sponsorat** (*sponsorship*)

sponsoriser (*vt*): parrainer, ou **sponsoriser**, des épreuves sportives (*sponsor*)

stage (*nm*): accomplir un **stage en entreprise** (*work experience placement*); le développement des **stages d'insertion à la vie professionnelle** (*training scheme [for young unemployed]*)

stagiaire (*nmf*): dessinateur **stagiaire** dans un cabinet d'architecte (*in-house trainee; probationer*)

statuer (*vi*): en dernier ressort, ce sera le tribunal qui **statuera** sur ce litige (*rule, give a ruling*)

statut (*nm*): les syndicats doivent déposer leurs **statuts** et les noms de leurs administrateurs (*articles of association*); SEE ALSO **revalorisation**

structure (*nf*): le ministre a visité une **structure d'accueil** pour personnes âgées (*shelter, refuge*)

structurel, -elle (*adj*): ne pas confondre le conjoncturel et le **structurel** (*structural; underlying*)

stupéfiant (*nm*): la législation sur les **stupéfiants** (*drug, narcotic*); l'affaire a été confiée à la **brigade des stupéfiants** (*drugs squad*)

subalterne (*adj*): dans des emplois **subalternes** (*junior, low-ranking*)

subir (*vt*): la ville a **subi** quelques dégâts (*sustain, suffer*); **subir une concurrence féroce** d'une société hongroise (*face fierce competition*); SEE ALSO **moins-value**, **sévices**

subornation (*nf*): la tentative de **subornation de témoin** dont il a fait l'objet (*bribing a witness*)

suborner (*vt*): essayer de **suborner** le témoin principal (*bribe*)

subside (*nm*): se battre pour obtenir plus de **subsides** de Bruxelles (*subsidies*); des personnes dépendant de **subsides publics** (*state subsidies*)

substitut (*nm*): le **substitut**, spécialement détaché à la section anti-terroriste (*deputy public prosecutor*)

subvenir (*vt*): des pays incapables de **subvenir à leurs propres besoins** (*be self-sufficient*)

subvention (*nf*): on débattra à Bruxelles des **subventions à l'agriculture** (*agricultural subsidies*)

subventionner (*vt*): l'agriculture est très largement **subventionnée** (*subsidize*)

succéder (*vt*): le ministre des Affaires étrangères **succède** au président à la tête du parti (*succeed, take over*); [**se**] (*vpr*): il compte bien **se succéder à lui-même** (*be re-elected, be returned to office*)

succession (*nf*): maire depuis 2001, il **brigue sa propre succession** en 2009 (*seek re-election*); 50% des héritiers ne paient aucun **droit de succession** (*inheritance tax; death duty*)

succursale (*nf*): les banques vont-elles fermer leurs **succursales** dans les petites communes? (*branch; agency*); SEE ALSO **magasin**

suffrage (*nm*): s'il veut rallier les **suffrages** des centristes (*vote*); le Président, élu au **suffrage universel** (*universal suffrage*); SEE ALSO **dépouillement**

suite (*nf*): le parquet **décidera des suites à donner** à l'affaire (*will decide what action to take*); SEE ALSO **classer**

suivi, -e (*adj/nm*): un mouvement de grève **peu suivi** (*poorly supported*); le débat sur le **suivi** des délinquants sexuels (*supervision; monitoring*); **assurer le suivi psychologique** des survivants (*provide counselling [for]*)

sujet (*adj/nm*): un **sujet** qui défrayait la chronique en 2006 (*topic, subject*); SEE ALSO **caution, conflictuel**

supercherie (*nf*): les documents étaient des **supercheries** (*fake*); inculpé pour avoir participé à la **supercherie** (*deception, deceit*)

suppléance (*nf*): il avait refusé la **suppléance de député** qui lui était offerte (*position of running mate in parliamentary elections*)

suppléant, -e (*adj/nm,f*): le **suppléant** à l'Assemblée du secrétaire d'Etat à la Jeunesse et aux Sports (*replacement, stand-in*)

suppléer (*vt*): **suppléer** un professeur absent pour cause de maladie (*stand in/supply for*)

supplétif, -ive (*adj/nm*): l'armée populaire, un **corps de supplétifs** de l'armée régulière (*reservist corps*)

suppression (*nf*): la **suppression** des subventions gouvernementales (*abolition*); un plan social avec 213 **suppressions de postes** (*job losses, redundancies*)

supprimer (*vt*): on **supprime les emplois** dans tous les secteurs (*cut jobs*)

surcapacité (*nf*): il faut réduire une **surcapacité** de 20% (*excess productive capacity*); la sidérurgie est **en surcapacité** de 30 millions de tonnes (*in a situation of overcapacity*)

surchauffe (*nf*): une reprise de l'inflation, due à une **surchauffe de l'économie** (*overheating of the economy*)

surconsommation (*nf*): pris dans un système de **surconsommation** et de technologies polluantes (*excessive consumption*)

surcoût (*nm*): le **surcoût** sera très important pour les petites entreprises (*additional cost*)

surcroît (*nm*): le **surcroît de travail** que cela occasionnerait (*additional workload; excess work*)

sureffectif (*nm*): la chasse aux **sureffectifs** (*overmanning*); des entreprises déjà **en sureffectifs** (*overstaffed, overmanned*)

surenchère (*nf*): préparer une **surenchère** à l'offre de l'industriel australien (*higher bid*); se lancer dans une **surenchère de violence** (*escalation of violence*); les syndicats **font de la surenchère** (*make extravagant demands*)

surenchérir (*vi*): obligé de **surenchérir**, ou de renoncer à son OPA (*raise the bid/offer*)

surendetté, -e (*adj*): 10% des ménages **surendettés** disposent de revenus inférieurs au Smic (*heavily in debt*)

surendettement (*nm*): le **surendettement**, un phénomène qui touche plus de 10.000 ménages (*overborrowing; debt burden*)

surendetter [se] (*vpr*): pouvoir rembourser sans **se surendetter** (*get heavily into debt*)

sûreté (*nf*): vers un accord sur la **sûreté** des centrales nucléaires (*safety*); des atteintes à la **sûreté de l'Etat** (*state security*); les policiers de la **sûreté** urbaine de Strasbourg (*[Fr] criminal investigation department*); condamné à quinze ans de réclusion avec une **période de sûreté de dix ans** (*with no release before ten years of sentence have been served*)

surface (*nf*): les **grandes surfaces** alimentaires dominent le marché (*large store; hypermarket*)

surimposer (*vt*): la nécessité de ne pas **surimposer** les artisans et les commerçants (*overtax*)

surimposition (*nf*): ayant payé une **surimposition**, il aura droit à un abattement sur la prochaine imposition (*excess tax*)

surnombre (*nm*): le problème des 1.500 salariés **en surnombre** (*excess, surplus*)

surpeuplé, -e (*adj*): les prisons toujours **surpeuplées** (*overcrowded*)

surpeuplement (*nm*): les gardiens sont les premières victimes du **surpeuplement carcéral** (*prison overcrowding*)

surpopulation (*nf*): le combat contre la **surpopulation des prisons** (*prison overcrowding*)

surseoir (*vi*): le maire a accepté de **surseoir à sa décision** (*defer/ postpone his decision*)

sursis (*nm*): aboutissant en général à des **peines de prison avec sursis** (*suspended prison sentence*); les jeunes Français peuvent bénéficier d'un **sursis d'incorporation** (*deferment of military call-up*)

sursitaire (*adj/nm*): en tant que **sursitaire**, il fera son service militaire plus tard (*deferred conscript*)

surveillance (*nf*): sous la **surveillance étroite** du ministère de la Santé (*close monitoring*); attaché à la **Direction de la surveillance du territoire** (DST) (*[Fr] counter-intelligence agency*)

susciter (*vt*): un discours qui a **suscité** bien des controverses (*cause, give rise to*); SEE ALSO **émoi**, **polémique**

sympathisant, -e (*nm,f*): affrontements entre manifestants de l'opposition et **sympathisants** du gouvernement (*supporter*)

syndic (*nm*): pour la reprise de la société, les **syndics** se sont prononcés pour le groupe belge (*official government receiver*)

syndical, -e *mpl* **-aux** (*adj*): la délégation **syndicale** CGT-FO (*[trade] union*); SEE ALSO **central**, **confédération**, **délégué**, **grogne**, **responsable**, **section**

syndicalisation (*nf*): avec le taux de **syndicalisation** le plus faible d'Europe (*union membership; unionization*)

syndicat (*nm*): les co-propriétaires groupés en un **syndicat** (*association*); appartenir à un **syndicat ouvrier** (*trade union*)

syndiqué, -e (*adj/nm,f*): un pays **syndiqué** où l'emploi est réglementé et cher (*unionized*); en 1979, les **syndiqués** y étaient encore au nombre de 12 millions (*member of a trade union*)

syndiquer [**se**] (*vpr*): les femmes de 30 à 40 ans **se syndiquent** plus fréquemment que leurs aînées (*join a union*)

système (*nm*): le **système de santé gratuit** est menacé (*free health service*); le Portugal veut privatiser son **système de soins** (*health care system*)

T

tabac (*nm*): le **passage à tabac** de jeunes immigrés, et autres bavures (*beating [up]; handling roughly [esp. by police]*); SEE ALSO **bureau**

tabagisme (*nm*): la lutte contre le **tabagisme** (*addiction to tobacco*)

tabassage (*nm*): les agresseurs présumés reconnaissent avoir participé au **tabassage** (*beating*)

tabasser (*vt*): le père d'un collégien **tabassé** dénonce l'inertie des autorités (*beat up*)

table (*nf*): retourner à la **table de négociation** (*negotiating table*); une **table ronde** entre pouvoirs publics, syndicats et élus (*round-table talks*); SEE ALSO **tour**

tableau *pl* **-x** (*nm*): des cartes et des **tableaux** comparatifs (*table, chart*)

tabler (*vi*): les experts **tablent** sur une baisse des prix des céréales de l'ordre de 15% (*assume, expect; count [upon]*)

taille (*nf*): la seule société française **de taille européenne** (*of European dimension*)

tailler (*vi*): il faudrait **tailler dans les aides à l'emploi** (*make big cuts in the social programmes*); [**se**] (*vpr*): **se tailler** une réputation d'incorruptible (*gain for oneself*)

tapage (*nm*): à l'écart du **tapage médiatique** (*media hype*); le **tapage nocturne** et autres troubles de voisinage (*disturbance of the peace [at night]*)

tarder (*vt*): si le gouvernement **tarde** à négocier avec les mineurs (*be slow to; delay*); aller de l'avant **sans tarder** (*without delay*)

tarif (*nm*): la guerre des **tarifs aériens** se rallume (*air fares*); les **tarifs douaniers** vont baisser de 40% environ (*customs tarifs/duties*); SEE ALSO **dépasser**

tarifaire (*adj*): une plus grande souplesse dans le domaine **tarifaire** (*pertaining to prices*)

tarifer (*vt*): le ministre a autorisé les banquiers à **tarifer** les chèques (*make a charge for*)

tarification (*nf*): les **tarifications réduites** proposées par la SNCF (*fare reductions*)

tas (*nm*): SEE **former**, **grève**

tassement (*nm*): hausse des exportations, **tassement** des importations (*drop; reduction*); un **tassement** de l'activité économique (*downturn, slowdown*)

tasser (*vt*): on, a beau **tasser les prix** (*squeeze prices*); [**se**] (*vpr*): les ventes vers les Etats-Unis **se sont tassées** en 2005 (*stagnate; slow down*)

taux (*nm*): le **taux de natalité** est partout en baisse (*birth rate*); une baisse des **taux d'intérêt** (*interest rates*); les banques relèvent leur **taux de base bancaire** (*base lending rate*); les variations des **taux de change** (*exchange rate*); SEE ALSO **abaisser**, **approbation**, **attractif**, **occupation**, **pratiquer**, **récidive**, **remonter**

taxation (*nf*): un alignement de la **taxation** du gasoil sur celle de l'essence (*taxation, taxing*)

taxe (*nf*): l'augmentation des **taxes sur les carburants** (*fuel tax*); la **taxe d'habitation** payée par tous les occupants d'immeubles (*tax on house occupancy; residence tax*); dans certaines communes, on doit payer une **taxe de séjour** (*tourist tax*); la ville reçoit 1,5 million d'euros de **taxe professionnelle** par an (*local tax levied on business*); SEE ALSO **foncier**

taxer (*vt*): les plus-values sont **taxées** à 15% (*tax*); **se voir taxé** de protectionnisme par les Etats-Unis (*be accused [of]*)

témoignage (*nm*): recevoir des **témoignages** de soutien et de solidarité (*expression*); de nouveaux **témoignages** sur les circonstances de la mort des otages (*testimony*); jugé pour **faux témoignage** et obstruction à la justice (*perjury, false witness*)

témoigner (*vi*): et s'il refusait de **témoigner en justice**? (*testify, give evidence in court*); ceci **témoigne** de l'importance que la France attache à ses rapports avec le Maroc (*testify [to], reflect*)

témoin (*nm*): un des suspects désignés par des **témoins oculaires** du lynchage (*eyewitness*); il y avait deux **témoins à charge** (*prosecution witness*); être requis comme **témoin à décharge** (*defence witness*); SEE ALSO **appel**, **audition**, **auditionner**, **citer**, **subornation**

temps (*nm*): la réduction du **temps de travail** (*work time*); le **temps partiel** contribue à la précarité des femmes (*part-time working*); les femmes souhaitant **travailler à temps plein** (*work full-time*); SEE ALSO **aménager, antenne**

tenant (*nm*): **tenants** et opposants de la peine de mort s'affrontent (*advocate, supporter*)

tendance (*nf*): la **tendance** était à une augmentation annuelle du nombre de chômeurs (*trend*); l'homme de la **tendance dure du parti** (*hardline tendency within the party*); SEE ALSO **confondre, hausse**

tendre [se] (*vpr*): les relations entre Washington et Pékin **se sont tendues** (*have become strained/tense*)

tendu, -e (*adj*): dans un contexte international **tendu** (*tense*)

tenir [se] (*vpr*): les élections **se tiennent** en juin (*take place*); le gouvernement **s'en tient** à la politique menée en Corée depuis 1988 (*keep to; continue*)

ténor (*nm*): de nombreux **ténors** républicains ont appelé à son départ (*leading personality, big name*)

tension (*nf*): tenter de dissiper les **tensions** entre Moscou et Washington (*tension*); SEE ALSO **aviver, foyer, regain, renouveau**

tentative (*nf*): une **tentative d'évasion** fait un mort et plusieurs blessés (*attempted escape*); en cas de vol ou de **tentative de vol** (*attempted theft*)

tenue (*nf*): la **tenue** d'une conférence sur le Moyen-Orient (*holding*); policiers **en tenue** et policiers en civil (*uniformed*)

tergiversation (*nf*): de longues **tergiversations** ont précédé l'adoption du projet (*prevarication, shilly-shallying*)

tergiverser (*vi*): Téhéran, après avoir **tergiversé**, répond à l'appel lancé par le Conseil de sécurité (*shilly-shally, play for time*)

terme (*nm*): **mettre un terme** à 40 ans de socialisme (*bring to an end*); son mandat, qui va **venir à terme** en juin (*expire; come to an end*); **aux termes de la loi**, l'employeur n'est pas obligé de le faire (*according to [the terms of] the law; legally*); SEE ALSO **mener**

terrain (*nm*): la pénurie de **terrains à bâtir** (*building plot/land*); des **terrains vagues** en bordure de la ville (*waste land*); vérifier **sur le terrain** la mise en œuvre de ses décisions (*on the ground*);

trouver un **terrain d'entente** (*common ground; basis for agreement*); SEE ALSO **étude, lotir**

terre (*nf*): le Gabon constitue une **terre d'asile** pour les régions limitrophes (*refuge; sanctuary*); la France, première **terre d'accueil** d'Europe (*haven; country of immigration*); SEE ALSO **morcellement, parcelle, privatisation, propriété**

tertiaire (*adj/nm*): l'industrie décline au profit du [secteur] **tertiaire** (*service industries; tertiary sector*)

tête (*nf*): **tête de liste** pour les élections municipales (*chief candidate [in list system of voting]*); SEE ALSO **article, peloton, turc**

texte (*nm*): voter un **texte** visant à réduire les pouvoirs du Président (*piece of legislation; bill*); amender un **texte de loi** (*law*)

thèse (*nf*): favorable aux **thèses** des séparatistes (*argument, thesis*); cette **thèse** ne convainc pas tout le monde (*theory, hypothesis*)

ticket (*nm*): ce **ticket modérateur** peut être partiellement remboursé par les mutuelles (*patient's contribution to cost of medical treatment*)

tiers, tierce (*adj/nm,f*): le troisième **tiers** de l'impôt sur le revenu (*third*); la pratique du **tiers payant** favorise une surconsommation médicale (*third party payment to doctor/ hospital by patient's insurers*); le **tiers provisionnel**, un acompte sur l'impôt sur le revenu (*interim tax payment [equal to one third of annual tax]*)

tiers-monde (*nm*): partisan de l'annulation de la **dette du tiers-monde** (*Third World debt*)

tiers-mondisme (*nm*): le **tiers-mondisme** cher à certains intellectuels (*belief that poverty in the Third World has been caused by the developed world*)

tiers-mondiste (*adj/nmf*): dix ans d'utopies **tiers-mondistes** (*Third World*)

tirage (*nm*): une baisse sensible des **tirages** (*circulation [press]*); les sujets préférés de la **presse à grand tirage** (*high-circulation press*)

tirer (*vt*): les exportations **tirent la croissance** dans l'industrie (*stimulate growth*); un quotidien qui **tire** à 400.000 exemplaires (*have a circulation of*); SEE ALSO **profit**

titre (*nm*): titulaires d'un **titre de séjour** en cours de validité (*residency permit*); un justificatif de domicile [un bail ou un **titre de propriété**] (*title deed*); 70.000 **titres** changèrent de main à la Bourse de Londres (*stock, share*); SEE ALSO **délivrer, expérimental, officieux, regroupement**

titrer (*vi*): *Le Monde* **titrait**: "Une victoire pour les eurosceptiques" (*run a headline*)

titulaire (*adj/nmf*): les **titulaires** de la double nationalité (*holder, person holding*)

titularisation (*nf*): le statut des enseignants qui n'optent pas pour la **titularisation** (*tenure; granting of tenure*)

titulariser (*vt*): **titularisé** à l'issue d'une période de stage de deux ans; en 1967, il fut **titularisé dans ses fonctions** (*confirm in post; establish*)

tollé (*nm*): ce fut un **tollé** de la part des syndicats (*outcry, protest*); SEE ALSO **déclencher**

tomber (*vi*): il menaçait de **faire tomber le gouvernement** sur ce projet (*bring down/overthrow the government*)

tort (*nm*): redresser un **tort** (*wrong*); une loi qui va **faire du tort** aux producteurs (*harm, hurt*); la Cour européenne **donne tort** à la France (*blame; find against*)

toucher (*vt*): le chômage **touche** 17% des actifs (*affect*); un pétrolier **touché** par un missile en Méditerranée (*hit, strike*); il aurait **touché** d'importantes sommes d'argent (*receive*); SEE ALSO **fouet, pot-de-vin**

tour (*nm*): lors du premier **tour** [du scrutin] (*electoral ballot/round*); (*nf*): la démolition des **tours** du quartier Rochambeau (*tower/high-rise housing block*)

tournant (*adj/nm*): l'Allemagne exerce la **présidence tournante** de l'UE (*revolving presidency*); un **tournant** dans l'évolution du PC (*turning point*); Irak: Paris circonspect face au **tournant** américain (*change of policy*); SEE ALSO **débrayage, plaque**

tournée (*nf*): terminant sa **tournée** diplomatique en Asie par une escale à Pékin (*round of visits*)

tourner (*vi*): les entreprises sont loin de **tourner** à pleine capacité (*run; operate, work*); (*vt*): les firmes d'armement **tournent** l'embargo vers le golfe Persique (*get round; find a loophole [in]*); SEE ALSO **court, dos, ralenti**

tract (*nm*): des **tracts** anonymes appelant à une grève générale; **diffuser des tracts** et affiches électoraux (*distribute tracts/ leaflets*)

tractation (*nf*): après six mois de **tractations**, les deux partis sont arrivés à un accord (*negotiation, bargaining*)

traduire (*vt*): sept personnes ont été **traduites en justice** (*bring before the courts*)

trafic (*nm*): la répression du **trafic illicite** des stupéfiants (*[illegal] trade, trafficking*); inculpé de corruption et de **trafic d'influence** (*trading of favours; bribery and corruption*)

train (*nm*): un **train de réformes** quasi continu d'ici au printemps 2010 (*batch of reforms*); la réduction du **train de vie** américain apparaît comme la seule issue (*lifestyle; standard of living*)

traite (*nf*): des accédants à la propriété étranglés par leurs **traites** (*[mortgage] repayment*)

traité (*nm*): aux termes du **traité de Rome** (*treaty of Rome*); il serait alors nécessaire de renégocier le **traité d'adhésion** (*membership treaty*); SEE ALSO **conclusion**

traitement (*nm*): les **traitements** dans le secteur du bâtiment restent stables (*wages, pay*); la collecte et le **traitement** des ordures ménagères (*treatment, processing*); mettre l'accent sur le **traitement social du chômage** (*social measures to combat unemployment*); les cas notifiés de **mauvais traitements à enfants** (*cruelty to children*); la réforme du **traitement pénal des mineurs** (*ways of dealing with juvenile crime*); SEE ALSO **convenir**

traiter (*vt*): on n'a pas pu **traiter** toutes les questions à l'ordre du jour (*discuss, deal with*); il **traita** l'auteur du livre d'affabulateur (*qualify, describe*)

tranche (*nf*): la première **tranche** du projet (*phase, stage*); l'augmentation du chômage a touchè toutes les **tranches d'âge** (*age bracket*); toutes les **tranches d'imposition** sont relevées (*tax band*)

trancher (*vt*): **trancher** des litiges (*settle, resolve*); le tribunal s'est donné jusqu'au 28 mai pour **trancher** (*decide; give a ruling*); le gouvernement pourra **trancher** dans les effectifs et les équipements (*make cuts*)

transalpin, -e (*adj/nm,f*): les services secrets **transalpins** y furent pour quelque chose (*transalpine; Italian*)

transférer (*vt*): **transférer** la production dans une autre usine (*transfer, relocate*)

transfert (*nm*): le **transfert des voix** entre les deux partis est de 1,7% au profit du Labour (*electoral swing*)

transfuge (*nmf*): **transfuge** du PS, qu'il quitta en 2002 (*defector*)

transiger (*vi*): c'est un principe sur lequel on ne peut **transiger** (*compromise*)

transitoire (*adj*): la mise en place de mesures **transitoires** (*transitional, provisional*)

transmettre (*vt*): **transmettre** seulement la nue-propriété et se réserver l'usufruit (*hand down, pass on*)

transmission (*nf*): organiser la **transmission** de son patrimoine (*transfer*)

transparence (*nf*): sa volonté d'assurer la **transparence** de sa gestion (*openness [esp. of government]*); le débat sur la **transparence du patrimoine** des élus (*full divulging of one's financial situation*)

transparent, -e (*adj*): **rendre plus transparentes** les compétences des collectivités territoriales (*clarify, define more clearly*)

travail *pl* **-aux** (*nm*): le **travail de nuit** des femmes dans l'industrie (*night working*); la lutte contre le **travail au noir** (*moonlighting*); les **grands travaux** ont l'avantage de créer des milliers d'emplois (*major building programme*); 400.000 personnes en stages, dont la moitié en TUC (**travaux d'utilité collective**) (*paid community work for young unemployed*); le parquet a requis 60 heures de **travail d'intérêt général** (TIG) contre les jeunes casseurs (*community service*); SEE ALSO **aménager, atelier, autorisation, biais, bourse, cessation, chaîne, droit, exécuter, groupe, hebdomadaire, inapte, incapacité, marché, partage, pénibilité, poste, reprendre, reprise, rétribuer, surcroît, temps**

travailler (*vi*): SEE **temps**

travailleur, -euse (*nm,f*): les **travailleurs sociaux** dans les quartiers réputés difficiles (*social worker*); SEE ALSO **clandestin, précaire**

travailliste (*adj/nmf*): les **Travaillistes** ont remporté deux élections partielles (*Labour*)

trésor (*nm*): c'est le **Trésor public** qui finance ces activités (*[Fr] government department in charge of public finance*)

trésorerie (*nf*): une baisse de sa **trésorerie** (*funds, cash reserves*); une **gestion de trésorerie** personnalisée et sans risque (*money management*)

trésorier, -ière (*nm,f*): le **trésorier** d'une association (*treasurer*); verser une somme à l'ordre du **trésorier (général)** (*[Fr] paymaster; head of* Trésor public *in each region*)

trêve (*nf*): une fragile **trêve** s'est instaurée entre Palestiniens et miliciens chiites (*truce*); le mouvement Hamas propose une **trêve sous conditions** (*conditional truce*)

triangulaire (*adj/nf*): dans une [élection] **triangulaire** au deuxième tour (*three-way election contest*)

tribunal *pl* **-aux** (*nm*): renvoyer une affaire devant un autre **tribunal** (*court*); il sera jugé par un **tribunal pour enfants** (*juvenile court*); le **tribunal de police** juge les contraventions (*police court*); les **tribunaux d'instance** ont remplacé les justices de paix (*[Fr] magistrate's court*); le **tribunal de grande instance** [TGI] siège au chef-lieu du département (*[Fr] county court*); SEE ALSO **citer, correctionnel, passible**

tribune (*nf*): organiser une **tribune** sur l'exclusion (*discussion, forum*); dans une **tribune libre** publiée en 2006 dans *Le Monde* (*newspaper opinion column*)

tributaire (*adj*): la progression des transports maritimes est **tributaire** de l'évolution de la conjoncture (*depend/be dependent [on]*)

tricolore (*adj/nm*): la plupart des grandes marques **tricolores** étaient représentées (*[Fr] French*); SEE ALSO **écharpe**

trimestre (*nm*): dès le premier **trimestre** de 2006 (*term; quarter*)

trimestriel, -ielle (*adj*): le paiement d'un loyer **trimestriel** (*quarterly*); un bulletin **trimestriel** (*end-of-term; termly*)

troc (*nm*): dans le cadre d'un accord de **troc** conclu récemment (*barter; exchange*)

troisième âge (*nm*): les promesses du candidat aux **personnes du troisième âge** (*elderly person; senior citizen*)

tronc (*nm*): les matières scolaires constituant le **tronc commun** (*common-core syllabus*)

trou (*nm*): le **trou** de la Sécurité sociale; le bilan cache un **trou** de 400 millions d'euros (*deficit*)

trouble (*adj/nm*): les innombrables dossiers **troubles** qui ont émaillé sa carrière (*shady, dubious*); **troubles** sanglants à la suite d'une manifestation anti-nucléaire (*disturbance, unrest*); les **troubles de comportement** chez les enfants (*behavioural problems*); un des symptômes d'un **trouble de la personnalité** (*personality disorder*); SEE ALSO **fauteur**

troubler (*vt*): ces gestes étaient de nature à **troubler l'ordre public** (*cause a breach of public order; disturb the peace*)

truand (*nm*): une bande de **truands** et de malfaiteurs (*gangster, crook*)

truchement (*nm*): l'Etat exerçait sa tutelle **par le truchement du préfet** (*through the intervention of the* préfet)

trust (*nm*): la mise en place de **législations anti-trust** (*anti-trust laws*)

truster (*vt*): ses supporters ont **trusté** les places au Congrès (*make a clean sweep of; monopolize*)

turpitude (*nf*): une enquête qui montrerait les **turpitudes** du pouvoir (*corruptness; corruption*)

tutelle (*nf*): la **tutelle** de l'enfant est alors attribuée aux grands-parents (*guardianship*); les départements sont soumis à la **tutelle** de Paris (*administrative supervision*)

tuteur, -trice (*nm,f*): le parent survivant devient **tuteur** légal des enfants (*guardian*)

U

ulcéré, -e (*adj*): il se déclara **ulcéré** par le retrait du projet de loi (*outraged*); **ulcéré** par les propos tenus par le ministre (*appalled, disgusted*)

ultime (*adj*): mais l'**ultime** séance de négociations n'a rien donné (*final*); SEE ALSO **cour**

ultra (*adj/nm*): les **ultras** de la mouvance islamiste (*extremist*); la surveillance des **milieux ultra de droite** (*extreme right-wing groups*);

un, une (*nm,f*): le **numéro un** mondial de l'informatique (*leader, number one*); le quotidien lui consacrait la **une** de son supplément dominical (*front page*); la visite **faisait la une des journaux** (*make the front page, be front page news*)

unanimité (*nf*): être réélu **à l'unanimité** (*unanimously*); on regrette que **l'unanimité ne se soit pas faite** à ce sujet (*there was not unanimous agreement*)

unicaméral, -e *mpl* **-aux** (*adj*): la Chambre du peuple [parlement **unicaméral**, 400 sièges] (*single-chamber*)

uninominal, -e *mpl* **-aux** (*adj*): on adoptera pour les législatives le **scrutin uninominal majoritaire** (*single candidate majority voting system*)

union (*nf*): il appelle la majorité à privilégier l'**union** (*unity*); le secrétaire de l'**union locale** CGT (*local interprofessional trade-union grouping*); les couples qui **vivent en union libre** (*cohabit*); un **contrat d'union civile** signé en mairie (*civil union/ partnership*); SEE ALSO **réaliser**

unique (*adj*): SEE **monnaie, parti, pensée**

unitaire (*adj*): une démarche **unitaire** de tous les écologistes (*unified, united*); appeler à un large **rassemblement unitaire** (*united alliance*)

unité (*nf*): la construction d'une nouvelle **unité** de 30 salariés (*production unit; factory*); une **unité de CRS** fait face aux émeutiers (*[Fr] unit of riot police*)

universel, -elle (*adj*): SEE **suffrage**

université (*nf*): cette deuxième journée de l'**université d'été** du RPR (*summer school/conference*)

urbain, -e (*adj*): les **urbains**, coupés du monde rural (*urban population*); Tours est peu de chose à côté des grands **centres urbains** (*urban centre*); SEE ALSO **émeute, insécurité, mal-être**

urbanisme (*nm*): un plan d'**urbanisme** et de résorption des bidonvilles (*town planning*); SEE ALSO **adjoint**

urbaniste (*nmf*): ancien **urbaniste** en chef de la ville de Lyon (*town planner*)

urgence (*nf*): l'**urgence** de rétablir un équilibre conventionnel en Europe (*urgent need*); demander une aide communautaire **d'urgence** (*emergency*); l'**état d'urgence** a été renouvelé pour six mois (*state of emergency*); des **centres d'urgence** pour accueillir les sans-abri (*hostel offering emergency accommodation*)

urne (*nf*): si on veut que les jeunes électeurs **se rendent aux urnes** (*vote, cast their vote*); beaucoup d'électeurs ont **boudé les urnes** (*abstain from voting*)

us (*nmpl*): celui qui n'est pas familier avec les **us et coutumes** du pays (*ways and customs*)

usage (*nm*): une résolution autorisant l'**usage de la force** pour faire respecter l'embargo (*use of force*); les policiers ont **fait usage de leurs armes** (*use their weapons*); **contraire aux usages** et au droit actuel de la mer (*contrary to custom*); SEE ALSO **faux**

usager (*nm*): grèves: les **usagers** mis à rude épreuve (*user of public service; general public*); la société Network Rail, soucieuse de **rassurer les usagers** (*reassure travellers*); SEE ALSO **gêne**

user (*vt*): il a prévenu qu'il **userait** de son droit de véto (*use, exercise*); une justification pour **user de la force** contre l'Iran (*use/employ force*)

usufruit (*nm*): il a l'**usufruit** du terrain, qui passera à son fils après sa mort (*use; usufruct*)

usufruitier, -ière (*adj/nm,f*): l'**usufruitier** a le droit d'user de la chose et d'en percevoir les revenus (*usufructuary, beneficial owner*)

usure (*nf*): le Parti socialiste, victime de la corruption et de l'**usure du pouvoir** (*wearing effect of the exercise of power*)

utile (*adj*): les partis qui préconisent le **vote utile** (*strategic voting*); SEE ALSO **voter**

utilité (*nf*): une association **déclarée d'utilité publique** (*state-approved*); SEE ALSO **travail**

V

vacance (*nf*): à cause de la **vacance** du poste de président (*becoming vacant*); assurer l'intérim **pendant la vacance du pouvoir** (*while there is no one officially in power*); SEE ALSO **étalement**

vacataire (*adj/nmf*): le **personnel vacataire** ne bénéficie pas de couverture sociale; des **vacataires**, payés à l'heure (*temporary employee*)

vacation (*nf*): son traitement d'instituteur et ses **vacations d'élu** (*parliamentary allowance*)

vagabond, -e (*adj/nm,f*): un lieu d'accueil pour sans-abri et **vagabonds** (*vagrant, vagabond*)

vagabondage (*nm*): le délit de **vagabondage** ayant été supprimé dans le nouveau code pénal (*vagrancy*); les gens qui ont contracté le virus par **vagabondage sexuel** (*sexual promiscuity*)

valeur (*nf*): pour la défense des **valeurs** traditionnelles (*values, attitudes*); hausse record des **valeurs** françaises (*stocks and shares*); le secteur public représente 30% de la **valeur ajoutée** industrielle (*added value*); la drogue, dont la **valeur marchande au détail** est estimée à 3 millions de dollars (*retail street value*); la région nantaise essaie de **mettre en valeur** sa production (*promote; exploit*); la **mise en valeur** du patrimoine industriel (*promotion; exploiting*); SEE ALSO **réclamer**

valider (*vt*): l'Assemblée **valide** la loi sur la bioéthique (*ratify [law]*); travail temporaire: **accord validé** (*an agreement has been ratified*)

validité (*nf*): avec un visa touristique **en cours de validité** (*valid*); une carte de résident **avec une durée de validité de trois ans** (*valid for three years*)

valoir (*vi*): les adversaires du projet **font valoir** qu'il sera très coûteux (*argue, point out*); **faire valoir ses droits** auprès de l'administration (*assert one's rights*); (*vt*): une opération manquée **qui lui a valu une peine de prison** (*which earned him a prison sentence*)

valorisant, -e (*adj*): une **fonction valorisante** et bien rémunérée (*post which brings personal satisfaction*)

valorisation (*nf*): la promotion et la **valorisation** de l'image de la marque (*promotion*); la **valorisation** des cités-ghettos et des quartiers dégradés (*renovation, redevelopment*)

valoriser (*vt*): sa proposition **valorise** la firme allemande à 850 millions d'euros (*value*); **valoriser** le patrimoine communal (*exploit, develop*); une société **qui valorise le mérite** (*which rewards achievement*); [**se**] (*vpr*): l'agroalimentaire, **un secteur qui se valorise** (*a growth sector*)

valse (*nf*): après les élections, ce fut la **valse des préfets** (*wholesale replacement of* préfets); la mesure a provoqué immédiatement une **valse des étiquettes** (*spiralling prices*)

vécu, -e (*adj/nm*): cet écart entre la statistique officielle et la **réalité vécue** (*real-life experience*); le **vécu** d'un SDF aujourd'hui (*day-to-day life/experience*)

vedette (*nf*): sa mort a **ravi la vedette** dans la presse outre-Rhin (*steal the headlines*)

véhiculer (*vt*): il **véhicule** ouvertement les obsessions racistes du parti (*promote; express*)

veiller (*vt*): la force qui sera chargée de **veiller** à l'application de l'accord de paix (*oversee; supervise*); SEE ALSO **sauvegarde**

veilleuse (*nf*): la **mise en veilleuse** du droit de vote des étrangers (*shelving [plan, reform]*)

velléitaire (*adj*): le gouvernement est très **velléitaire** sur ce chapitre (*indecisive*)

velléité (*nf*): refroidir les **velléités guerrières américaines** (*warlike impulses on the part of the Americans*); pour étouffer **toute velléité de révolte** (*any thought of revolt*)

venir (*vi*): **venir en aide** aux plus démunis (*help, bring help*); une proposition qui a peu de chances de **venir à bout de la grogne des syndicats** (*overcome trade union hostility*); SEE also **secours**, **terme**

vente (*nf*): la **mise en vente** de 55% de son capital (*offering for sale*); la **vente au privé** de Saint-Gobain (*privatization*); SEE ALSO **adjudication**, **armement**, **point**, **prix**

venue (*nf*): encourager la **venue** d'activités nouvelles (*arrival; setting-up*); depuis sa **venue au pouvoir** il y a cinq ans (*coming to power*)

verbaliser (*vt*): l'agent **verbalisait** pour stationnement non-autorisé (*report a motorist for a traffic offence*)

verdict (*nm*): rendre un **verdict à la majorité** (*majority verdict*); SEE ALSO **contester, énoncé, prononcé**

véreux, -euse (*adj*): des opportunistes et des hommes d'affaires **véreux** (*crooked, corrupt*); encore une affaire de **policiers véreux** (*police corruption*)

vérification (*nf*): Désarmement: le problème de la **vérification** (*inspection, checking*); procéder à des **vérifications d'identité** (*identity check*)

vérifier (*vt*): contrôler les véhicules et **vérifier** les identités (*check, verify*); [**se**] (*vpr*): si les prévisions de fréquentation **se vérifient** (*turn out to be true/accurate*)

vérité (*nf*): Bruxelles exige la **vérité des prix** (*fair/realistic prices*); SEE ALSO **épreuve**

verrou (*nm*): 64.000 personnes sont actuellement **sous les verrous** en France (*behind bars; imprison*)

verrouillage (*nm*): le **verrouillage** de la frontière orientale avec l'Irak (*sealing*)

verrouiller (*vt*): la police a **verrouillé** le quartier (*cordon off, seal*); le parti **verrouille les postes clés** en région parisienne (*hold/ monopolize the key posts*)

versement (*nm*): après le **versement** d'une caution (*payment*); payable en 12 **versements** annuels (*instalment*); SEE ALSO **commission, dessous**

verser (*vi*): **verser** dans la délinquance (*lapse/fall into*); (*vt*): des sommes **versées** sur un compte en banque (*pay [in], deposit*); SEE ALSO **arrhes**

vert, -e (*adj*): l'**Europe verte** sera à l'ordre du jour du sommet (*farming within the EU*); un vendredi noir pour le **billet vert** (*dollar, greenback*); le **tourisme vert**, une panacée pour revitaliser la campagne (*rural tourism*); distinguer entre zones d'aménagement et **espaces verts** (*green areas, open spaces*); (*nmpl*) tous, les **Verts** et les écologistes compris (*[Fr] Green party*); SEE ALSO **ceinture, livre, numéro**

vertigineux, -euse (*adj*): la **hausse vertigineuse** du dollar (*spectacular rise*)

véto (*nm*): la France n'hésitera pas à user de son **droit de véto** (*right of veto*); le Président va pouvoir **opposer son véto** à la loi sur le commerce (*veto*)

vétuste (*adj*): la nécessité de renouveler les installations **vétustes** (*old, dilapidated*)

vétusté (*nf*): en raison de la **vétusté** de nombreux établissements (*dilapidated state [buildings/premises]*)

veuf, veuve (*adj/nm,f*): la veuve ou le **veuf** d'un conjoint assuré au régime général (*widower*); l'attribution d'une **pension de veuve de guerre** (*war widow's pension*)

veuvage (*nm*): l'**allocation-veuvage**, une allocation de la Sécurité sociale destinée au conjoint survivant (*widow's allowance/ pension*)

viabilisation (*nf*): le coût de la **viabilisation** de la zone [voirie, alimentation en eau potable] (*equipping with mains services*)

viabiliser (*vt*): acquérir et **viabiliser** des terrains (*equip with mains services*)

viabilité (*nf*): ainsi la **viabilité** de l'entreprise serait compromise (*viability*)

viable (*adj*): des entreprises pourtant économiquement **viables** (*viable, healthy*)

viager, -ère (*adj/nm*): une possibilité: **vendre en viager** la ferme et le cheptel (*dispose of [property] in return for a life annuity*); SEE ALSO **rente**

vice (*nm*): la demande fut rejetée pour **vice de forme** (*legal flaw, irregularity*); le jugement fut cassé **pour vice de procédure** (*on a procedural irregularity*)

vide (*nm*): un **vide** politique dangereux (*vacuum*); bénéficiant d'un incroyable **vide juridique** (*gap in the law*)

vie (*nf*): la lutte des travailleurs contre la **vie chère** (*high prices/ cost of living*); être en âge d'**entrer dans la vie active** (*enter employment*); SEE ALSO **associatif, cadre, couple, durée, espérance, pronostic, train**

vieillesse (*nf*): le financement de la branche **vieillesse** (*state pension scheme*); le **minimum vieillesse** garanti à toute personne âgée (*minimum old-age pension*)

vieillir (*vi*): mieux vaut **vieillir** chez soi que dans une institution (*grow old*); dans un pays **vieillissant** comme la France (*ageing*)

vieillissement (*nm*): en raison du **vieillissement de la population** (*ageing population*)

vierge (*adj/nf*): SEE **casier**

vif, vive (*adj*): faire l'objet de **vifs débats** (*lively debate/discussion*)

vigile (*nm*): des affrontements entre les jeunes du quartier, les **vigiles** et la police (*security guard; vigilante*)

vignette (*nf*): les impôts indirects tels que la **vignette automobile** (*road fund licence, [Brit] tax disc*)

vigueur (*nf*): les taux de cotisation **en vigueur** au 1er novembre 1996 (*in force/operation*); l'**entrée en vigueur** du cessez-le-feu (*coming into force; implementation*); la nouvelle Constitution **entre en vigueur** le 4 décembre (*come into force*)

vilipender (*vt*): 500 manifestants ont **vilipendé** le ministre (*vilify*)

viol (*nm*): pour **viol** des règlements nationaux et internationaux (*violation*); trois adolescents inculpés de **viol en réunion** (*gang rape*)

violation (*nf*): en **violation** des résolutions votées par le Conseil de sécurité (*violation, breach*); porter plainte pour **violation de domicile** (*forcible entry [into person's home]*)

violence (*nf*): interrogé sur l'origine de la **violence au foyer** (*domestic violence*); les **violences racistes** sont restées stables en France en 2007 (*racial violence*); mis en examen pour viol et **violences sexuelles** (*sexual violence*); SEE ALSO **juguler, provocation**

violenter (*vt*): une jeune mère de famille **violentée** par deux hommes masqués (*sexually assault; rape*)

violer (*vt*): Bonn accuse Moscou de **violer** les droits de l'homme (*violate, infringe*); **violer la loi**, et payer le prix (*break the law*); une jeune Ivoirienne tue son employeur qui la **violait** (*rape*)

violeur (*nm*): le ravisseur et **violeur** présumé déféré au parquet de Lille (*rapist*)

virage (*nm*): un **virage** dans la politique hongroise (*change of direction*); l'élan Sarkozy est sans doute le reflet d'un **virage à droite** de la société française (*turn to the right*)

virement (*nm*): le transfert de fonds s'est effectué par **virement bancaire** (*bank transfer*)

virer (*vi*): la province canadienne de l'Ontario **vire à droite** (*swing to the right*); (*vt*): la somme a été **virée** sur un compte de dépôt (*transfer*); le chef d'état-major brésilien **viré** pour avoir trop parlé (*fired, sacked*)

visa (*nm*): obtenir un **visa de sortie** (*exit visa*); la suppression des **visas d'entrée** en France (*entry visa*)

visée (*nf*): la Russie alimente les **visées sécessionnistes** de cette région de la Géorgie (*secessionist aims*); les **visées expansionnistes** d'Israël (*expansionist policy*)

viser (*vt*): une vague d'arrestations **vise** l'opposition au Bangladesh (*target*); il faut **faire viser** le formulaire à la mairie (*have [document] visaed*); le texte **vise à garantir** les droits des petits épargnants (*seek to protect*)

vivre (*vi*): le Liban a **vécu** une journée noire (*experience, live through*); le service national dans sa formule actuelle **aura vécu** (*will be a thing of the past*); SEE ALSO **aide**, **mal**, **union**

vocation (*nf*): la **vocation agricole** de la région risque de s'estomper, voire de disparaître (*agricultural identity*)

vœu *pl* **-x** (*nm*): la presse reçoit les **vœux** du Premier ministre (*good wishes*); le changement de régime qu'un grand nombre de Russes **appellent de leurs vœux** (*ardently hope for*)

voie (*nf*): en empruntant la **voie rapide** (*expressway*); les **voies d'eau** pourraient être mieux utilisées (*waterways*); une procédure judiciaire pour outrage et **voies de fait** (*violence against the person*); pour toute décision de justice, il existe une **voie de recours** (*appeal procedure*); dans le cas des **pays en voie de développement** (*developing countries*); SEE ALSO **hiérarchique**, **liaison**, **racolage**, **référendum**

voile (*nm*): le port du **voile** dans les écoles publiques (*[Islamic] veil*)

voirie (*nf*): les routes ont été dégagées par la **voirie** municipale (*roads/maintenance department*); mettre un article au rebut, ou l'envoyer à la **voirie** (*refuse dump*); SEE ALSO **entretien**

voix (*nf*): la **voix prépondérante** du président (*casting vote*); le projet sera **mis aux voix** le 16 juin (*vote on; put to the vote*); SEE ALSO **comptage**, **déplacement**, **transfert**

vol (*nm*): son inculpation pour **vol à l'étalage** (*shoplifting*); deux cambrioleurs inculpés de **vol avec effraction** (*burglary; theft with breaking and entering*); SEE ALSO **tentative**

volet (*nm*): un compromis américano-européen sur le **volet agricole** (*agricultural chapter*); le **volet social** du traité de Maastricht (*social chapter*)

volontaire (*adj/nmf*): inculpé de coups et blessures **volontaires** sur un enfant âgé de moins de quinze ans (*deliberate, intentional*); une politique d'immigration très **volontaire** (*firm, determined*); un réseau national de 3.500 **volontaires** (*volunteer*); SEE ALSO **départ**, **homicide**

volontairement (*adv*): le Japon limite **volontairement** ses ventes aux Etats-Unis (*voluntarily*); accusées d'avoir innoculé **volontairement** le sida à des enfants libyens (*deliberately*)

volontariat (*nm*): une journée de travail en **volontariat** (*unpaid work*); les départs se sont faits **sur la base du volontariat** (*on a voluntary basis*)

volontarisme (*nm*): le Premier ministre prône un **volontarisme industriel** (*vigorous industrial policy*)

volontariste (*adj*): pour une politique **volontariste** de l'environnement (*determined, vigorous*)

volonté (*nf*): il a affirmé sa **volonté** de voir la Turquie entrer dans l'UE (*will, determination*); l'absence de **volonté de démocratisation** du pays (*desire for democratic institutions*); pour signaler à la Chine sa **volonté de dialogue** (*willingness to talk*)

volte-face (*nf*): Privatisations: la **volte-face** du gouvernement (*volte-face; U-turn*)

votant,-e (*nm,f*): l'élément déterminant du choix des **votants** (*voter*)

vote (*nm*): le **vote** du budget (*vote on*); le **vote agricole** reste conservateur (*agricultural electorate*); une des raisons des **votes protestataires** (*protest vote*); SEE ALSO **consigne**, **défiance**, **gré**, **intention**, **pondéré**, **privation**

voter (*vt*): le Sénat **votera** le projet de loi en première lecture (*vote on*); le groupe centriste n'a pas **voté** la motion de censure (*vote; vote in favour of*); les électeurs seront plus enclins à **voter utile** (*vote tactically*)

vouloir [**se**] (*vpr*): **se vouloir** un champion de l'ouverture (*claim [to be]*); le ministre de l'Economie et de l'Emploi **s'est voulu rassurant** (*tried to sound reassuring*)

vu (*prep*): **vu** l'article 126 du code pénal (*in view of*)

vue (*nf*): SEE **garde**

X

X (*nm*): déposer plainte contre **X** (*a person/persons unknown*); confier la direction commerciale à un **X** (*graduate of the* Ecole polytechnique)

xénophobe (*adj/nmf*): une campagne ouvertement **xénophobe** (*xenophobic*)

xénophobie (*nf*): manifester contre la **xénophobie** et le racisme (*xenophobia*)

Z

zélateur, -trice (*nm,f*): les **zélateurs** de cette solution étaient nombreux (*advocate, supporter*)

zèle (*nm*): appliquer **avec zèle** la législation sur la maîtrise de l'immigration (*zealously. enthusiastically*); SEE ALSO **grève**

zénith (*nm*): il est **au zénith de sa popularité** (*at the height of his popularity*)

zéro (*nm*): des prêts **à taux zéro** (*at zero per cent*)

zizanie (*nf*): un diviseur qui **crée la zizanie** au sein du parti (*stir up ill-feeling*); cette affaire **sème la zizanie** au conseil municipal (*create ill-feeling*)

zone (*nf*): un enfant d'immigrés, né dans la **zone** (*slum belt*); des entreprises nouvelles installées sur les **zones d'activités** du district (*business park, enterprise zone*); on réclame l'instauration d'une **zone de conversion** (*redevelopment area*); le collège est un **établissement de zone sensible** (*school in a designated problem area*); la **zone d'exclusion** autour de la capitale bosniaque (*exclusion zone*); sept communes du Nord sont déclarées **zone sinistrée** (*disaster area*); SEE ALSO **abattement, non-droit, pavillonnaire, rural**